SLAVERY & THE INVENTION OF DUTCH ART

SLAVERY &

THE INVENTION *of* DUTCH ART

CAROLINE FOWLER

DUKE UNIVERSITY PRESS · DURHAM AND LONDON · 2025

Printed in the United States of America on acid-free paper ∞
Project Editor: Lisa Lawley
Designed by Matthew Tauch
Typeset in Garamond Premier Pro and Real Head Pro
by Copperline Book Services

Library of Congress Cataloging-in-Publication Data
Names: Fowler, Caroline O., author.
Title: Slavery and the invention of Dutch art / Caroline Fowler.
Description: Durham : Duke University Press, 2025. | Includes
bibliographical references and index.
Identifiers: LCCN 2024023464 (print)
LCCN 2024023465 (ebook)
ISBN 9781478031321 (paperback)
ISBN 9781478028093 (hardcover)
ISBN 9781478060314 (ebook)
Subjects: LCSH: Painting, Dutch—17th century—Themes, motives. | Art and
society—Netherlands—History—17th century. | Transatlantic slave trade—
History—Sources. | Art, Dutch—Economic aspects. | Slavery—Economic
aspects—Netherlands. | Slavery in art.
Classification: LCC ND646 .F69 2025 (print) | LCC ND646 (ebook) |
DDC 759.949209/032—dc23/eng/20240826
LC record available at https://lccn.loc.gov/2024023464
LC ebook record available at https://lccn.loc.gov/2024023465

Cover art: Rembrandt van Rijn, *Two Men of African Descent*, 1661.
Oil on canvas. Courtesy of Mauritshuis, The Hague.

CONTENTS

ACKNOWLEDGMENTS

This book came into its own while I was running the Research and Academic Program at the Clark Art Institute, and I would like to thank the scholars, thinkers, and artists who have come to Williamstown and, in exchanges on race, art history, and aesthetics, deeply influenced my thinking and work, including Rachel Ama Asaa Engmann, Anna Arabindan-Kesson, Jennifer Bajorek, Jill Casid, Adrienne Childs, Christa Clarke, Roberto Conduru, Vashti Dubois, Cheryl Finley, Jonathan Flatley, Turry Flucker, Sora Han, Erica Moiah James, Joan Kee, Anne Lafont, Tsedaye Makonnen, Keisha Oliver, Kailani Polzak, Igor Simões, Ellen Tani, and Jared Sexton.

I also must thank Gage McWeeney and Stephen Best, for a workshop on description that informed the early stages of this project; Robert Wiesenberger, for conversations on ecology, art, and possibility; Shawn Michelle Smith, for her grace and wisdom; Jeremy Melius, for our mutual love of writing; Wayne Modest, for maintaining the importance of joy; Stephanie O'Rourke and Sam Rose, for a generous invitation to speak at Saint Andrews; and Paul Jaskot, for an invitation to share part of this work at Duke University, as well as the respective audiences for stimulating and important questions. Colleagues in the field of early modern art have been invaluable interlocutors, particularly Shira Brisman, Jennifer Nelson, and Stephanie Porras. This book would also be impossible without my closest intellectual collaborator, Caitlin Woolsey. And I also must thank Sara Houghteling, who encouraged me to stick with the conclusion that I wanted to write.

This work grows from teaching with Emmelyn Butter-field-Rosen, and everything that she said about this manuscript was correct, wisdom from a beloved friend. Alexander Bevilacqua gave invaluable feedback, for which the manuscript is infinitely improved. Vanessa Lyon's engagement with these ideas while writing our state of the field essay deeply informed the structure of this book, not to mention that this work evolved from our conversations and friendship. The minds and hearts with whom I most closely shared these ideas over the years have been those of my students at Williams College, and I am particularly indebted to Eliza Dermott, Armanis Fuentes, Kailyn Gibson, Charles Keiffer, Claire L'Heureux, and Byron Otis.

I am infinitely grateful to Ken Wissoker for taking on this project and overseeing it with such kindness, humor, and intellectual generosity. Ryan Kendall's precision and oversight have been invaluable in completing the manuscript. The reviewers for this manuscript were also models of generative feedback that made the book stronger.

Finally, this book would be impossible without the work of all the scholars who have been writing these histories of plantation economies, race, archives, visibility, and invisibility for generations. This book would not exist without their work and their brilliance.

SLAVERY & THE INVENTION OF DUTCH ART

Transubstantiation across Atlantic Worlds

In January 1619, tobacco planter John Rolfe described "a Dutch man of Warr" that landed in Chesapeake Bay carrying about twenty Africans from Angola, whom the governor had bought in exchange for food and water.[1] This brief account is widely cited as the origin point for slavery in North America, an exchange between the ship's captain and the governor in which lives were treated as commodities. Surviving documents trace the journey, which began with a Portuguese ship, the *São João Bautista*, on the west African coast. While the ship was bound for Mexico, an English privateer, who was sailing under a Dutch letter of marque, intercepted the vessel. The letter of marque, issued by Prince Johan Maurits van Nassau-Siegen in the Dutch Republic, sanctioned the raiding of ships sailing under sovereign flags of countries with whom the Dutch were at war, therefore legalizing what would have otherwise been considered an act of piracy. Instead of gold, silver, pearls, or sugar, the captain seized kidnapped men and women from Angola and brought the captives to the Chesapeake shore in exchange for provisions.[2] The slippage between the nations—between the Dutch and the English—and the ability of an English privateer to carry out legalized piracy in open waters under a Dutch letter granting him the right to attack were products of the intertangled histories of emerging nation-states. The Dutch role in the arrival of slavery to North America illustrates the longer history of the Dutch relationship to the transatlantic slave trade, a narrative that has often been obscured by the illegalization of slavery within the Dutch Republic and a historiography that celebrated the Dutch as emblems of tolerance, free markets, and freedom from the tyranny of the Spanish monarchy.[3]

The arrival in 1619 of a ship carrying men, women and children from Angola into Chesapeake Bay marked the landscape, so that the twentieth-century American poet Lucille Clifton would write about a desire to celebrate "grass and how the blue / in the sky can flow green or red / and the waters lean against the / chesapeake shore like familiar / love poems about nature and landscape."[4] Yet instead of a nature poem celebrating sea and shore, Clifton recalls knotted oaks, and she evokes the American history of lynching, a violence that makes it impossible to stand on that shoreline and write a "love poem." The forests, soil, coastlines, and swamps witnessed the emergence of a new world defined across racial lines in ways that continue to shape America today. In conclusion, Clifton asks: "why / is there under that poem always / an other poem?"

This book is about that other poem and the seventeenth-century visualization of a transatlantic space, across which a Middle Passage was born that transformed oceans into burial grounds, while sovereign nations battled for economic control over waterways, claiming the ocean as a neutral, ahistorical, empty space. At the center of seventeenth-century Dutch pictorial production was a struggle with depicting the transubstantiation of personhood into property, a visual labor that defied figuration. The rise of the plantation economy in the seventeenth century can be understood through the visualization of not only bodies and selves but also the sites where lives are discussed but not depicted, imagined but obscured, alluded to but refused pictorialization. The refusal to depict the violence of early racialization and enslavement in seventeenth-century Dutch pictorial production is as important a subject as are the rare instances of its representation. This book predominantly focuses on a period during which the transformation of individual lives into property and units of labor was in the process of legal establishment, while the perceived relationship between skin color, personhood, and enslavement remained fluid in ways that would rapidly diminish by the end of the seventeenth century, as the pigment of one's skin became increasingly perceived in relation to one's right to claim property in one's own person.[5]

While this early history exists in documents—ship manifests, correspondence, and legal letters—the visual record is sparse in the seventeenth-century Dutch Republic.[6] The Dutch were prodigious in their development of maritime painting as a genre, yet the seascapes refuse any visibility to the lives that were carried, born, and died across the expanse of ocean between Africa and the Americas. There are noted exceptions, and certain artists obliquely pictured sanitized renditions of plantations in the Americas, artists such as Frans Post, Albert Eckhout, and Dirk Valkenburg.[7] Recently, scholars have made evident the role of the Dutch in the rise of plantation economies and their impact on seventeenth-century visual production.[8] There has also been an increase in attention to the role of Black figures as central to the history of Dutch portraiture, works in which "black figures were often deployed and read as pure surface, as bodies without presence or interiority, whose value lay solely in their role as a formal, symbolic, and semiotic prop."[9] And rare paintings exist of the free Afro-Dutch community in Amsterdam, such as Rembrandt van Rijn's portrait of two young men (plate 1).[10] In contemporary art, many artists turn to this history of European painting so as to "shift the gaze," or to recognize blind spots within the discipline of art history.[11] In the words of artist Peter Brathwaite, who restages canonical works of European Black portraiture, this process of engaging with the racialized history of European painting allowed him to "construct a Black narrative on my own terms."[12]

Most of the case studies in this book, however, examine images in which the role of figuration remains peripheral or absent. Nevertheless, this figural absence does not necessarily indicate complete absence within the visual archive of the seventeenth and early eighteenth centuries. Instead, this book considers the ongoing and surviving presence of the Middle Passage and its aftermath within histories of Dutch painting, as well as the ways in which this visual narrative traveled beside works often read as indicators of erasure or absence. For histories of seventeenth-century painting and slavery, scholarship often pivots around figural representation in portraiture, history painting, still life, and staffage. When human figural presence is absent (or almost completely abstracted), there has been presumed a critical formation around eradication. While acknowledging the fundamental necessity of this work, early modern art histories of the plantation economy must look beyond representations of bodies, for the act of transforming life into property defies depiction and the world of sense. In one of the most trenchant critiques of art history's grappling with the early modern visual culture around slavery, Charmaine Nelson notes that the scholarship tends to focus "on the human subject" and assumes that the subject "needs to be black (or at least not white)."[13] As Nelson points out, this means that scholarship does not examine the construction of whiteness, or definitions of what might connote the figural, or human, subject. The early modern visual archive around the development of the transatlantic slave trade is often read in terms of absence and erasure, producing a historiography that evades confrontation with the direct presence of enslavement within the archive and with dominant narratives around tolerance, free markets, and global expansion. As a discipline, art history is complicit in maintaining these mythologies instead of writing about the inventories, notes, marginalia, and historiographic texts that overtly acknowledged the role of the plantation economy in the construction of seventeenth-century Dutch painting.

To engage with the period in which transatlantic slavery becomes central to the European (not only Dutch) economy, it is necessary to consider an extant body of inventories, records, and texts that delineate a crisis of picturing the transformation of life into commodity.[14] For it was not only salt, sugar, pepper, and mace that became abstracted into prices on an index, to be exchanged as paper contracts in the Amsterdam Bourse; human life also became reduced to prices in a merchant's log, bills of sale, insurance contracts. Across the case studies in this book, seventeenth-century Dutch pictorial production (and its historiography) is structured by a fundamental struggle with depicting the transformation of life into property, as artists grappled with denying, obscuring, and representing that transformation. This history is particular to the Dutch Republic, as it was marked by discourses around economic and political freedom, tolerance, and a rapidly expansive globalized economy that demanded the abstraction of life into paper and numbers for a stock exchange. Reframing the history of seventeenth-century Dutch painting in relationship to the emergence of the transatlantic slave does not only mean attending to the representations of Black individuals in Dutch painting, or considering more closely work created within the colonies, or examining the economic connections and trade routes of materials or wealth—although all these methods are necessary points of departure. There must also be a reexamination of the theoretical foundation of Dutch pictorial production in relation to the impossibility of figuration, a crisis that emerged in the wake of an iconoclastic Reformation, which stripped churches of altarpieces to replace them with white walls and maritime monuments, creating a visual field for imagining citizenship within an emerging nation-state.

Artistic developments in the seventeenth-century Dutch Republic are attributed to various factors on the European continent evolving from the Eighty Years' War between the nascent Dutch Republic and the Spanish

Hapsburg monarchy, a conflict about church and state, religion and taxes, governance and nobility. At the end of the sixteenth century, iconoclastic riots destroyed altarpieces, and artists fled from the Southern Netherlands to the Northern Netherlands to escape religious and financial persecution at the hands of the Spanish monarchy. The Dutch Republic became celebrated for its tolerance (in contrast to the Holy Roman Empire), as well as becoming an innovative site for artists to experiment and thrive, as the domain of religious painting for the church was challenged. While the word of God was celebrated over the picturing of divinity, and churches remained stripped of their images, artists innovated in other genres: landscape, seascape, and urban scenes.

One of the central theological debates of this period was the doctrine of transubstantiation, a contestation that instigated religious wars and led to mass migrations, new theories of the image, and an emerging empiricism countering the belief that a wafer and wine could transform into the body and blood of Christ.[15] Disagreement about this word and its meaning brought on theological strife, so that new sects of Lutheranism and Calvinism splintered from the church (and one another), as they debated Real Presence, consubstantiation, and whether the act of communion was in memory of a Christ now absent. The work of René Descartes was placed on the list of forbidden books because his understanding of corporeality defied the Catholic reasoning over transubstantiation.[16] For over 150 years, the Eucharistic wafer determined the European religious and political landscape, so that the "eucharist was fought over regionally and nationally, personally as well as communally, and became a touchstone of attitudes toward community, family, virtue, and politics."[17] These debates over transubstantiation would continue into the seventeenth century (as evidenced in the banning of Descartes's writings), yet they also reached a tenuous accord with the Peace of Westphalia in 1648.

As Kwame Nimako and Glenn Willemsen maintain, the Peace of Westphalia, which brought an end to both the Eighty Years' and the Thirty Years' Wars, created a new European order that was fundamental for the ongoing trade in lives as chattel property. The Spanish ended their hostility toward the Dutch Republic and recognized it as a sovereign nation, and monarchs officially adopted state religions, defining countries as centers of either Protestantism or Catholicism. In turn, the Peace of Westphalia set the parameters for trade and economic development.[18] European states were forced to recognize their mutual sovereign borders and rights, including in open waters, where ships sailing under state flags represented the borders of their territories on land. In turn, European states formalized their investment in the slave trade, recognizing the sovereignty of one another as they dismissed the sovereignty of territories peripheral to the Peace of Westphalia.

This was a period of religious conflict, war, and disagreement on the nature of presence and absence, the ability of images to mediate divinity, the rapid desecularization of property, the replacement of real value (land and gold) with paper bills of sale, and mass migrations caused by internal European religious strife that extended into their colonial enterprises. Historically, however, these revolutions on the Continent have appeared separate from the Middle Passage. Yet the arrival of some of the first Angolans in Chesapeake Bay demonstrates that the intertwined economic and political interests of European sovereign powers during this period were pivotal to the slave trade. The whitewashed walls of the Reformed churches in the sixteenth century were the visual predecessors to a legal theory that would define the ocean as a site of erasure, on which no ship could leave a trace (according to many seventeenth-century jurists). In parallel to this legal theory, artists created a new genre of painting—the seascape—dedicated to depicting the ocean as a reflective surface with no depth on which privateers could act as pirates with impunity. The religious images and altarpieces of the sixteenth century were replaced by an art market selling landscapes, seascapes, and still lifes, a pictorial world dependent on oceanic control and the economic success of the plantation economy of the Americas and elsewhere. The crises of the religious wars and iconoclasm in the sixteenth century created the necessary impetus for new genres, such as landscape and seascape, in the seventeenth century.[19] These narratives have not, however, grappled with the ongoing legacy of racial capitalism and its earliest formation in the early modern period, with the role of artists mediating a world in which life transfigured into property.[20] While the sixteenth century was determined by theological debates about representing Christ and his divinity, the seventeenth century engaged in a continuing crisis of representation, around not only the religious image but also the emergent image of human life transubstantiated into property and the uncertainty of markets and wealth built from futures trading.

Central to this history is the movement of speculation and faith from the altar to the marketplace. The crises around sense and knowledge that the wafer and wine of the Eucharist addressed—how could a thin, dry white wafer embody the presence of Christ—transferred to an economy in which wealth was built from trading in goods that would never touch one's lips, requiring a new faith in paper and stocks. Transubstantiation—the ability of one thing to become another, of one material world to denote the presence of another material world—did not disappear. Stocks, paper currency, and bonds could hold the Real Presence of wealth as much as land and gold. The Dutch Republic was built on faith in this act of economic transubstantiation while lives in this period were transformed into paper for exchange. In the nineteenth century, Karl Marx also recognized the centrality of transubstantiation to explain the process of a commodity becoming money. In discussing the value of a material, such as iron, Marx writes that iron must "quit its bodily shape" and "transform itself from mere imaginary into real gold," and he describes this process as a "transubstantiation."[21] To receive a fixed price, iron must become not only equivalent to but also capable of transforming into gold. Marx imagines how iron loses its sensual qualities—not to mention its direct links to the earth and mining—to receive a value founded in gold on the system of exchange.

The demand that a life also "quit its bodily shape" to become an abstracted value of labor and production on a document, ship manifest, or insurance contract also transforms bodies, minds, psyches, and their sensate and sensual qualities from real lives into imaginary units of labor. As the contemporary poet M. NourbeSe Philip recognized, the transformation of human life into property is an act of transubstantiation, so that "the conversion of human into chattel becomes an act of transubstantiation the equal of the metamorphosis of the eucharistic bread and wine into the body and blood of Christ. Like a magic wand the law erases all ties—linguistic, societal, cultural, familial, parental, and spiritual."[22] Instead of referring to the wafer and wine of the Eucharist, which embodies the miraculous presence of Christ so as to bring his followers into communion, Philip cites the central rite of the Catholic Church to describe a reverse, anticommunion on the human psyche and body. This transubstantiation reduces life to a matter of capital devoid of sentient form, severing the bonds that make communion possible, disconnecting life from universe and being. The word *transubstantiation* in Philip's writing becomes the means by which to understand turning a life into a value on a ledger sheet, a loss of bodily form that cannot be conveyed by the sensory apparatus of aesthetic and knowledge production. The loss extends beyond the corporeal and into the interconnections among selves, earth, and spirit that define, create, nourish, and sustain the body and its eventual passing. Transubstantiation introduces a metaphysical term by which to think about the limited role of our sensory apparatus in grasping knowledge, from the ability to sense divinity in the mundane foodstuff of wafer and wine to comprehending the violence brought on bodies, lives, and psyches through an economy dependent on trading humans as though chattel property. Philip's employment of this phrase brings to the reader's attention that this movement of life into property is no less stupefying of sensate experience than the transformation of wafer and wine into body and blood. It brings to awareness a crisis of sense at the center of this economic system.

Often terms such as *erasure* are employed to define the absence of the Middle Passage and the violence of the plantation economy in the works of this period, such as Frans Post's landscapes depicting sugar plantations in Brazil. Yet this was an economic moment in which merchants and seamen, bankers and politicians, watched as a new paper economy and revolution emerged, so that commodities and goods (including human lives) became translated into wealth on paper. For many in the Dutch Republic, this transformation and these lives—just like the shipments of nutmeg and cloves from Asia—might not ever actually pass through their physical hands but were represented through a stock exchange and financial market. For the markets to work, merchants had to believe in the Real Presence of these commodities, not their memory or possibility. In terms of transforming a life into chattel property, as Philip recognizes, this is no less a metaphysical feat than the doctrine of transubstantiation. Instead of examining how this history was erased, this book considers the visual sites in which the emergence of the transatlantic slave trade is present, but in ways that are unexpected, overlooked, or abstracted: a marginal note on a drawing; an inventory; a maritime monument; a church interior; a palimpsest of texts and images that demonstrate the pervasive presence of this new trade in determining the visual landscape of seventeenth-century Holland. As Paul Gilroy has remarked, the visibility of Blackness often exists as a "series of bitter negotiations over terms and conditions of visibility."[23] Just as European artists struggled for centuries with denoting the absence and presence of Christ within images, artists in the seventeenth-century Dutch Republic also confronted, with the rise of this new economy founded on economic transubstantiation, the presence and absence of a new violence at the center of their economic miracle. The transference of transubstantiation from the altar to the marketplace, from the body and blood of Christ to the body and blood of enslaved men and women across the emergent Dutch colonial world, defined the visual production of Dutch artists confronting and obviating this history.

This crisis is captured by Rembrandt van Rijn in one of the most frequently discussed portraits of two Black men, possibly sailors, living within the free Afro-Dutch community of Amsterdam (plate 1). A disjunctive painting, one man directly addresses the viewer while the other presents a recalcitrance about being made visible. This withdrawal suggests a mode that Tina Campt defines as "a tense grammar" of "vulnerability twinned with proud defiance."[24] The man places his chin over the shoulder of a fellow model, an intimate gesture. With his eyes downcast, he projects a sense of exhaustion coupled with an inner state that remains denied to the viewer. This posture of both affection toward his fellow man and avoidance of the viewer directly counters that of the other model, who poses in an antique costume. The juxtaposition between these two men forms the tension within the composition. The gentle touch of one man's chin on his friend's shoulder transforms the work from a study for a history painting (implied by the costume in the foregrounded figure) to a consideration of the relationship between the two men, their differing moods, one extroverted, the other introverted, one engaging the viewer, the other resisting.[25]

The presence of the second man challenges the viewer. While the man in the foreground embraces his portrait, the man standing behind him rejects this process, thereby also questioning the transformation of himself into an image within Rembrandt's workshop. The second man refuses the viewer's gaze, positioning himself in relation to his fellow model. Rembrandt captures the repudiation of the model toward him, painting the model's ambivalence about standing before him—a rarity for Rembrandt, who was celebrated as a portraitist. Before racialized conceptions became entrenched in the Euro-American imaginary, and epidermal identification and enslavement became intertwined, Rembrandt considered the doubt of a model, recognizing the transference of his being to an image-as-property. Rembrandt's speculations were intertwined with the emergence of the plantation economy in the Americas, and it is difficult to imagine that, although these two men were free on Dutch soil, Rembrandt was not aware that their legal status could be different if they were in the Caribbean. He was an artist acutely aware of his own transformation of personhood into a market commodity, and this transubstantiation of person into property fascinated and repulsed him, as he was both financially made and ruined by speculative financial markets.

Moreover, the rejection of the viewer by the model also asks if finding his identity in the archives is an act of decolonization. The model specifically articulates his self in relation to his fellow model, fostering an intimacy that exists between them alone. His presence does not invite the viewer. If anything, his stance rejects the beholder's gaze. This raises the question whether searching for his identity in the archives is justified or runs the risk of continuing histories of forced visibility. He does not need contemporary historical inquiry to determine the value of his existence, which was realized in his contemporary relationships, one articulated in the portrait. To assign an uncertain identity to an individual in an effort to further educate ourselves in the present about the racist structures of museums places a form of labor on an individual who remains firmly rooted in a quality of inward life that never necessarily asked to be made perceptible. This is not to undermine the importance of bringing the presence of the Afro-Dutch community in seventeenth-century Amsterdam into contemporary scholarship, or of examining an archive in which voices have been historically omitted. Instead, as in the portrait of the two men, it is to hold in tension a recognition of the necessary work that remains within the archive while also realizing that making visible runs the risk of turning the complexity of a life into an image for marketing, and for museum diversity campaigns.

For Philip, it is precisely in the empty nonfigural expanses of the page and silences that she gathers the possibility of communion, as she employs the term *transubstantiation* in an essay following *Zong!*—a poetry collection built from the written decision for a late eighteenth-century legal case, *Gregson v. Gilbert. Zong* refers to an eighteenth-century merchant ship, originally named *Zorg* (the Dutch word for "care"), which was seized by the British off the coast of Africa. In 1781, the captain, Luke Collingwood, and his crew cast 132 enslaved individuals overboard to secure an insurance payment for the ship's owners in Liverpool.[26] Attempting to ration provisions and maintain profit, Collingwood and his crew committed an act known now as the Zong massacre, assuming that the maritime insurance company would compensate the owners for the 132 human beings cast into the ocean as though inanimate ballast from the ship's hold.[27]

This act demonstrates how financial speculation on paper drove the transatlantic slave trade, a form of finance and "trading in the wind" that developed in Amsterdam. The ship's crew drowned the African men, women, and children, as their value was determined by not only the auction block in Jamaica but also the paper insurance contract in Liverpool.[28] The marine insurance industry, which began in the thirteenth century in the Mediterranean and became, in seventeenth-century Amsterdam, a profitable business, made the development of a global economy possible, as shareholders could protect themselves against lost cargoes, sunk ships, and piracy.[29] The industry culminates in this moment of financial speculation, in which the kidnapped were cast into the ocean while maintaining their value within the contractual obligations of the transatlantic markets.

This act is not singular in the history of the Middle Passage, and there are other examples from Dutch maritime history. The *Leusden* foundered on a sandbank at the mouth of a river in Suriname. The crew locked the enslaved Africans in the ship's hold while the ship sank, drowning the majority of captives to prevent an insurrection.[30] In 1750 on the *Middelburgs Welvaren*, the crew repressed a revolt of enslaved Africans also by locking them in the hold and thereby suffocating 231 individuals. Like the Zong massacre, this latter case led to a debate between the insurer and the insured about the validity of claiming insurance on the murdered. The morality was never debated, merely the extent of the claim for damages.[31] Even in the case of the Zong massacre, which was pivotal to the rise of the abolitionist movement in England, Collingwood was never held responsible for the individual lives. The trial centered on the insurance claim made by the ship's owner (Gregson) and the refusal of the underwriter (Gilbert) to pay the claim.

Philip takes the language and words of this legal case as it survives in the archives and fragments, disperses, and creates a new work, writing the "other poem" from the legal case document. Philip draws into relationship the white empty space of the page and the printed letters, so that the spaces between the letters and the words—between one clause and another, between one name and another, between a single article and another— reverberate. The paper takes on a physical presence in Philip's spacing of the words, in her rearrangement, reframing, and building of an ode to a history that exists within and between the lines of the legal document. Philip reverberates the empty space of the page so that it is imbued with the presence of not only words but also breath, palpitation, and the hum of existence in the veins. The reader of her work therefore must attend not only to the text but also to the ellipses, and to the areas where nothing exists but the whiteness of the ground. This ground commingles all the lives, grief, crimes, and injustices that are within *Gregson v. Gilbert* yet never directly articulated. Through the physical material of the printed page, Philip makes palpable the "other" poem that Clifton cites. Fragmenting the legal account into verse strategically dispersed across the paper (figure I.1), Philip visualizes an institutional archive that historically omitted the voices of the enslaved, only to bring them back as specters, between the

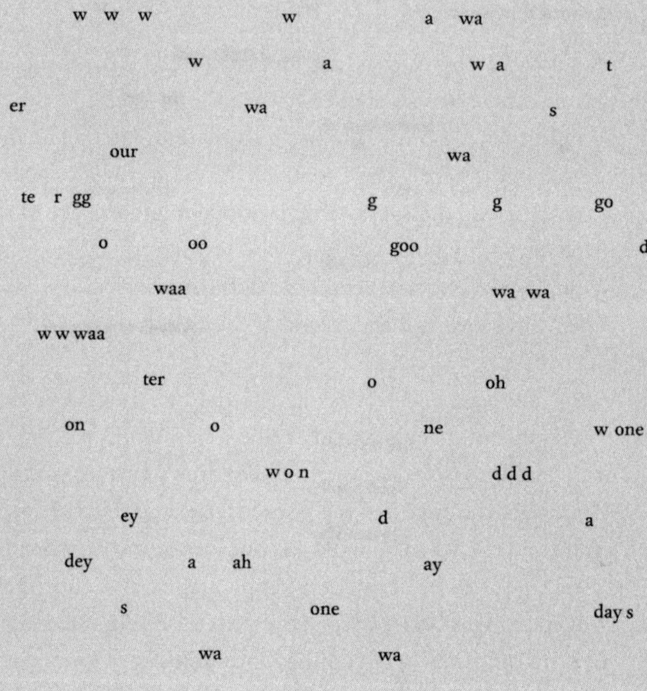

1.1 M. NourbeSe Philip, "Zong! #1," from *Zong!* (Middletown, CT: Wesleyan University Press, 2008).

lines, in the margins. Within this collection of verse, Philip places the miracle of transubstantiation at the center to determine how individual lives become reduced to speculative financial futures on sheets of paper.

Yet within these empty spaces, resounding with their beats, stretches of expanse that howl in the absence of words, Philip also draws together a new possibility of communion, as readers of Philip suggest that her poetics creates "a gathering of black life and writing wherein is found another communion (a together-in-nothingness) in openness and multiplicity."[32] Philip's verse, therefore, and the commingling of printed testimonies wrested from the historical archive on the white page present the possibility of an intimacy founded on the relational lives of African descendants lost across the Middle Passage, a history that continues to structure contemporary societies. This displacement of transubstantiation from the altar to the marketplace forms the structure of this book, which is based primarily in the seventeenth-century economic capital of Amsterdam and the emergent plantation economies in the Atlantic world. The loose federation of provinces known today as the Netherlands was the home not only of the Reformed Church but also of one of the first global economies. This history of Dutch painting focuses on the emergence of maritime space—coastlines, seascapes, monuments, natural history—considering how the transatlantic slave trade coexisted beside a pictorial record that predominantly absented the violence of the emergent plantation economies and the Middle Passage, although it remains resolutely present within the ellipses, the open spaces, the resonant surfaces within Dutch pictorial practice.

A Brief Historiography

Beginning with Georg Wilhelm Friedrich Hegel, Dutch painting has been equated with freedom. In his teleological narrative of the limits of painting in the wake of the dissolution of Christianity, Hegel takes particular delight in the surfaces of Dutch painting and their enigmatic portrayal of everyday life. He grounds the tradition of Dutch painting in the Eighty Years' War and Spanish tyranny, arguing that following this conflict, the Dutch created a form of art that reveled in freedom and daily existence:

> By resolution, endurance, and courage, townsmen and countrymen alike threw off the Spanish dominion of Philip II, son of Charles V (that mighty King of the World), and by fighting won for themselves

freedom in political life and in religious life too in the religion of freedom. This citizenship, this love of enterprise, in small things as in great, in their own land as on the high seas, this painstaking as well as cleanly and neat well-being, this joy and exuberance in their own sense that for all this they have their own activity to thank, all this is what constitutes the general content of their pictures.[33]

For Hegel, Dutch painters were masters in depicting the "prose of everyday life," capturing the ephemeral moments of existence—the reflection in a metal surface, a quick smile—so that it becomes suspended on the canvas. The paintings invite the ability to reflect on the skill of the artist to capture the fleetingness of life and consciousness. For Hegel, this attention to quotidian surfaces was a product of a specific political situation and history, namely, the Dutch celebration of *vrijheid* (freedom or liberty) from Spanish tyranny. The pleasure found in the reflective surfaces of Dutch painting is inseparable from the hard-wrought freedoms won from Spanish tyranny, from the massacres that Spain inflicted on the Low Countries as they sought religious and economic freedom (both necessarily intertwined). Importantly, Hegel employs the word *citizenship* to describe the coming together of a people who took delight in "small things," "their own land," and "the high seas," recognizing the centrality of emergent ideas of citizenship in Dutch urban life to a view of the world that celebrated fleeting surfaces of light and nothingness.[34]

Hegel did not consider the paradoxical relationship between Dutch Republican *vrijheid* and the emerging dependence on enslaved labor, an absence in the historiography that has provided a foundation on which mythologies around freedom, tolerance, and Dutch painting have been constructed. While examining Hegel's writings on Dutch painting in relation to the Dutch colonies might be considered a twenty-first century mode, historians have demonstrated Hegel's acute awareness in his writing of other colonial histories, particularly the Haitian revolution.[35] Knowledge of the Dutch as violent enslavers and their role in the Caribbean was central to the abolitionist rhetoric of the eighteenth and nineteenth centuries, particularly after John Stedman's account of Suriname and William Blake's accompanying illustrations.[36] Certain traditions of Dutch landscape, seascapes, natural history, and monuments developed to define citizenship, personhood, interiority, and the natural world as a site of refuge. This was an active pictorial project, and there is an abstraction central to seventeenth-century Dutch painting, which is not the divine subsumed into the natural world, but instead the transfiguration of lives and the natural world into commodities for exchange—a transformation visually realized in an acute attention to detail and surfaces. Hegel recognized this effervescent attention to detail, realizing that it was born from a desire to pictorially articulate a vision defined by political and economic freedom for the citizens who belonged within that world, to the exclusion of others.

While there has been attention to the brushwork that achieved particular qualities of Dutch painting and its surfaces, these effects are mostly accomplished in a pictorial tradition celebrated as a direct portrait of an emergent middle-class life, founded on an urban culture dedicated to civic virtue, tolerance, and a celebration of republicanism (as opposed to monarchy). Nineteenth-century French critic Eugène Fromentin described the Dutch Republic as "a nation of burghers, practical, unimaginative, busy, not in the least mystical, of anti-Latin mind, with traditions destroyed, with a workshop without images, and parsimonious habits, to find an art which should please it, that should seize its conventionalities, and represent it."[37] While scholars could challenge the broad characterization, Dutch painters did forge a visual vocabulary for a class of collectors that was neither clergy nor aristocracy. Moreover, the dominance of an art market driven by the wealth of merchants frames a history of painting created in tandem with an economy built from global economic expansion. As Fromentin wrote, Dutch painting is the "portrait of Holland, its exterior image, faithful, exact, complete, and like, with no embellishment."[38] Although one might dismiss Fromentin's characterization nearly two centuries later, this trope of the "faithful" image that reflects the world persists. Interpretations of Dutch painting have been caught between taking pleasure in the quality of the painting—the brushwork, the surface, the effect—and arguing that these are paintings about everyday life, the interior self, the quotidian delight in light falling through a window. They are paintings about the pleasure of art.[39]

One of the most formative historical engagements of this transcriptional, photographic-like quality to Dutch painting remains Svetlana Alpers's *The Art of Describing*, which moves the discipline away from tired methods of iconography and hidden symbolism. Alpers likened the canvas to the surface of the eye's retina, drawing a parallel between Dutch picturing practices and seventeenth-century concepts of vision and optics, explicating a quality of this particular school of painting that has struck viewers since Fromentin: the appearance of a direct reflection, unmediated by author, hand, viewer. Her scholarship reinforces a sense that this history of picturing presents the world as though passively, as though fragmented, as though a momentary reflection of the eye, suggesting that the view of the world is an immediate unmediated picture.[40]

The assumptions around an immediately evident form of picture making have reinforced a pictorial practice in which the emergent plantation economies were erased from the historical record, so that art historians for generations abdicated an engagement with enslavement and its role in the rise of a modern global economy. Until recently, little attention has been paid to this textual discourse in art history, for the attention to the picture-plane-as-surface has created a tradition around the coextensive relationship between text and image, so that, as Louis Marin summarized in regard to Dutch painting, "the picture is thus a surface of description that is exactly co-extensive with and perfectly transparent to the descriptive discourse that utters it and which it exhausts in a smooth 'tautology' between image and language."[41] Yet the accounts of the rise of the transatlantic slave trade in records, inventories, and inscriptions, when read beside the pictorial tradition, disrupt this smooth surface, introducing a textual history that reveals the epistemic dangers of reinforcing a reading of the canvas as a direct, passive, unmediated reflection of the world.

In Julie Hochstrasser's account of Dutch still-life painting and the impact of slavery, sugar, and plantations on artists, she writes: "What is to be seen of the grisly realities of sugar production in all of the images of seventeenth-century Dutch art? Precisely nothing."[42] Geoff Quilley and Kay Dian Kriz argue that in the long eighteenth century, "these cataclysmic events [the Middle Passage] became almost invisible and virtually unrepresentable (completely so within the formal structures of many artistic genres) for western modernity."[43] Other scholars agree with Jean Michel Massing's assessment that there was no depiction of "the excesses and cruelty of slavery and, more generally, social inequalities," because they "were hardly ever the subject of any painting before the anti-slavery imagery of the eighteenth and nineteenth centuries."[44]

Philip describes how the narrative unfolds in the "space where it's not told—literally in the margins of the text, a sort of negative space, a space not so much of non-meaning as anti-meaning."[45] Philip literalizes this in her visual juxtaposition between words placed in configurations across the pages, drawing attention to the ellipses, empty space, ground, and the construction of the paper book itself as support. Drawing on Philip's account of the negative space as holding meaning, this book examines visual histories that might be considered void of content, particularly regarding the history of the transatlantic slave trade: sea surfaces disturbed only by wind, coastal profiles against blank sea and sky, canvas grounds, marble slabs, armor, and blue skies. In these sites, which scholars have often described as "pictorial," "pleasant," and "beautiful," I consider how the specter of the plantation economy in the Americas overflows into these nondescript spaces, surfaces that seem to offer little more than a reflection of a still world.

As a visual corollary to Philip's engagement with the space of the paper and its capacity to gather meaning within negative space, there is a seventeenth-century drawing by the artist Gesina ter Borch, in which the paper enigmatically palpitates with a presence that surrounds her drawing of two Black children, who face each other (plate 2).[46] One child sits in a chair while the other stands, looking directly at each other. They are both barefoot, and the standing figure casts a shadow, while the seated child's chair is attended to with great specificity, outlining the simple woodwork carving and a leather seat. This chair and its detailed execution draws attention to the strangeness of the composition, as the child sits on an object from an interior scene in a drawing devoid of interior. Typically, Gesina ter Borch delighted in placing her figural subjects within domestic spaces, often attending as closely to the surrounding details of home as to the figures themselves. Yet in this rendition of two children, she pictures a chair—suggesting an interior scene—while leaving the children perpetually placed outside a domicile. Instead, the empty space of the paper becomes the ground, walls, and landscape, so that they arrive here in the realm of representation devoid of any context beyond a European chair, typical seventeenth-century Dutch clothing, and bare feet.

The only other context provided is a date, September 11, 1654, and the scrawled words *nae 't leven*—indicating that she drew this picture after life. *Nae 't leven* could be used in the context of the artist's studio, to indicate drawing the human figure (often nude) after life, or in the context of botanical or zoological illustration. In using this terminology, Ter Borch places these children within the context of natural history illustration, the foreign oddity that she witnessed. The empty paper speaks to the children's domestic spaces and interiors left unpictured by Ter Borch. The lives of the two children become reduced to the empty space of the paper, across which one boy casts his shadow, giving this nonfigurative realm weight. Obliquely, the paper's ground makes present that the domestic space for the children is absent, as they stand and sit in their bare feet, facing each other across a divide. Unlike the intimacy between the two men of African descent that Rembrandt captured in his painting, these two children are denied a clear relationality. The caricaturized representation of their facial features suggests that Ter Borch struggled to delineate one child from the other, so that the difference between two selves is demarcated by their clothing. Yet the lack of distinction between their facial features almost suggests that it is one child, doubled and reimagined in another pose and another outfit. The children are therefore posited as infinitely replicable, models to be copied and inserted into other works—like studies of botanical and zoological specimens to be integrated into later paintings and landscapes. The empty white paper represents Ter Borch's inability and lack of desire to imagine these two children as part of a domestic space. The empty white paper surrounding the children demonstrates strategies of representation that made it possible to deny citizenship and belonging, and it is precisely this white space of the page, which has so often been a space of refusal, denial, and occlusion, that Philip transforms into a world for gathering, commingling, and remembering.

Dutchness

This book adheres to a tradition of "Dutch" painting, which is also a construct. For example, Maria Sibylla Merian (1647–1717), who is the focus of the fourth chapter, is technically a German-born artist, although her life was informed by living in the Dutch Republic and its colonies. This was also a period in which citizenship was more closely bound to local urban identities—Amsterdam, Haarlem, Leiden—rather than to the Dutch Republic itself.[47] Moreover, as many scholars have argued, and as discussed in greater depth throughout the book, the Atlantic economy defies national narratives.[48] Although the Dutch were often at war with the Spanish and English (among others), they also depended on them for economic prosperity. The interconnections among the Portuguese planters in Brazil and the Sephardic communities in Amsterdam are central to this history. Not to mention that the crews on ships sailing under the flag of the Dutch Republic were often manned by a migrant labor force of sailors, fishermen, and dockworkers coming from the Baltic and Germanic states, France, Africa, and elsewhere.[49]

Nevertheless, the *idea* of a school of Dutch painting and its persistent mythos in museums, curatorial hires, and surveys of European art have created a tradition associated with a small country built from the sea, which economically dominated the world in the seventeenth century. A specific intellectual history formed in the Dutch Republic around citizenship, Republicanism, virtue, and freedom from Spanish tyranny that is central to the specificity of the transatlantic slave trade's development and its impact on Dutch visual culture.[50] The merchants in the Dutch Republic built on an economic system forged by Italian, Portuguese, and Genoese bankers that would culminate in the British Industrial Revolution. Intrinsic to this historical moment is the work of painters, such as Rembrandt van Rijn, whose work must be understood in the context of a new economic system that formed ideas of property, self, and the right to property-of-the-self, which would ultimately become intrinsic to ideologies of whiteness.

The first chapter engages with the rise of an art market built on financial speculation. In the economic boom of seventeenth-century Amsterdam, artists participated in one of the first open art markets, driven by middle-class consumption as opposed to patronage from church and state. Scholars are only beginning to consider, however, how the Dutch economic miracle was inseparable from the rise of the transatlantic slave trade. Examining the works of Hercules Segers (1589–1638) and Rembrandt van Rijn (1606–69), I assert that this emergent world of financial speculation founded on enslaved labor haunts their work. In turn, the rise of the artists' conception of self and property, as often discussed in the products of Rembrandt's workshop, cannot be separated from the simultaneous development of the trade in humans as chattel property.

The second chapter examines the Atlantic crossing, shifting perspectives, and what it means to think about the archive of slavery beside the visual record. Engaging with the famous paintings of Frans Post (1612–80), this chapter explores both his coastal studies of salt mining in the Cape Verde islands and his depiction of the Brazilian sugar plantations in relation to the account books, inventories, and written records that traveled beside his pictorial record. Typically, his work is described as scientific, atmospheric, observational, and beautiful. Yet an extensive archive of texts that traveled beside these pictorial accounts recounts the violence of enslavement. By examining the textual accounts of the emergent slave trade beside the pictorial record produced by Post, this chapter demonstrates how painters struggled with translating the reduction of human life into an abstraction of property and value, a transformation at the heart of Dutch picturing.

The third chapter considers the rise of the Dutch maritime monument within the empty whitewashed interiors of the Reformed Church.

In seventeenth-century texts, there are two scenes of oceanic space. One is a material history of the ocean dominated by the enslaved and Indigenous divers, whose bodies became crucial to natural philosophers' understanding of water, air, pressure, gas, and the corporeal system, thereby existing at a crux of discourses exploring the physicality of oceanic ecospheres and their depths. The other discourse describes the ocean as an immaterial site of erasure and oblivion, a surface—or highway—for trade, in the legal writings of Hugo Grotius (1583–1645), and the rise of international law. This chapter juxtaposes these two histories to demonstrate how an urban ideal of citizenship was built from creating a monumental visual language dedicated to Dutch naval heroes, a phenomenon that structured ideas of citizenship and noncitizenship so that the Dutch naval monument built in the empty space of Reformed churches formed a particular view of the ocean as a no-place space devoid of history.

The fourth chapter examines Maria Sibylla Merian, a female naturalist who traveled to Suriname to study local plants and insects, who recounts in a study of the peacock flower that Indigenous and enslaved women used the specimen to perform abortions, as they did not want their children born into slavery. This chapter confronts Merian's celebration as a female pioneer in art history while examining her inextricable role in the plantation economy of Suriname. Merian's study of plants and insects is dedicated to generation, but scholars have yet to consider how the fascination with insect reproduction in seventeenth-century natural history and visual culture occurred in tandem with a series of crises around human reproduction in the Americas. Merian's illustrations and text engage with a crisis in domestic interiors in the plantation.

While the majority of these chapters engage with crises in figuration, the final chapter turns to a specific moment in the history of Dutch art and its historiography, namely Rembrandt's picturing of a young Black man at the beheading of John the Baptist. This man, although overlooked in the historiography on Alois Riegl, was central to his articulation of attention, subordination, and Dutch group portraiture. Riegl's engagement with the child demonstrates the centrality of state violence to the emergence of the modern inward self. While this historiographic turn has been fundamentally ignored by art historians, it was central to Derek Walcott in his final poem, *The Prodigal,* in which Rembrandt's *Syndics of the Drapers' Guild* and Riegl's reading of it are the cornerstones by which Walcott examines the history of Dutch painting and its realization and undoing through its relationships to the Caribbean, the plantation economy, and the transatlantic slave trade. In conclusion, this book examines the ground and the texts surrounding Dutch painting and its mythological foundations, and the ways in which these mythologies continue today in our understanding of capitalism, global trade, the art market, and figuration. These micro-histories unfold in the space between, the words unspoken, the paintings left unpainted. In the words of Lucille Clifton, this book is about an other poem.

CHAPTER ONE

Art Markets and Futures Speculation

Painting in the seventeenth-century Dutch Republic is inseparable from the emergence of a new art market, funded by capital traversing the oceanic highways. Instead of working under a patronage system for state and church, artists developed innovative styles, techniques, and genres, often in consideration of the shifting economic demands of a market formed as much through collectors, auction sales, and dealers as the contingent winds and uncertainties of price, labor, and value.[1] "Real" wealth determined by silver, gold, agriculture, and landed property was increasingly replaced by paper contracts, bonds, bills of sale, shares in overseas trading companies, and the shifting fluctuations of prices on the stock exchange for mace, sugar, pepper, and other goods. With this new trade, the national income per capita rose about 50 percent in Holland between 1580 and 1650.[2] Although the role of the slave trade in generating wealth and the economy in seventeenth-and eighteenth-century Holland has been debated, recently historians have pointed out that the trade led to economic stimulus and profits in parallel sectors, such as shipbuilding, wages for ship crews, and insurance, regardless of direct profits in the global trading companies.[3] Moreover, the new economy was determined by a transformation of labor and commodities into prices on an index. These fundamental shifts in wealth and value transformed seventeenth-century artistic practice as artists' livelihoods were increasingly part of an economy intertwined with plantations in the Americas and the contingent circumstances of stocks and trade. In a short period, Amsterdam transformed from an economy built on Baltic trade and raw materials among northern European states Spain and Portugal to become a central force in an emerging global economy of sugar, spices, textiles, metals, and enslaved labor.[4] As one scholar remarks, Amsterdam went from being a "fishing port" to a "global power" in a matter of decades.[5] Soon the Dutch Republic displayed certain aspects of a modern economy, defined by a competitive market in staple goods, an attention to property rights (for some), and a desire by government and business to support and increase market-oriented consumer behavior.[6]

The wealth of the young republic was founded on innovations in financing long-distance trade. By creating a corporation, the Verenigde Oost-Indische Compagnie (VOC), in 1602, merchants in Amsterdam formed a model that shared the cost and risk of long-haul journeys into Southeast Asia, which also offered a common promise of wealth. Trade in Asia was more expensive than the relatively shorter runs in the Baltic or Atlantic, and the voyages could take years, so investors had to wait to see a return. The formation of the VOC made the ability to invest in the market open to a wider public, and soon after the company was formed, shareholders began selling their shares before even seeing a profit from the initial investment. There were also established rules on ownership and transfer, and subscribers did not have to pay immediately for their shares, thereby allowing greater speculation on future profits.[7] The company also did not immediately pay its shareholders dividends, but continually reinvested the profits of their overseas ventures.

In 1621, the Geoctrooieerde Westindische Compagnie (WIC) was founded to establish dominance over the profitable plantations in Brazil, the Caribbean, and North America, and a triangular trade developed between the VOC and WIC, in which cottons, textiles, and cowrie shells from Southeast Asia became primary goods exchanged for enslaved persons on the west coast of Africa. Between the founding of these two companies, the Amsterdam Bourse was established in 1611, and the Dutch Republic became a bastion of futures trading, or what was known as *windhandel* (trading in the winds). By the eighteenth century, *windhandel* was visually depicted in the export trade through satirical commentary. Two porcelain plates exported from China for Dutch consumers show figures from commedia dell'arte, one of them slapping his bare bottom (figure 1.1). The plates read: *By God, I lost all my shares / Shit shares and fart trade* (*windhandel*).[8] The import of these porcelain wares was made possible by the

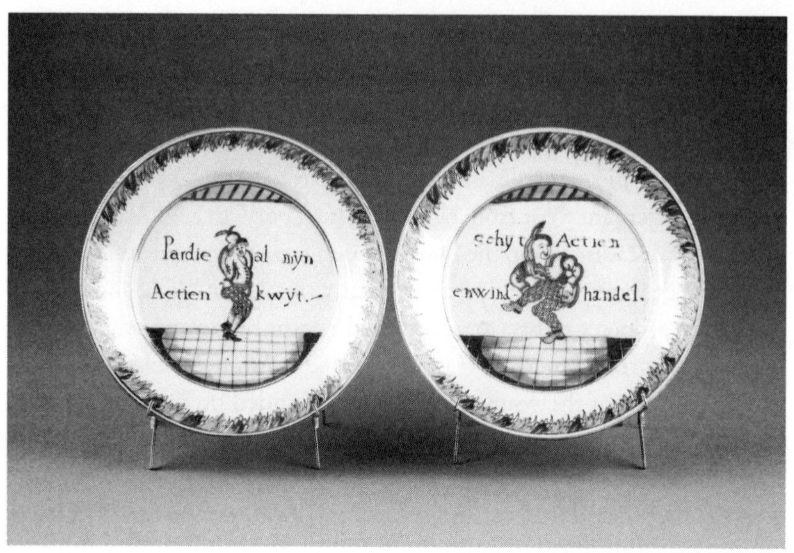

1.1 Anonymous, *Fart Shares and Shit Trade*, ca. 1720. Porcelain plates decorated in underglaze blue, with overglaze colors and gilding. China, Qing dynasty, made for the Netherlandish market (photo: Mohr, Jens, Hallwylska Museet/SHM [CC BY 4.0]/Hallwyl Museum, Stockholm).

economic ventures of the VOC in Asia. In turn, the economic failures of the shareholders and directors of the Dutch East India Company became integrated into the market, so that the satirical exported plates became part of the commodity cycles that created the shit shares and fart trade.

The plates critique *windhandel* while also being part of the circulation of commodities that depended on the economic ventures of uncertain capital for their existence. Yet before these later crises, *windhandel* was a central catalyst of the Dutch economy, primarily developed around speculation on commodities.[9] This uncertainty in value between the imaginary and the real becomes the subject of anxiety in merchant Joseph de la Vega's *Confusión de confusiones* (*Confusion of Confusions*), which was published in Amsterdam in 1688. In his book, de la Vega tells the origin story of the Amsterdam stock market through a series of dialogues among a merchant, philosopher, and shareholder. As the shareholder explains to his companions on the origins of the stock market: "Several ships were built and in 1604 were sent out to seek adventure Quixote-like in the East Indies.... The ships sailed their courses without encountering windmills or enchanted giants. Their successful voyages, their victorious conquests, and the rich return of the cargoes meant that Caesar's *veni, vidi, vici* was surpassed and that a tidy profit was made—which became a stimulus to further undertakings."[10] In this dialogue, the shareholder explains: "You should not come to the conclusion that the movements of the stock exchange are inexplicable and that nothing is firm[;] take note and realize that there are three causes of a rise in prices on the exchange and three of a fall: the conditions in India, European politics, and opinion on the stock exchange itself." Moreover, the shareholder clarifies the interrelated economies of the slave trade and stocks when he describes how "a few Dutch merchants" transport from Curaçao "as many Negroes as the Company is able to carry from the coast of Guinea" to sell to the Spanish in the West Indies. The Spanish were necessary for the success of this trade, as the share price depended on peace and "the security of the state."[11] De la Vega's text stands as the first history of the stock market, capturing the financial uncertainty of the seventeenth-century republic as mobile property, stocks, bonds, and shares began to replace historical models of landed or real property. Recently, scholars have begun to consider the role of the slave trade in the economic boom that catapulted Holland into becoming one of the first "modern economies."[12]

During this critical period, shareholders and the stock exchange came to dominate the art market, introducing radical shifts in property and value to artistic practice. One artist in particular, Hercules Segers (ca. 1589–ca. 1638), directly engaged with the specter of maritime capital in his artistic output. In turn, his contemporary biographer displayed an artist struggling to adapt to a new economic system. A consideration of the specter of maritime space in Segers's work engages with how the emerging liquid economy impacted art as an asset in relation to the novel financial models underpinned by a developing plantation economy. Most importantly, the careers of Segers and his successor Rembrandt illustrate the contradictions in a republican society founded on the ideal of freedom and liberty (both from the tyranny of the Spanish and the development of free trade) while also engaging in empire building, which depended on suppression and enslavement.[13] The economic downturns of both Segers's and Rembrandt's careers reveal the complications of a new form of artistic identity that developed in relation to the art market and free trade, a commodification of personhood that occurred in tandem with the rise of the transatlantic slave trade.

In a series of printed images, the hulls and masts of ships are lodged within mountainous geological landscapes. In one etching, a ship's hull is caught in the mountains, like a marine fossil. The smooth and curved lines of wooden planks project against the sky (plate 3).[14] The ship exists as a palimpsestic presence in the landscape, a form from a previous etching that persisted when Segers cut a larger plate into smaller matrices. Segers reused the precious copper, but he did not entirely efface the earlier etching, and traces of the ship persist in the new landscape, so that maritime capital haunts the desolate mountains. The palimpsestic printing of ships in landscape runs as a minor theme throughout his surviving work, as he played with layering fragments of maritime scenes into mountainous landscapes. In another etching, Segers left the rigging of a ship in a moss-laden tree (plate 4).[15] The ravaged remains of a fence mark the foreground. In the fallow field, the geometric lines of the rigging are lodged within the branches of a tree, morphing into lichen. The tree itself intrudes, out of scale, not planted but placed incongruously atop a hillock. And from its stumpy trunk—at once blurred and textured—emerge branches scribbled with moss, entangled with a ship's rigging. In another etching, *Landscape with a Waterfall*, Segers cuts the surface of the matrix with the parabola of the sail and the taut lines of mast and ropes, so that the geometric precision of the maritime world interrupts the geological density of the landscape (plate 5).[16] From these surviving works, the oceanic world and its piratical excesses haunt Segers's prints, like a ghost, a body that refuses to dematerialize. The human precision of ship construction contrasts with the random rhythm of geology, reminding the viewer of the precise lines cast by grids, mariners, and sea charts.

The images of displaced and destroyed ships are not only analogical forms of failed conveyance but also physical realities portending financial ruin on the stock exchange, a turn of *fortuna* that structures Segers's seventeenth-century biography by Samuel van Hoogstraten (1627–78), "How an Artist Should Conduct Himself against the Blows of Fortune."[17] With this title, Hoogstraten situates Segers within an uncertain maritime economy, in which fortunes were easily won and lost. Reading Van Hoogstraten's biography of Segers beside this collection of palimpsestic maritime prints, in which the seaborne economy of Amsterdam haunts his landscapes, reveals a narrative about the impact of capital's emergent power on the artistic persona. The manmade heterotopic wooden atoms that crossed the seas, becoming the primary vehicle in Amsterdam's economic rise as a global power, haunt Segers's landscapes, pointing toward the repeated trials to make visible a labor and market that was increasingly invisible and contingent as the Dutch Republic transformed from a local to a global economy.

While it may be easy to dismiss the survival of these prints haunted by naval excess as accidental, they demand further examination. The maritime world influenced the financial markets and created precarious existences defined by the vagaries of speculation on imaginary goods, as well as on a dematerialization of labor, commodities, and the surface on which they all traversed: the ocean. Segers and his fellow artists were actively engaged in the transition to a model of wealth founded on the art market as a form of speculation, as Segers was also an active art dealer. Jaap van der Veen speculates that his own works formed a significant part of his stock, although he also traded in other artists.[18] In 1631, Segers sold a collection of paintings to the merchant Jean Antonio Romiti, who likely sold this same lot of works (137 paintings) to another merchant, Johannes de Renialme, in 1640. In turn, a second document survives from the end of Segers's life also involving a large transaction of paintings; both documents point toward his work as an art dealer, although "apparently with little success."[19]

Segers was celebrated, however, as an innovator in process and an exemplar of economic ingenuity. Historian John Michael Montias describes the art market in Amsterdam within the model of "process and product innovation." Painting and printmaking (like any other commodity) transforms "labor, capital, land" into an object for the market, in which the economic value is determined by supply and demand.[20] Product innovation creates an entirely new object, like the invention of small, portable landscape paintings. In turn, process innovation finds new ways to efficiently produce the new commodity, as in the seventeenth-century painter Jan van Goyen's investment in cheaper pigments and ground preparation to make paintings defined by muted tones and rapidly sketched skies, land, and seas. In the seventeenth-century art market, works that saved on the expense of labor and materials were, perhaps paradoxically, increasingly valued.[21] Huigen Leeflang maintains that Segers was an innovator in process, as his prints imitated popular watercolors that dominated the art market in Amsterdam, a genre imported from the Southern Netherlands by Flemish immigrants, fleeing economic collapse and religious intolerance.[22] Instead of painting watercolors, Segers emulated these watercolors by printing reproductions that he made unique through the variation of applied paint, color, and ground, mimicking the aesthetic of the popular watercolors. Art theorist Van Hoogstraten specifically mentions Segers in this capacity: "And it is understandable, if it were possible to print finished paintings, as Hercules Segers has done with landscapes in our time, that it would no longer be easy to find anyone who would want to devote much labor and time to producing his works."[23] Van Hoogstraten valued Segers's works not for the time and labor necessary to produce the final commodity but instead for the innovative processes that they represented in creating difference through economically efficient repetition.

Segers's palimpsestic images of ships are often understood within this context, as scholars maintain that he would have painted over the intrusive ships had he not died. Instead of taking the time to burnish the original copper plate, he allowed the deeply etched forms to impress into his new landscapes, knowing that he would erase them with paint in the final image.[24] Yet even if these landscapes haunted by ships are unfinished, they remain (like the ships themselves) as spectral embodiments of his artistic practice.[25] While it might be easy to dismiss the survival of these prints haunted by naval and artistic excess as accidental, they engage with the specter of seafaring finance and capital in the young republic. For it is within this world of commodities and financial speculation that Van Hoogstraten presents Segers's prints as moving in relation to other goods. In one of the most oft-quoted lines from the biography, Van Hoogstraten writes: "No one wanted to look at his works in his lifetime: the printers took his prints by the basketful to the sellers of fats to wrap butter and soap, and most of them ended up as twists for pepper." In his equation of Segers's prints to wrapping paper and the paper used to package other goods, such as butter, soap, and pepper, Van Hoogstraten extends the economic capital of Segers's prints beyond the art market into fats and spices, a circle of exchange, in which scraps of paper were continually reused to light pipes, wipe shit, and wrap other goods.[26] He also situates Segers's prints within the culture of iconoclasm brought on by the Reformation, in which defaced and torn pages from religious manuscripts and books were often used to serve cakes, scrub candlesticks, clean boots, and, as with Segers's prints, sold to the grocers as wrapping paper.[27]

Segers's inability to realize the value of his prints on the art market, however, becomes clear in the biography's final excerpt, as Van Hoogstraten explains that Segers took his plate to an art dealer only to discover that there was no market for his works: "Eventually he showed a plate, his ultimate masterpiece, to an art dealer in Amsterdam, offering it for very little money, but what happened? The dealer complained that there was no market for his works, and hardly thought it worthwhile even to pay the price of the copper. The wretched Hercules had to go home, disconsolate, taking his plate with him. After pulling a few prints from it, he cut it into pieces, saying that art lovers would come and would pay four times more for one impression than he had asked for the whole plate."[28] The recycling of the copper plate becomes not only a means to economize on materials but also a method by which to create market scarcity for his printed works, thereby increasing their value. Here, Segers speculates on a future in which his prints would become valuable, partially because the matrix was destroyed and they existed in limited quantities. It is tempting to connect this passage to his maritime shipwreck prints, which are created from a matrix cut into pieces. This suggestion remains tendentious, yet the biography offers a model by which to understand his palimpsestic prints within the context of the art market. His recycled matrix becomes more than a workshop practice founded in efficient methods of production. By making the original print barely visible, Segers alludes to a destroyed matrix, an unattainable print surfacing within the layers of the current impression. Through the palimpsestic print, he imagines a market in which collectors will pay huge sums for singular impressions—a market mirrored in ships wrecked or lodged at the bottom of the ocean. Like ships and their precious cargoes lost at sea, the absence of those commodities could increase the value of the goods in circulation. In turn, Segers's destruction of his original matrix was akin to a shipwreck, removing from circulation certain goods (printed reproductions) to drive up the value of the prints in circulation. The ghostly image of a previous work that no longer exists creates a desire for an unattainable print, driving up the value of his work in circulation.

The bodies of the shipwrecked vessels also allude to the other commodities lost, just as the original matrix and its accompanying impressions were destroyed. The haul of goods, such as the *Witte Leeuw* porcelain, sank to the ocean floor only to become transformed by the sea life residing beyond the oxygenated atmosphere of humans, a metamorphosis revealed when the shipwreck's cargo was brought to the surface in the twentieth century bearing the salty sea and encrustations of barnacles (figure 1.2). Segers's palimpsestic prints make visible an economy founded on the precarity of speculation on the future return of goods that may be destroyed, lost, or transformed, an economy dependent on the paper insurance contract. Segers's foresight in destroying his matrix realizes an economic market

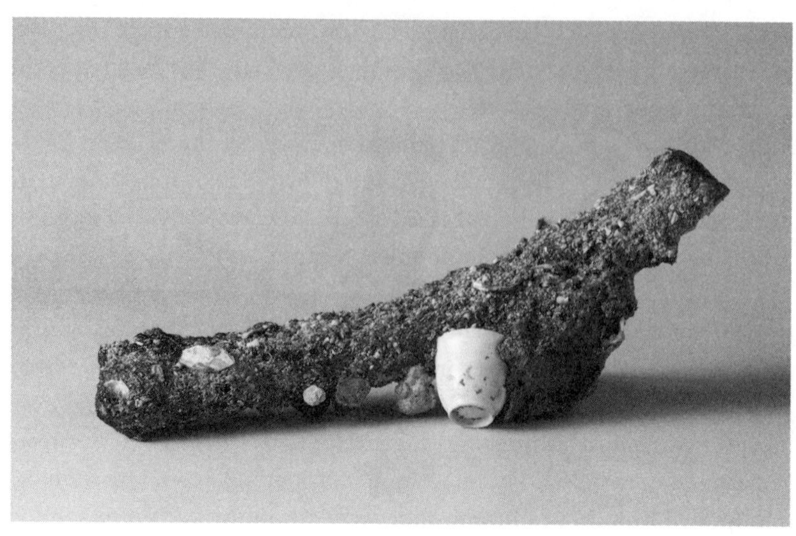

1.2 Anonymous (time and the sea), *Porcelain and Pepper from the VOC-Trading Ship the* Witte Leeuw, before 1613 (Rijksmuseum, Amsterdam).

in which the paper goods in circulation outweigh in value the commodities of copper, pepper, sugar, and lives. Segers speculated on his future self as a valuable commodity that would be worth more than the cost of materials, such as copper, particularly in death. He realized the speculative financial possibilities of death.

In his own lifetime, however, the economic mobility of his prints as commodities demonstrates the difficulty in transforming from an economy based on real property (land and gold) to one founded on the imaginary value of stocks, bonds, bills of exchange, and insured property. In Segers's biography, print becomes another good to be speculated on, traded, and valued. The haunting maritime seascapes buried in his landscapes materialize the futures trading founded on ocean commerce. As the bodies and lives of people, goods, and labor were increasingly divested of their materiality to become goods on an open exchange and prices on an index for speculation, profit, and shareholding, the traces of Segers's process in his palimpsestic prints refused the erasure of his labor. Yet where Segers failed during his lifetime to make his work economically viable (according to his biographer), his successor Rembrandt succeeded. Nevertheless, Rembrandt was also economically ruined by poor business decisions and "losses at sea." The translation of artistic practice to an art market that was part of an economy based on free trade has been formative to interpretations of Rembrandt's workshop. Yet the tension between free trade and enslavement, while recognized in the seventeenth century, has yet to be considered for the development of the art market in the young republic and its impact on artistic models of competition and innovation.

Freedom

The term *vrijheid* (translated as freedom or liberty) was central to seventeenth-century Dutch political language, as the republic celebrated its freedom from the Spanish monarchy and its tyranny. The rhetoric surrounding the Spanish occupation often likened the Dutch to the enslaved and the Spanish to tyrannical overlords. In the Treaty of the Union from 1579, the Spaniards "bring these provinces wholly or partly into subjection under their tyrannical government and into slavery."[29] Or as the Prince of Orange wrote to the king of Spain in 1573, "we would rather die an honest death for the freedom and prosperity of our fatherland than be reduced to slavery and be trampled on by wanton foreigners, who have always displayed hatred and displeasure towards us."[30] In turn, Dutch humanists and later political theorists drew parallels between the Spanish occupation of the Americas and the occupation of the Low Countries, realizing the ethical danger of conquest and its constriction on liberty. Justus Lipsius, for example, decried Spanish conquest of the Americas as central to the monarchy's downfall and cupidity.[31] In Caspar Barlaeus's panegyric to the brief Dutch occupation of Brazil, he also recognized the contradiction of decrying tyranny while engaging in the trade of humans as chattel property: "We as well have returned to the practice of buying and selling man, even though he is the image of God and redeemed by Christ, the master of the universe, and anything but a slave because of a fault of nature or intellect."[32] The humanists and later political theorists of the Dutch Republic, therefore, were not oblivious to the tension in their own rhetoric between freedom and enslavement or to an economy increasingly dependent on the enslavement of others in distant plantations. Nevertheless, the free market ideology of the young republic has been written about as a model for artistic innovation by contemporary historians.

While the contradiction of a free market dependent on enslaved labor was discussed in some writings, others depended on antique models of enslavement by which to extrapolate on their political position while ignoring contemporary economic realities. Pieter de la Court (1618–85), who argued for limited governmental regulation of trade, likened the monarch to the Egyptians who enslaved Moses and his people. By contrast, De la Court celebrated the Sydonians who set their city on fire instead of being enslaved by the Persians. Like many prominent Dutch merchants, De la Court had familial ties to the plantations in the Americas, as his cousin Nicolaas was based in Curaçao, a stronghold of the Dutch slave trade. Yet the contemporaneity of the slave trade remains absent in his political rhetoric, based within a European republican tradition of decrying monarchy, often through the figure of the enslaved in antiquity.

This model of economic freedom celebrated by De la Court, in which the contemporary reality of slavery for the plantation economies in the Americas remains absent, was formative for Svetlana Alpers in her reading of Rembrandt's workshop.[33] Often citing De la Court in her reading of Rembrandt and his interpretation of *vrijheid*, Alpers maintained that the market was a system of representation, a process of dematerializing and abstracting the physical world only to remodel it into a new system of forms that could stand in for the physical world: "If, understood one way, the market is an emptying out, understood another way it marks the establishment of a system of representation." Rembrandt formed this new system by creating a "brand," an innovative process of efficient production realized in his workshop that still plays out in the art market today, as connoisseurs and auction houses debate attributions to Rembrandt, to one of his students, or to Rembrandt and Workshop. In creating a corporation of his self, Alpers argues, Rembrandt made John Locke's right to "property in one's own person" central not only to himself but also to "the center of his art—the center, even, of Art."[34] While scholars have argued with Alpers's reading, it remains a brilliant interpretation and relevant for the field of seventeenth-century Dutch painting, which is often celebrated as the first art market and global economy. Yet this reading of property in "one's own person" cannot be disentangled from an economy dependent on also denying the rights of property in one's own person to certain populations.

Rembrandt, in particular, is famous for his bankruptcy, which according to the legal documents was "losses suffered in business, as well as damages and losses at sea." Montias postulates that these losses at sea occurred in conjunction with Rembrandt's investment in a shipping venture with the auction buyer Marten van den Broeck, who traded pearls, cloth, and paintings (including at least four of Rembrandt's) for shipping equipment.[35] In return, Van den Broeck invested in tobacco in Barbados and land on Staten

Island near Nieuw Amsterdam. Montias's suggestion demonstrates how paintings moved in tandem with other goods and land in the Americas, revealing the close economic connections of Rembrandt's collectors and patrons with the plantation economies in the Americas, literally trading Rembrandt's paintings for shares in tobacco plantations. While Segers's prints circulated in an economy of butter and pepper, Rembrandt's paintings were traded in a circuit of goods extant with tobacco, Indigenous land, and enslaved individuals.[36] The elusive model of representation offered by the markets in Holland created a chimera world of commodities and exchange in which valuable and singular prints became wrapping paper for butter and pepper, and paintings moved in a network of exchange with pearls and tobacco. This constantly shifting world of value was born in relation to the plantation economies of the Americas and Asia, part of an economic system that dematerialized labor, even artistic practice, ultimately making the violence of the emergent economy almost, but never completely, imperceptible.

Segers's or Rembrandt's awareness of the ethical and human cost of enslavement remains uncertain, although their contemporaries, such as Barlaeus, condemned the practice of slavery. Its role in forming the art markets to which both artists were indebted was also likely invisible to them, although Rembrandt possibly speculated in commodities produced through enslaved labor. Yet the historiography of both artists, from Van Hoogstraten to Alpers, engages with the impact of novel economic models on artistic practice. Nevertheless, Alpers's celebration of the free market as central to Rembrandt's creation of the artistic self demonstrates a blind spot in studies of seventeenth-century Dutch art, which have not grappled with how the liberty given to artists in the new art markets was indebted to the rise of trading humans as chattel property. The invention of artistic freedom and the right to monetize the self cannot be disentangled from the historical period in which enslavement informed the main European economies. This history, in which art became a means to market the artist for public enjoyment to circulate in relation to other stocks, bonds, and commodities, commences in the biographies of Segers and Rembrandt. The historiography surrounding both artists demonstrates the cost of working for the first art market determined by a global economy, a practice in which fortune remains fickle, and freedom and enslavement are the Janus-faced coin of history.

CHAPTER TWO

Seascapes and Landscapes

In a sixteenth-century treatise on navigation, *Circles of Proportion*, English mathematician William Oughtred (1574–1660) states that pilots should collaborate with artists to record "the secret motions or agitations of the seas, when they begin and how long they continue, how farre they extend, and with what inequality."[1] In one of the most well-known surviving seventeenth-century maritime sketchbooks, this process of discernment and collaboration is displayed, as Frans Post and a cotraveler with some nautical knowledge document the sea and the surrounding atmosphere.[2]

The drawings are a mastery of pen and wash while also containing rudimentary mistakes in ship portraiture and other details that would have been known to a maritime draftsman. In turn, each paper has an inscription with information specific to a pilot's logbook, such as mileage or the type of wind blowing. Although he did not sign the surviving drawings, they have been attributed to Post, while the annotator remains anonymous. The drawings testify to the limits of visibility at sea, as both artist and copilot engaged with their specific tools to determine the landmasses rising up before them as they sailed along the coastal waters of the Canary Islands, Tenerife, and Cape Verde. With ink and watered pigment, Post formed nebulous bodies of land and cloud. In turn, the inscriptions temporally and spatially situate the draftsman and the annotator as they track their perceptions over the space of about two weeks.

The drawings were produced from December 1636 into January 1637 as Johan Maurits (1604–79) and his crew sailed across the Atlantic to control the lucrative sugar plantations in the northeast of Brazil.[3] Post and his pilot were likely producing coastal surveys for their patron Maurits, documenting islands and waters of strategic interest.[4] Both the Canary Islands and Cape Verde were controlled by the Portuguese and Spanish and played vital roles in the emergence of the transatlantic slave trade and the movement of valuable commodities, such as salt, also called white gold. In 1637, Johan Maurits captured Elmina, a fort on Africa's Gold Coast that was central to the Portuguese slave trade. In 1641, he captured Luanda and Sâo Tomé and thereby solidified the Dutch as a central transatlantic power. The Dutch retained control of the Angolan territory for only a year, but they maintained their stronghold on Elmina until 1872, when they sold it to the British.

While this history is central to contextualizing the maritime drawings, it also refutes a clear alignment with the tradition of the drawn military survey and coastal map, for the drawings are a failure according to the standards set in many prominent handbooks, such as Lucas Jansz. Wagenaer's *Der Spieghel der Zeevaerdt* (1583–84), in which he stresses the necessity of clarity in illustrations, so that "every mark on the land may be clearly and evidently perceived." In contrast, the sketchbook captures the meteoric conditions that informed the lack of visibility at sea, the opaque fluctuating clouds that obscured the fixed bodies of land while the mariner demarcated distances, depths, and winds with nautical instruments. This sketchbook presents the unstable perception of land, water, and air, demonstrating how the process of vision while sailing in coastal waters is a constant interchange of movement, in which monuments and markers come in and out of sight.[5]

In the first drawing of the series, the volcanic crust of Madeira (figure 2.1) emerges against the horizon. The sketch would verge on the formless were it not for the accompanying inscription: *Eerste Ghesicht van Madera* (*First Sight of Madeira*), a title that names the low-profile stretch of form contrasted with stronger striations of gray wash demarcating water. From this first marking of earth, Post tracked the island's perceptibility throughout the day. The accompanying inscription on the third drawing (figure 2.2) explains that the island was only partially visible because of the movements of clouds: "On 19th December, we approached Madeira Island, and it was partially covered by clouds to the southeast, as portrayed here."

The tension between meteoric conditions and visibility continues throughout the day, as evidenced by the next sketch (figure 2.3): "On the

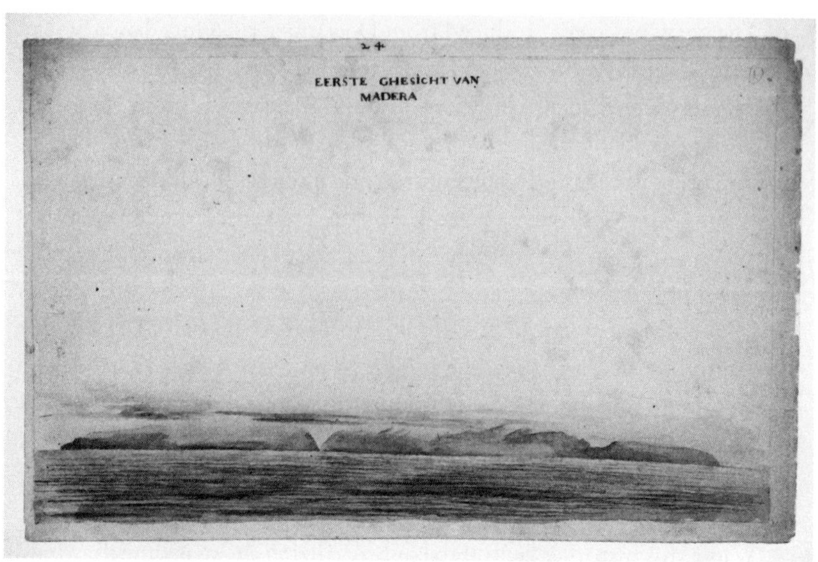

2.1 Frans Post and copilot, *First Sight of Madeira*, pen and black wash on paper, 1636, object number A.3457(01) (Het Scheepvaartmuseum/ National Maritime Museum, Amsterdam).

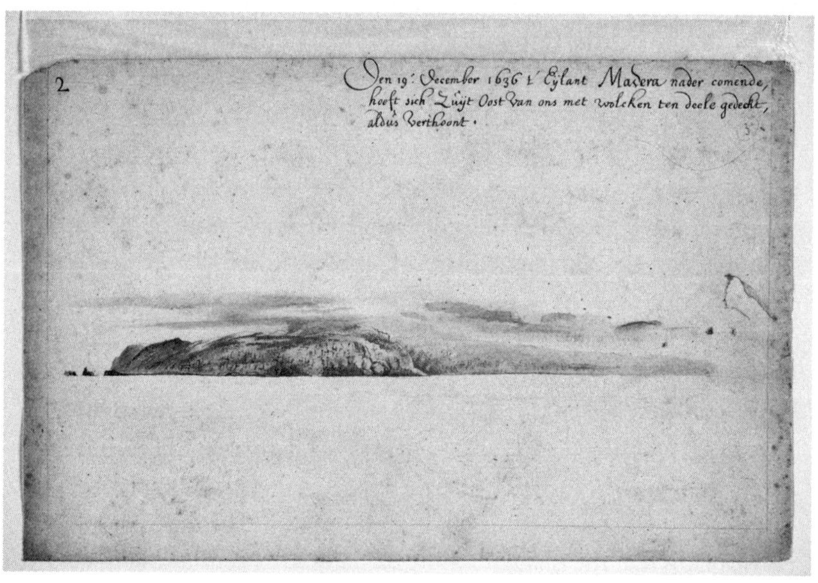

2.2 Frans Post and copilot, *Madeira Partially Covered in Clouds*, 1636. Pen and black wash on paper, object number A.3457(03) (Het Scheepvaartmuseum/ National Maritime Museum, Amsterdam).

same day, Madeira Island was totally covered by clouds." In this drawing, however, Post did not draw an island made invisible by clouds. Instead, he smudged a band of translucent wash through the island's center while rendering a more detailed rendition of its outer peripheries. This slight difference between the annotation and the drawing demonstrates the process by which two different perceptions come together on a single page. The discrepancy between the drawing and the inscription, while slight, points toward the temporal progression of losing or gaining sight as details emerge against the blur marking the island's center. The veiling of the islands through cloud banks continued on December 22, as the ship approached Palma (figure 2.4): "Position at 28 degrees, 46 minutes, approximately 15 miles out to sea, the island is covered by clouds." On December 25 the pilot writes, "We saw the Island of Grand Canary, situated at 28 degrees, 14 miles and 20 minutes to our east, totally covered by clouds" (figure 2.5).

These drawings belong to an established tradition of maritime draftsmanship known as the rutter, a manual dedicated to coastal seafaring. In 1520 Pierre Garcie published the first printed rutter with woodblock illustrations of coastlines (figure 2.6). Although the thick black lines of Garcie's prints differ from Post's drawings, they both confront the difficulty of seeing at sea. As David Waters argues, the profile views in Garcie's book are exaggerated caricatures to "impress on the seaman's eye."[6] The overemphasis of form was necessary, as the pilot would consult the illustrations under conditions of poor visibility, like those recorded by Post's copilot. Nevertheless, unlike the fixed renditions in Garcie's manual, Post's and his pilot's drawings show a fascination with the lack of fixity at sea. In the sketches made during Post's journey to Brazil, he and his cotraveler present the gathering of knowledge at sea as fragmentary, uncertain, and often obscured. The pilot and draftsman documented their partial observations to form a more complete view, demonstrating how contestations around depth, salinity, and phosphorescence demanded multiple forms of investigation. The sketches were produced not only by Post's eye and hand with paper and graphite, but also with the navigational tools of the pilot: compasses and deadweights, knowledge of stars and winds.[7] The two forms of notation exist beside each other, but they do not form a single work. The materials of the draftsman, dominated by watery gray wash and charcoal, are distinct from the linear scrawl of the pilot's pen.

As the seemingly infinite and borderless horizon of oceanic space began to dominate legal and trade discourse of the seventeenth century, it also became a site by which to extrapolate on the uncertainty of knowledge.

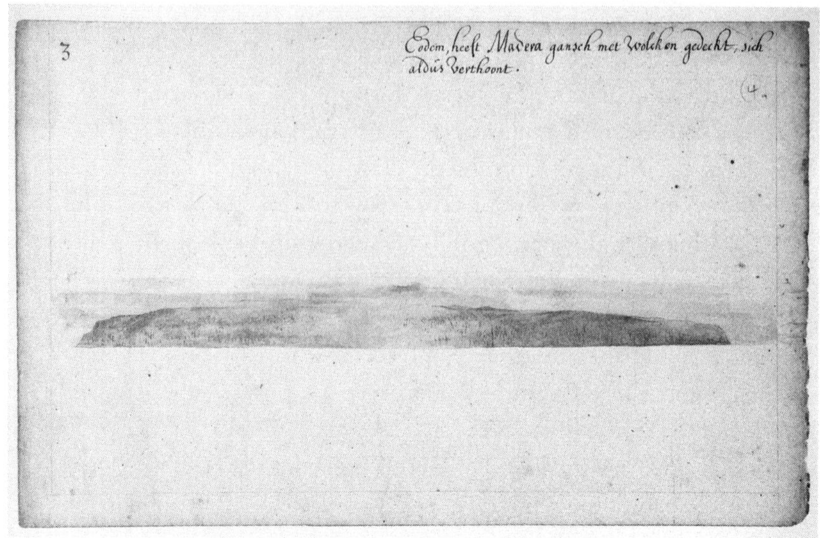

2.3 Frans Post and copilot, *Madeira Completely Covered in Clouds*, 1636. Pen and black wash on paper, object number A.3457(04) (Het Scheepvaartmuseum/ National Maritime Museum, Amsterdam).

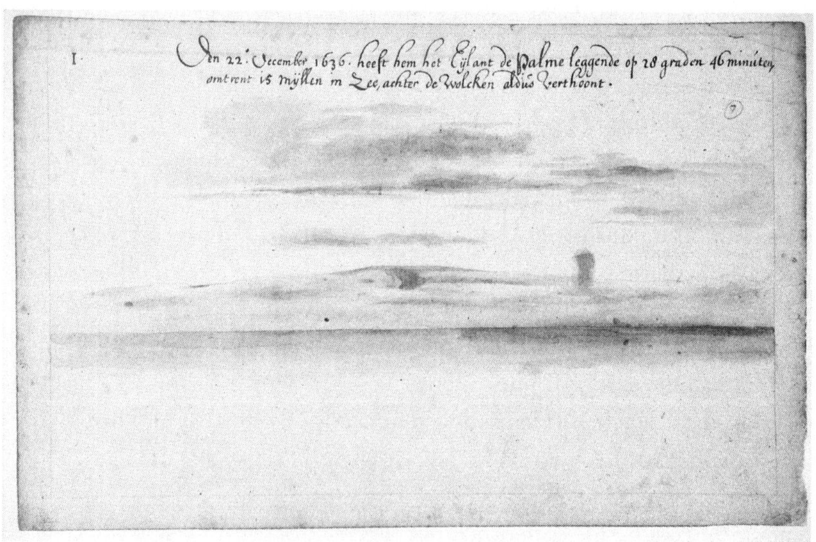

2.4 Frans Post and copilot, *Palma Completely Covered in Clouds*, 1636. Pen and black wash on paper, object number A.3457(07) (Het Scheepvaartmuseum/ National Maritime Museum, Amsterdam).

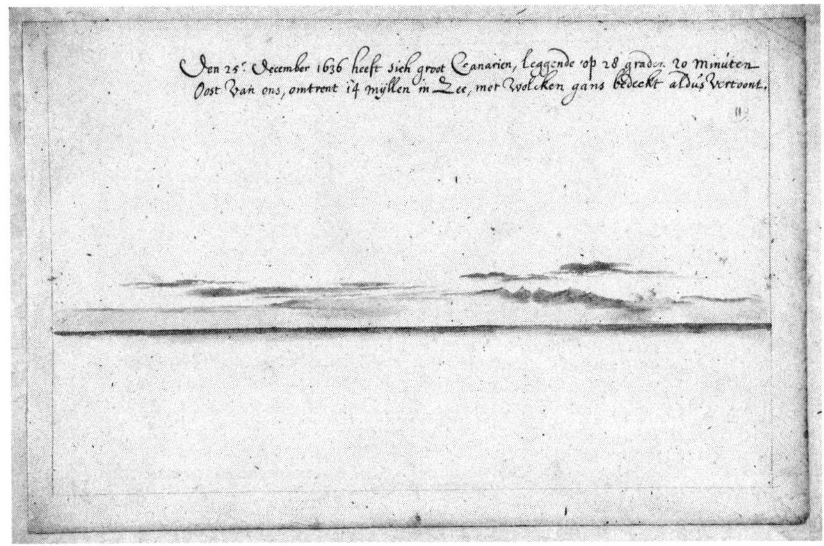

2.5 Frans Post and copilot, *Grand Canary Completely Covered in Clouds*, 1636. Pen and black wash on paper, object number A.3457(11) (Het Scheepvaartmuseum/ National Maritime Museum, Amsterdam).

In a treatise, *The Hidden Qualities of the Air*, Robert Boyle (1627–91) frequently draws on the knowledge gathered at sea to problematize the acquisition of facts collected through the faulty apparatus of human perception.[8] The level of the sea, for example, made the measurement of mountains uncertain. Although Tenerife was thought to have the highest mountain peak, Boyle realized that the measurement of mountains was relative to the height of the ground (or water) on which one stands: "And so the pic of *Teneriff* being looked upon from the level of the sea, may be much less high than some other hills, which yet protuberating above the level part of some country, which is itself generally exceeding high, may have its top more remote from the centre of the earth, than that of the pic, and would appear higher that it, if as well the one as the other were looked upon from the same superficies of the sea." In turn, Boyle likened scientific trial to navigation, so that the young scientist becomes a pilot in unknown seas. Boyle defines vision at sea as an uncertain process, noting that when pilots "first discerned something obscure near the horizon, at a great distance off, have often doubted, whether what they had so imperfect a sight of, were a cloud, or an island, or a mountain." This imperfect sight must be pursued, however, in hopes of discovery: "for if it were a deluding meteor, they

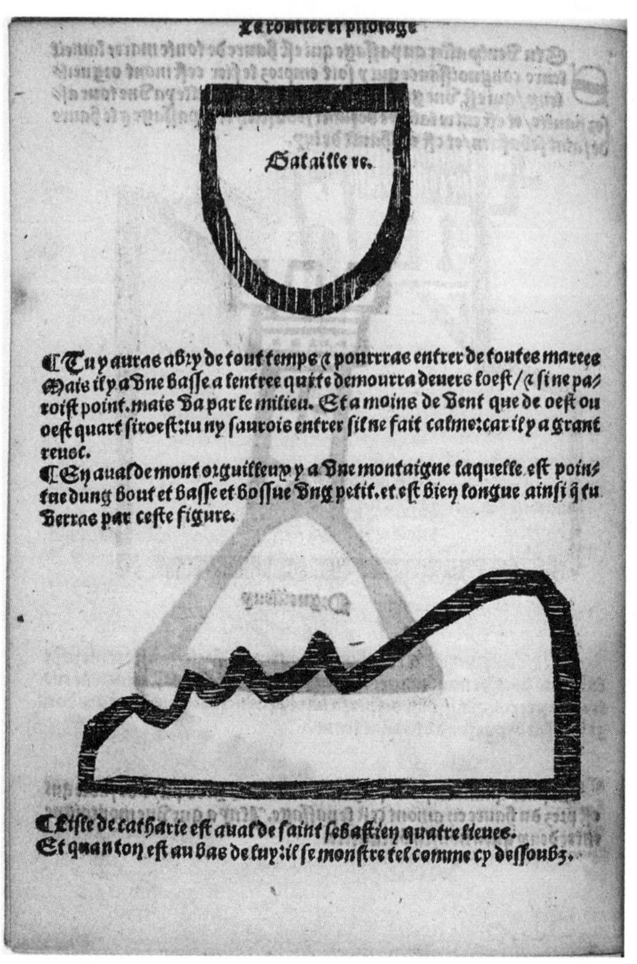

2.6 Pierre Garcie, *Le Grant routier et pilotage et enseignement pour ancrer tant ès ports, havres que autres lieux de la mer* (Rouen: J. Burges, 1531; Bibliothèque nationale de France).

would not however sustain so great a loss in that of a little labour, as, in case it were a country, they would in the loss of what might prove a rich discovery: and if they desisted not too soon from their curiosity, they could not rationally satisfy themselves, whether they sighted a cloud, or a neglected a country."[9] In Boyle's writing, the insights of natural philosophy are likened to the capital won from the exploitation of a "neglected" country's soil, labor, and resources, displaying no separation among the merchant's trade, exploitation, and the natural philosopher. Boyle also captures a crisis in sensory perception at sea. The ability to measure land becomes relative

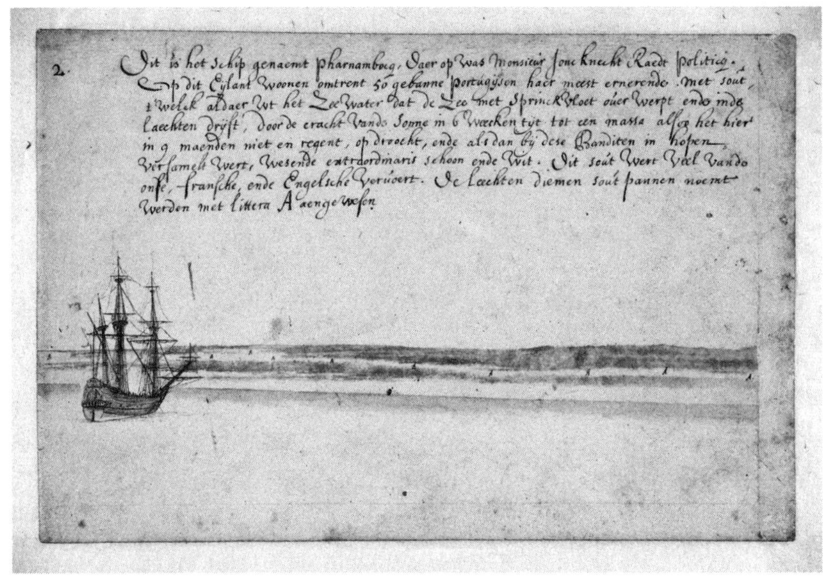

2.7 Frans Post and copilot, *Salt Flats*, 1636. Pen and black wash on paper, object number A.3490(05) (Het Scheepvaartmuseum/National Maritime Museum, Amsterdam).

depending on the position of the surveyor, and the act of coastal seafaring creates a set of conditions in which clouds and land become interchangeable, both rising and descending into the surface of the sea.

Drafted earlier in the seventeenth century, Post's drawings capture the uncertainty between clouds and "neglected countries." This crux of Post's representational practice coalesces within a drawing depicting the salt flats on the island of Maio, an inhospitable landscape home to an exiled labor force. Post and his copilot were no doubt acutely aware that the salt flats were a desired colonial outpost for the Dutch to control the salt trade. Nevertheless, Post's drawing practice grounds itself within the atmosphere, while allowing his cotraveler to record the economic and labor conditions of the island. In this drawing, Post renders a ship anchored off the coast, while repetitions of the letter *A* demarcate the salt pans (figure 2.7). The inscription states: "About 50 banished Portuguese live on the island, most of whom work with salt washed ashore during high tides and drained into the lagoons. Due to the intense heat, in six weeks this high-salt water is transformed into a dry mass—since it hasn't rained in nine months on the island—and the remaining salt is collected on to piles by the outlaws. The salt is extraordinarily clean and white, and it is transported by us, by the

French and the English. The lagoons, called salt pans, are marked with the letter 'A.'"[10]

The accurate depiction of cultivating salt by forced labor is absented from the languid execution of land. Without the inscription, the drawing would illustrate a ship anchored off a coastline. With the textual addition, the drawing becomes a picture of the lucrative salt industry and the forced labor that made it possible. In the empty space between the writing and the drawing, the salt industry becomes unrepresentable (demarcated by the letter *A*), and salt translates into an invisible commodity moving along the empty space of the waters, as frictionless and white as the paper itself, dissolved into the oceanic space that formed the waterways toward Dutch prosperity. The demarcation across the drawing with the letter *A* belongs within a tradition of landscape, print, and mapmaking, in which letters often marked coordinates and textual interpolations that would become integral to a final printed version. Yet this drawing was never printed, and conditions of forced labor for exiled populations were rarely, if ever, widely circulated in early modern landscape prints.

This drawing also portends the enslaved labor for salt that would come to define the Caribbean and New World economies for the Dutch in the later seventeenth century, and that already defined the economy in the Cape Verde islands.[11] Post's attention to the coastlines derived from the strategic potential and importance of the islands to Dutch interests in dominating the transatlantic trade in sugar, salt, and slaves. During Post's lifetime, the Spanish refused the Dutch access to the salt and sugar markets in the early decades of the seventeenth century, only increasing the desire for overseas expansion and the motivation for settler-colonial ventures, such as Johan Maurits's tenure in Brazil.[12] Post's drawings of the archipelagoes and their coastlines on the journey to Brazil are not neutral accounts of landscape profiles but belong within a larger history of art that grapples with the corrosive impact of salt mining and enslaved labor across the Caribbean diaspora.

This history comes full circle in the work of contemporary artist Ellen Gallagher, who engages with her family's history in the Cape Verde islands, where her grandparents were born. In works such as *Bird in Hand*, Gallagher forms the mythological figure of a pirate, with not only oil paint and canvas but also gold and salt, making materially palpable two commodities that dominated European economic interest in West Africa and its islands (plate 6). The body of the seafarer is built from encrustations of paper, rock salt, and gold, his corporeal composition refusing the transubstantiation that Marx postulated as central to capital. Instead, the materials of salt and gold do not transform into an indexical value or become reduced to a letter on a picture—such as the letter *A* in Post's drawing. Their material form refuses to disintegrate on the final pictorial plane. Gallagher concretizes in salt and gold a history of labor and exploitation that was abstracted into a study of atmospheric conditions and the uncertainty of perception in Post's drawings.[13]

Post's sketchbook with both drawings and anonymous notations articulates the ways in which images, information, and data could travel in the early modern world beside one another. The barely there renderings of sighted land in Post's drawings become grounded in time and space with the notations of his copilot. The textual additions to the drawings explicate while also offering detailed accounts of landscape, labor, and conditions, which remain omitted within Post's drawings. In this planar understanding, I draw on Eve Kosofsky Sedgwick's concept of *besideness*, which evokes not an equality among the finite parts but a variety of relations.[14] In besideness, Sedgwick makes room for a formation of ideas grounded in an ambivalent materialization of multiple desires and aversions that coexist. For Post, his perception of the sea and the land is inscribed within the relationship between his eye and hand, a register that reveals his frequent inability to demarcate land from cloud. In turn, the pilot remains at the level of linguistic and mathematical notation, taking in the wind, water, stars, and their position in regard to the ship and his own body. The sketches capture a tension between the pilot and the draftsman as they relegate their perceptual experiences of the islands to their respective media of charcoal, wash, paper, and time, winds, and depth. The notations of the copilot and of Post share the same page, but they are also discrete modes of note taking. They could exist separated from one another (as drawing and as data), yet they share the same page. The goals of Post and the pilot are removed from one another, as the draftsman captures the immediate, intuitive perception of the island's profile, while the pilot measures depths, distances, and meteoric conditions. Although Post's desire to see is blocked by the weather, the pilot's tools and nautical knowledge allow for a clearer assessment of the conditions. Moreover, to sail along coastlines is a matter of working beside the land, which demands an ever-changing point of view as the ship orients itself against the constellations, the winds, and the tides. Sailing along coastlines is a navigational besideness, using the shapes of landmasses to pilot, a form of mapping that requires an ability to think beside: both ship beside land and draftsman beside pilot, as competing views come in and out of sight.[15] The texts offer eyewitness testimony, yet they do not form a unified account with their accompanying illustration. Instead, the textual and pictorial accounts challenge each other. Besideness allows for the co-existence of two authors, and two discrete accounts, two distinct perspectives, hands, and embodied positions.

To exist beside one another is to share a spatial and temporal ambivalence. Post and the pilot, the drawing and the data, the land and the ship are all distinct ontological structures, yet thinking them beside each other allows myriad relationships to open up and to foreclose. To think two works beside each other is to allow each its own presence, temporality, and even audience while also considering that they only come into view from the vantage point of the other, as the view onto the land's profile is realized by the ship's movement. This sketchbook makes maritime draftsmanship collaborative, as the relationality between Post's drafting and the pilot's recording allowed Post to develop the atmospheric qualities of his practice while leaving the inscription of detail aside. In turn, Post's drawings became a tool for the pilot to visually gesture toward a set of conditions that were finally conveyed in detail within the text. For the historiography of Dutch art, works that traveled beside one another also articulate shifting perspectives, demonstrating how historians have chosen not to see certain textual records that accompanied the pictorial account. The drawing of salt production on Maio is a relatively minor work in Post's oeuvre, and it is perhaps not surprising that scholars have chosen to shift their perspective from the text to the drawing. Yet this refusal to turn one's attention to other textual histories that traveled beside Post's paintings becomes more striking in the history of his landscapes and depiction of sugar plantations in Brazil. In particular, a seventeenth-century inventory that was drawn up to accompany Post's paintings to the court of Louis XIV remains unremarked on in Post scholarship, although it clearly enumerates the violence negotiated within Post's portrayal of the emerging plantation economies.

The Inventory

In 1679, long after Johan Maurits's return from his brief governorship of Brazil, he sent to the king of France Louis XIV representative works from his foreign sojourn, likely either in hopes of receiving financial compensation, or as a diplomatic gesture following the Franco-Dutch War.[16] To accompany his gift, Maurits wanted someone who had been in Brazil to

2.8 Frans Post, paper inscription on back of canvas, *Planter's House and Village*, 1644. Oil on canvas (Musée du Louvre, Paris).

travel with the paintings to elucidate the pictures for the royal audience. Jacob Cohen, Maurits's financial agent, was unable to find "a Brazilian that would be able to explain the paintings, since most of them have died—the Brazilian sojourn having been more than twenty-five years ago." Cohen raised the possibility of Post traveling with the works, but acknowledged that "he has become a trembling drunk."[17] Maurits's request that someone travel with the paintings illuminates how works such as Post's often took part in larger ephemeral staging of colonialist desires, performances and oral stories whose traces may be gleaned in archival documents.[18] Cohen's letter also demonstrates that the visual record did not stand alone, as Maurits desired a witness to the Brazilian sojourn who could expand on the pictorial account for the French court.

In the absence of a "Brazilian" for the journey, Johan Maurits had an inventory drawn up that would contextualize the paintings. Many of the inventory records survive, not only within a document but also as paper labels affixed to the backs of the canvases, which describe the paintings in brief sentences (figure 2.8). For example, a work in the Louvre has the following inscription on its back (plate 7): "The dwelling of a worker, or better saying that one who is involved with something other than growing sugar cane. N.B. The yellow color one sees in the region are the sugar cane fields from where the sugar is extracted."

In the account provided for the eighth work on the list—a painting of a sugar mill—the author includes a report on the violence that the system of *engenhos* supported:

A Sugar Mill powered by water, with Kilns, where the syrup is extracted
from the Cane for the making of sugar. In the mouth of the kiln the fire
is so hot that the Negro slaves prefer to die, and for this reason they
poison themselves when they are able, suffering as they do with that
heat. The Portuguese, to prevent them from escaping, cut their ten-
dons. Others, who have smallpox, come to this kiln to cure themselves.
At the top of the Mountain is the Chapel, lower down is the house of
the sugar mill's owner. N.B. Everything seen in the region with a yellowish colour is the Sugarcane, from which the Sugar is extracted.[19]

The final lines of the paragraph are repeated throughout the inventory:
"N.B. Everything in the region with a yellowish colour is the Sugarcane,
from which the sugar is extracted," a refrain that tries to control the bodily
maiming, epidemics, and enslavement with an empirical cadence, placing
the atrocities on the same level of interest as the color of sugarcane and
the placement of buildings within the landscape. Scholars are uncertain
about the exact painting that the inventory describes because the gift to
Louis XIV was dispersed throughout the eighteenth century. Two surviving paintings, however, closely adhere to the description. In one, signed
and dated 1668, the painted view looks down on the valley floor, where
the sugar mill is situated in the low-rising hillsides. According to the main
monograph on Post, this painting, which is now in a private collection,
"twice broke auction price records for a Frans Post work during the 20th
century," a financial assessment attributed to "many of the most seductive
qualities that made Post famous in the 1660s."[20] The other surviving painting from Post's oeuvre that closely pertains to the inventory description
(plate 8) is written about as one "of the finest and most charming sugar
mills painted by Frans Post," with "one of the richest and most detailed
descriptions" of the sugar mills.[21] The ekphrasis of a painting as a "rich
and detailed description" for a scene that purposefully omits significant
details about the functioning of an emergent plantation system dependent
on enslaved labor reveals how the discipline of art history has chosen to attend to one register of description—the atmospheric—while refusing to
engage with another.

The horizon line and sky dominate the canvas, situating the figures and
their labor within an expansive perspective that focuses on distant hori-
zons. He gives over the pictorial surface to the ephemeral ever-changing
movement of the clouds against a blurred horizon. Lakes and ponds populate the midground, providing reflective surfaces for light, further drawing

the viewer's eye away from the activity of the sugar mill in the foreground and toward the sea. In the foreground, Post captures the yellow fire of the kilns, which visually rhymes with the yellow tones of the sugarcane fields, repeatedly described throughout the inventory descriptions. The attention to the thatched roof and the arched structure of the sugar mill gives the effect of detail while ultimately withholding it. The precision of palm leaves, a protruding pineapple, and clouds allows for the perception of an accurate rendering of place while subsuming it into an evocation of blue skies, foreign fauna, and a yellow ember light that is both fire and cane.

Yet as the inventory reveals, although the violence of the *engenhos* remained omitted from the paintings, it traveled beside the visual works (or perhaps even affixed with strips of paper to the canvases). Although twentieth-century scholars might have chosen to ignore the record of enslavement in order to delineate Post's picturesque qualities, the presence of the inventory as likely affixed to the backs of paintings suggests that for seventeenth-century viewers, the violence was central to the construction of the landscape. While one could argue that this inventory points toward the cruelty of the Portuguese and not the Dutch, the Dutch hired the Portuguese to run their sugar mills during their brief tenure in Brazil, and the Dutch colonizers depended on the Portuguese for profits. This inventory explains the painting with an open recognition of the brutality that was necessary to maintain the wealth accumulated through enslavement and claiming inhabited land in the Americas as property of European governments. Almost a century later, in Voltaire's *Candide*, a person working in the sugar mill describes the Dutch owners: "When we work at the sugarcanes, and the mill snatches hold of a finger, they cut off the hand; and when we attempt to run away, they cut off the leg."[22] The slippage between Portuguese and Dutch over the course of a century also points to the transatlantic slave trade as integral to most early modern European economies, as the various sea powers made treaties to profit beside one another across Africa and the Americas.[23]

The inventory was specifically written to accompany, expand on, and travel beside the painting. Both the inventory and the painting rely on different rhetorical methods to create distance between the report and the content. The horror evoked in the inventory is immediately dulled into the descriptive rhythm of the sugarcane fields, and Post presents a scene in which the plantation is distilled into the single yellow light of the kiln. In Post's paintings, he presents sweeping landscape vistas, in which figures and architectural structures are often minute details within a vista of mountains, clouds, and sea.[24] Post's views adhere to a tradition of European landscape painting, perhaps most famously innovated by Pieter Brueghel, in which the viewer is positioned at a distance, conveying a mastery of their gaze over the expanse of the landscape unfolding. This distance served Post to picture sugar mills and plantations while withholding the details enumerated in the inventory. Nevertheless, within certain of Post's landscapes, the fire of the kiln discussed in the inventory burns bright against the ephemeral architectural structures of the mill. In the context of the inventory, these moments of luminescence provide an entry point for the knowledgeable viewer of the painting to discuss the conditions of enslaved life on the plantation. As the inventory was meant to accompany the paintings in place of an oral narration, the inventory's language was intended to fill a void within the painting, to extrapolate on those insistent blurred patches of yellow paint, stubborn signifiers of detail that would remain opaque to most viewers unless further explained. The painting and its depiction of the burning fire of the kiln as a barely distinguishable flicker does not ask the viewer to feel, to understand, or to enter the figural, affective, or imagined space of the enslaved. Instead, it offers a minute detail, a spark for the reader of the inventory, for the court audience, to engage and recognize the history emblazoned within that flame, a narrative of the cost, labor, sickness, and death that accompanied and was inseparable from creating that commanding view over the landscape that suggested it could be owned and conquered. The presence of this inventory demonstrates how the seventeenth-century plantation paintings for elite audiences traveled beside a record that revealed the violence necessary for its pictorialization.[25]

In turn, the distance achieved in Post's painting is also mimicked in the inventory. While the words enumerate the brutalities of the European presence in the Americas, the author includes this information within the genre of the inventory, offering neither moral recrimination nor ethical reflection. Instead, words demarcating the position of the chapel and the plantation master's house move the reader immediately toward problems of mapping and geographic orientation within the painting, suggesting that the details of corporal punishment, fugitivity, and death are of the same quality as the positioning of the architectural structures in relation to one another. There is a distance prescribed in both the painting and the inventory, offering a visual model and reference by which to conceive of creating a legal structure that would allow for the metamorphosis of lives into property as a condition of economies and of European claims for land.

The painting and its accompanying inventory arrived at the French court directly preceding the drafting of the Code Noir by Jean-Baptiste Colbert, the finance minister of King Louis XIV of France, who was also an active patron of the arts. The Code Noir became law in 1685, after Colbert's death in 1683, enshrining a set of legal codes for the treatment of slaves in the French colonies, as slavery was deemed "necessary," and the means by which living human beings and their kin could be determined another man's property.[26] Although some scholars have argued that the Code Noir limited the barbarity of practices on plantations in the French colonies, as Saidiya Hartman points out, "the barbarism of slavery did not express itself singularly in the constitution of the slave as object but also in the forms of subjectivity and circumscribed humanity imputed to the enslaved."[27] The basis of the laws created a legal structure to define the transformation of life into chattel property. Moreover, the punishments enumerated in the Code Noir for fugitives are similar to those described within the inventory for the Post painting. Per the Code Noir, a fugitive would have their ear cut off and receive a fleur-de-lis branding after their first capture; their hamstring would be cut after their second attempt; and they would be put to death after their third attempt.[28] Post's painting and its attendant inventory entered into the French court at a moment during which the structures of enslavement were under debate. Works such as Post's painting and its accompanying inventory expanding on details—like shining flames of burning kilns—served as sites by which members at the court could discuss the role of slavery in the colonies and determine the necessary conditions of the plantations for labor. The flame of the kiln in Post's painting represents both the gathering of life and its extinction, as the furnace for the sugarcane economy, and as a bare limit of figuration gesturing toward the violence necessary to maintain control over the view, the landscape, the sugarcane, and the global economy. The burning fire of the kiln is intrinsic to the painting, and it is moreover not an erasure of the violence of the emerging plantation systems. The yellow smear of paint offered a vehicle by which to discuss, subsume, and defend the transformation of life into property, and it also offered an abstraction of bodies, lives, hearts, relationships, and intellects into a fire for consumption. The painting and its inventory did not erase the violence of the plantation. It transfigured the violence into a single flame, an abstraction that was mirrored within the production of the Code Noir and other legal documents that determined the lives and fates of many as though they were abstract units of value and property.

Although the inventory is central to the historical context in which the painting was received at the French court, it remains invisible in Post scholarship, despite existing in plain view within the main monograph on the artist.[29] Post's painting with an attendant inventory describing the punishment meted out to fugitives in the Dutch colonies offered a visual and textual window for ministers such as Colbert to imagine the legal structures of enslavement in the Americas. The distance inscribed into the rhetoric of Post's painting—the slight visibility to the flame of the kiln—visualizes an emergent sense of property, violence, and land that can be structured, coded, legalized, and controlled. Though some scholars assume that slavery's cruelties would not be depicted in the seventeenth century because this period occurred before abolitionist movements, this assumption ignores the contemporaneous history in the seventeenth century that actively codified a legal structure for the practices of the transatlantic slave trade.[30] Acts of cruelty and the transformation of life into property in this historical moment were central to ministers such as Colbert, who was in the process of defining the legislation for the French state in the Caribbean. Attending to the seventeenth-century inventory of the painting orients us. It says: See this. It is not the capybara. It is not the anteater. It is not the pineapple, or the bright blue sky, or the thin white clouds. It is the heat of the fire in the kiln. The heat that burned bodies and that was thought to save those ravaged by European smallpox. In the relationship between the inventory and the painting, the textual legislation of enslavement and its rendering into landscape and clouds, land and property claims, elisions between land and bodies, property and selves, lives and fire, become evident.

Acknowledging the presence of the inventory and the painting as coexisting—possibly as a single object, glued to one another—demonstrates that the painting was contingent on knowing about the heat of the kiln, about the pandemics, the forced labor, and the resistance. The inventory suggests that the painting was always about seeing it—at least within the context of the court, the site of power and colonial expansion—as a sanitized record that necessarily coexisted beside a history of coercion, fugitivity, resistance, and brutality inscribed within the diaries, logbooks, letters, and legal code carried across the Atlantic, enforcing the conditions of the plantations in the Americas. In the coexistence of the bureaucratic description and the visualization of landscape, the painting emerges. Post's painting offered a visual language that made evident the possibility for imagining a legal code to structure and defend the transformation of life into property.

Account books, legal codes, inventories, and written records are crucial to understanding the visual production of seventeenth-century Dutch painting and its relationship to the emergence of the transatlantic slave trade. Artists such as Post were engaged in a complicated negotiation with the abstraction, figuration, and imaging of laboring bodies transformed into property through violent means that refused their intellect and being. The presence of Post's painting and its attendant inventory at the French court during a period in which the legal structures for plantations in the French Caribbean were under discussion is not insignificant. Paintings such as Post's offered a visual language to imagine, tolerate, and defend the formation of laws that would structure the bare humanity granted to the enslaved populations of Africans and Indigenous people, a visibility realized in the flickering flame of the kiln rhyming with the yellow of the sugarcane.

CHAPTER THREE

Monuments and Architectural Painting

In the poem "The Sea Is History," the Saint-Lucian poet Derek Walcott (1930–2017) opens with a question: "Where are your monuments, your battles, martyrs? Where is your tribal memory?" To which he responds: "Sirs, in that grey vault. The sea."

Walcott speaks here to the communities of the African diaspora, and to the ancestors lost during the Atlantic passage, presenting a history encrusted within underwater barnacled caves, a natural architectonic monument that counters a narrative constructed on land with cathedrals, marble sculptures, historical battlefields, and textbooks. Against these structures, Walcott pictures the sea as forged in the transatlantic slave trade, a period in which its invisible depths became the site of mourning and remembrance. These histories cannot so easily be brought to the surface, so instead he takes his reader down to the "bones soldered to coral," conjuring watery graves, turning the ocean into its own monument and battlefield.

Walcott's account of the sea counters a western European visual history, starting in the early modern period, in which the ocean is "an empty space to be crossed by atomistic ships."[1] Or as one recent historian remarks, for much of Western history, the sea has been "empty: a space not a place. The sea is not somewhere with 'history,' at least not recorded history."[2] Instead,

Walcott's poem demands recognition for a liturgy of lamentation founded on and below the sea's surface, recognizing a history erased as ships crossed the ocean's highways in the name of free trade, capital, and God.

Writing more than two centuries earlier from a slave fort on the West African coast, Dutch merchant Willem Bosman (1672–1703) remarks that the sea is the "considerable support of human life; without which it were impossible to subsist here," and continues on to describe the local fishing industry.[3] In his account of natural resources within the African coastal waters, Bosman also describes the inability of the local communities to bury and mourn their dead, who were kidnapped and traded as chattel property. He remarks that Africans boarded on the ships often disappeared into the ocean, as their corpses were fed to the sharks that swam next to the ships, so that "not the least particle is left."[4] Bosman's brief remark inadvertently reveals the ontologies of community and mourning disrupted when these rites of burial are denied. Elsewhere in the text, he describes local burial practices, citing building a small house over the deceased, planting rice, and placing "earthen images" on the graves, likely referring to the tradition of terra-cotta funerary sculpture.[5] He comments in closing that the inhabitants "are strangely fond of being buried in their own country."[6]

Bosman's text embodies the dehumanization that pervades European early modern accounts of enslavement. It demonstrates how slave traders depended on the ocean to obliterate the violence of their profession while inadvertently capturing what the contemporary scholar Stephanie Smallwood observes as forming a cycle of trauma established in the inability to grieve as a society.[7] As Valérie Loichot remarks, "The stripping of rituals is a fundamental attempt to uncouple humans from their humanity."[8] This is not to suggest that African funerary and burial practices did not continue within the diaspora, but it evokes the attempted obliteration of ritual and mourning enacted through both casting off corpses at sea and writing dismissive texts such as Bosman's that describe local artistic practices as "earthen images," dismissing complex visual cultures as idolatry. The combined erasure of lives and images are the lost "tribal memory" that, for Walcott, remains locked in the sea's grey vault.[9]

Bosman's text is not the only early modern account of oceanic ecosystems and their impact on the bodies of the enslaved. In a manuscript held in the collections of the Morgan Library, known as the "Histoire naturelle des Indes," an anonymous chronicler documents pearl diving off the coast of Peru (figure 3.1). The narrator focuses on the lucrative trade and depicts a man on the verge of suffocation by a manta ray, writing: "This fish is very

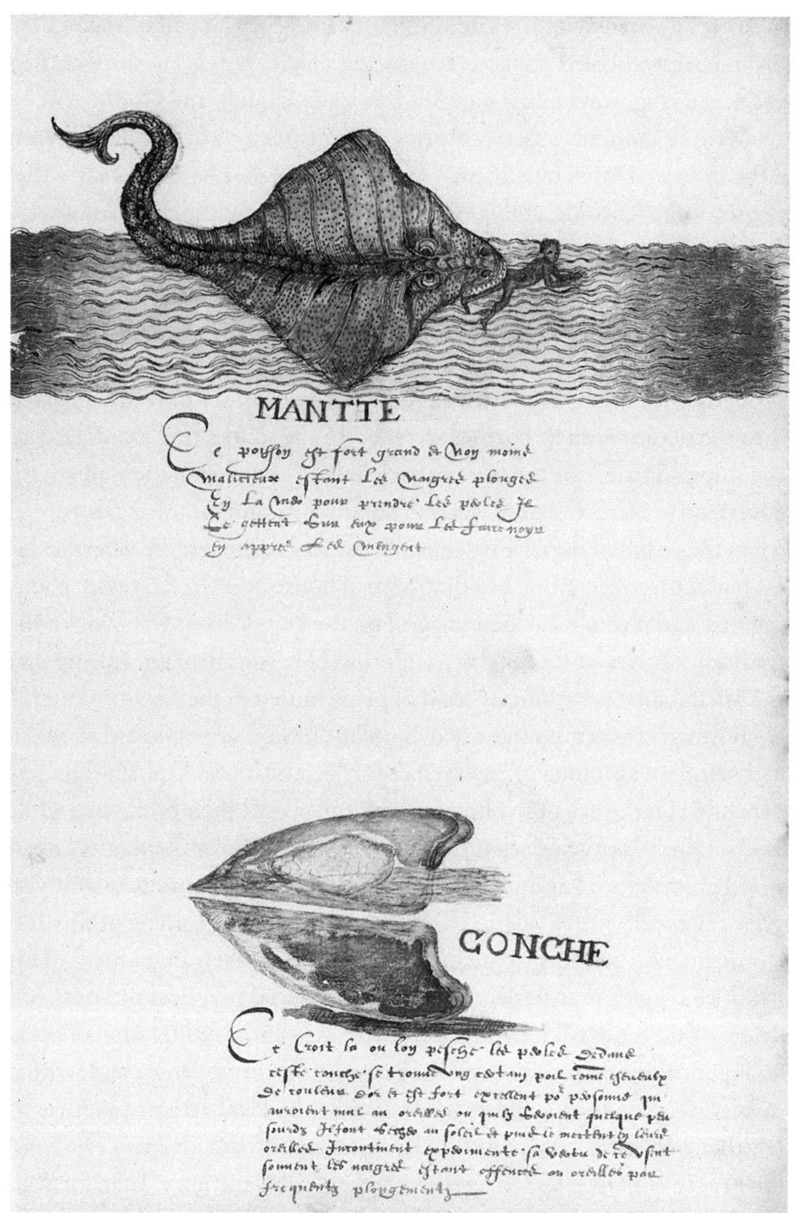

3.1 Anonymous, fol. 47r, "Histoire naturelle des Indes," illustrated manuscript, 1586 (Morgan Library and Museum, New York).

large and no less vicious. When the negroes dive in the seas for pearls it jumps on them and makes them drown and afterward eats them." The accompanying illustration depicts black sea animals with large eyes staring out at the viewer while the diver's eyes are empty sockets. The amphibious animal is granted a confrontation with the viewer while the diver remains incapable of sight. The manta ray attack is also a mythological digression, as the creatures primarily subsist on plankton and do not suffocate swimmers. Yet this fantastic animal and its attendant lore obliquely contend with the disappearance of Black lives into the Atlantic.

The narrator also captures the extraordinary conditions under which the individuals dove for pearls, explaining that the divers scraped the bottom of the sea soil where the oysters lived, and that "the deeper they descend in the water, the larger are the pearls they find. Not being able to hold their breath longer than a quarter of an hour, they come up again." In the accompanying watercolor, naked men and women swim in the waves, while others jump off the boat, feet in the air, grasping baskets while plunging for the ocean floor (figure 3.2). The passage captures the skill required to hold one's breath for the necessary time to mine for pearls. In turn, the pressure and its undue stress on the body are mentioned in a passage regarding the conch shell, in which the author notes that it holds hairs that provide relief for the pearl divers, who "often use it, their ears being hurt by frequent dives." The text documents the forced transformation of a terrestrial body into an aquatic one, from the increased capacity of the lungs to earaches and accompanying deafness.

Yet the diver is not only associated with forced labor. He also becomes a metaphorical figure for the process of gaining knowledge through experimentation. Natural philosopher and chemist Robert Boyle likens the exploration of natural philosophers to the gathering of pearls and coral: "An Experimental Philosopher may be compar'd to a *skilful Diver*, that cannot only fetch those things that lye upon the Surface of the Sea, but make his way to the very Bottom of it; and thence fetch up Pearls, Corals, and other precious things, that in those Depths lye conceal'd from other men's Sight and Reach."[10] The diver was prominent for Boyle to illuminate a world of observation that exists beyond the surface, and he no doubt had this imagery at hand, as it was central to his treatise *An Hydrostatical Discourse* (1672), which considers the properties of solids, liquid, and air.

Boyle recognized that liquid is distinct from air or solids in the force that it exerts on a body. He relied on travelers' accounts of pearl diving to illustrate how the corporeal body—a structure formed by elastic organs,

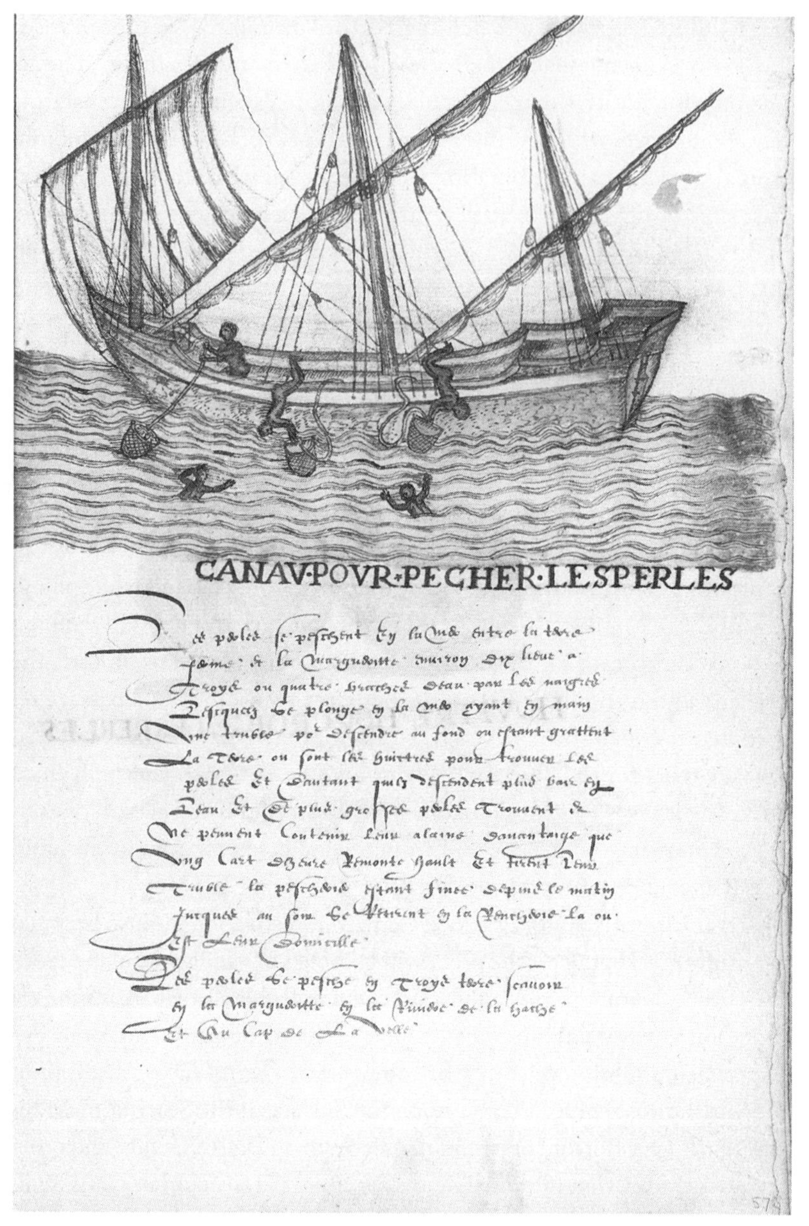

3.2 Anonymous, fol. 57r, "Histoire naturelle des Indes," illustrated manuscript, 1586 (Morgan Library and Museum, New York).

breath, and air—interacted with the pressure and weight of water. These narratives were central to expanding his own observations as they offered eyewitness testimony to the impact of water pressure on the internal fluid system of the body. Boyle notes that according to a Spanish prelate, Indigenous divers in the Americas commonly experienced "blood at the mouth, and of the bloody flux caused by the stomach." He quotes an official for the English East India Company, who described female divers whose "eyes by continually diving grew as red as blood."[11] Boyle also quotes an account of pearl diving in Cuba, in which Indigenous divers would tie stones to their bodies to aid in the descent, and then release the rocks at the bottom of the ocean to ascend to the surface. As he remarked, this innovation was due to the "aery substance" at the sea floor.[12]

In both Boyle's work and "Histoire naturelle des Indes," the lives of Indigenous and African enslaved are written about in the context of natural history and corporeal experimentation, suggesting "human" as a contingent category for the diver. The divers in these treatises become enfolded into an ocean ecology in which there is not a clear delimitation among animal, aquatic, and human. As Zakiyyah Iman Jackson argues, the Enlightenment denial of "humanity" did not form racial categorization, but instead "the fleshy being of blackness is experimented with as if it were infinitely malleable lexical and biological matter."[13] Prior to the Enlightenment in these early modern texts, the diver embodies this ontological fleshiness, becoming a site of experiment as the corporeal form takes on physical changes enforced on it through extensive labor underwater, demonstrating itself as malleable, distinct from the aquatic life only in its capacity for transformation brought on by forced, excessive, constant, traumatic encounters between the space of the sea and the bipedal human body. The divers' bodies illustrate interactions among pressure, air, and water under discrete circumstances. Yet the divers themselves, and their testimonies, remain absent from the community of experimental philosophers, for Boyle complains that what is commonly reported about diving is obtained from "slaves and ignorant men" who do not "make over-accurate observations."[14] Boyle's deployment of the divers' bodies divested of their own voices created a social space in which Indigenous and Black knowledge was denied, along with many other voices, within the rarefied world of seventeenth-century Restoration philosophy. Instead, the divers' bodies become part of a discourse for experimentation, while the ability to observe, describe, and contribute phenomenological knowledge is refused.

In Steven Shapin and Simon Schaffer's work on the social place of experiment and politics in seventeenth-century Restoration natural philosophy, they demonstrate that experimental philosophy was built on "collective witnessing," a process determined by accessibility and credibility. The "experimental community" was "a model of the ideal polity."[15] Although they never discuss Boyle's references to pearl diving, Shapin and Schaffer's account contextualizes the ramifications of Boyle's refusal of the enslaved divers to witness, as their narratives would challenge the model of the ideal polity. Allowing for the testimonies of the divers themselves would endow them with an intellectual and moral capability that would undermine the economy of slavery, threatening the construction of an "ideal polity" in the social space of the experimental philosopher, as well as the categorization by which citizens were allowed into this utopic space. Yet inadvertently, Boyle's references to bleeding lungs and bloodshot eyes register the impact of the ocean economy on the divers' bodies. Moreover, this attention to travelers' accounts and oceanic space extends the social space of experiment beyond England and the European continent and into the burgeoning colonial empire. Distinct from land, maritime space becomes central to demarcating the limits of the human body as a corpuscular machine, its fluid core of blood, water, organs, and liquids acted on and reactive to the outside pressure of oceans and rivers. The body that encapsulated this particular form of knowledge production was the diver, the men and women who scraped the ocean floor for pearls and corals, producing not only economic wealth but also testimonies to the body as a system of fluids, affected and formed in relation to other bodies of water.

These brief accounts demonstrate how the early modern construction of oceanic space, and in turn the body as a fluid structure, was inseparable from the development of the transatlantic slave trade. These natural history accounts and Boyle's philosophy recognize the sea as a material space, formed by fluid waters both bodily and oceanic, a ground to be mined for pearls and coral. Yet this material knowledge is gained by enslaved labor and an accompanying erasure through mythological manta rays. While the abstraction of the diver is a metaphor for knowledge, the divers themselves are dismissed as ignorant and refused citizenship to the "ideal polity" of experiment.

In contrast to these early modern accounts, contemporary philosophers and theorists, particularly those working in the African diaspora, articulate a materialization of the sea that realizes the role of Black and Indigenous labor, lives, and knowledge as central to the ocean.[16] Christina Sharpe, for example, demonstrates that contra Bosman, the anonymous lives buried at sea continue within the ocean ecosystem. Sharpe points out that "the atoms of those people who were thrown overboard are out there in the ocean even today. They were eaten, organisms processed them, and those organisms were in turn eaten and processed, and the cycle continues."[17] Calling on the concept of residence time, Sharpe demarcates the period in which a substance enters and leaves the ocean, noting that for human bodies, this can be up to 260 million years. This acknowledgment of the Atlantic as a physical space of burial and of the regeneration of aquatic life to continue the presence of histories erased at sea stands in stark contrast to the image of oceanic space created in both legal discourse and painting in the seventeenth-century Dutch Republic, as the transatlantic slave trade became increasingly vital to its economy. To apprehend the attempted eradication of lives during the Atlantic passage throughout the early modern period, it is necessary to understand how the sea became framed as a site of oblivion and erasure, a place with no history, an impossible burial ground open to the sky.

Accounts such as Bosman's illustrate the difficulty in narrating histories of race and enslavement in early modern art through studies of the human figure and portraiture, as bodies were made to disappear into the ocean. While the history of Black portraiture and figure studies in early modern art is a necessary lens, historians must also contend with how writing early modern histories of race and enslavement through the figurative runs the risk of overlooking the transformation of the corporeal into the fungible, and its centrality to the seventeenth-century development of the slave trade. For contemporary scholars, this process has been understood as "the liquidation of Black life too."[18] Rinaldo Walcott articulates how the fluid nature of oceanic space is inseparable from the liquidity of capital and its accumulation. The enslaved diver realizes this dynamic as her body becomes a site of experimentation to document pressure and fluidity while her labor mining the ocean floor contributes to an expanding global economy. In turn, the language around oceanic fluidity is the basis on which seventeenth-century legal scholars defined the ocean as a common pathway for all nations to trade, allowing for "the liquidation of Black life too." Accompanying this discourse, painters created an image of the ocean and sea as a mirrorlike surface, an infinite horizon, a space devoid of character, defined by its capacity for obliteration.

Seventeenth-century Dutch painting of the sea is a pictorialization of light on water, ships crossing aquatic highways, anchored in coastal areas, docked in ports. Artists such as Jan van de Cappelle (1626–79), Jan van Goyen (1596–1656), and Willem van de Velde the Elder (1610/11–93) and the Younger (1633–1707) produced seascapes of ships in storms, cargo arriving in calm ocean bays, parades of warships anchored off coasts, and many battle scenes. In some paintings, light casts off mirrorlike surfaces as fluffy white clouds populate the skies. In Van de Cappelle's *The Home Fleet Saluting the State Barge* (figure 3.3), the water's surface reflects the ceremonial cannon fire and the puffs of gray clouds as men gather, an embodiment of an emerging Dutch national consciousness. In other works—for example, the *penwercken* by the Van de Veldes—the canvas imitates the monochromatic scale of an engraving, with a white-painted ground on which inked lines mimic the curves of the engraver's burin, a monumental printed painting (figure 3.4). Some artists, such as Van Goyen, rapidly employed translucent washes of paint to a panel, so that the grain of the wooden support becomes visually part of the final work (plate 9). Seascapes are at once repetitive and innovative. Artists engaged with many compositional tropes and monotonous motifs while also experimenting technically. The technical investigations allowed for market innovation and rapid production (as in Van Goyen's thin washes), and the ubiquity of the compositional devices and the subjects reinforced through a consistent repetition created a pictorial vocabulary around the depiction of maritime space that continues into the current century.

One of the most important facets of this visual rhetoric is the attention to surface, rendering a world in which power is made evident by controlling the surface of things. As Roland Barthes wrote about Dutch seascapes, it is "a ground you could walk on, the sea completely urbanized."[19] The colonization of the land over the sea is not only a visual metaphor but also references the system of dikes, dunes, and polders that created the physical landscape in the Dutch Republic, an early modern feat of engineering that wrested arable land from salt water, creating the necessary topography for agriculture and housing. The attention to surface in Dutch painting, therefore, is not a superficial conceit but an understanding, wrought from their own engineered land, that power rests in the ability to define the surface of the world. This is also mirrored in the depiction of ships, with a focus on detailed renderings of architecture, figureheads, and flags declaring

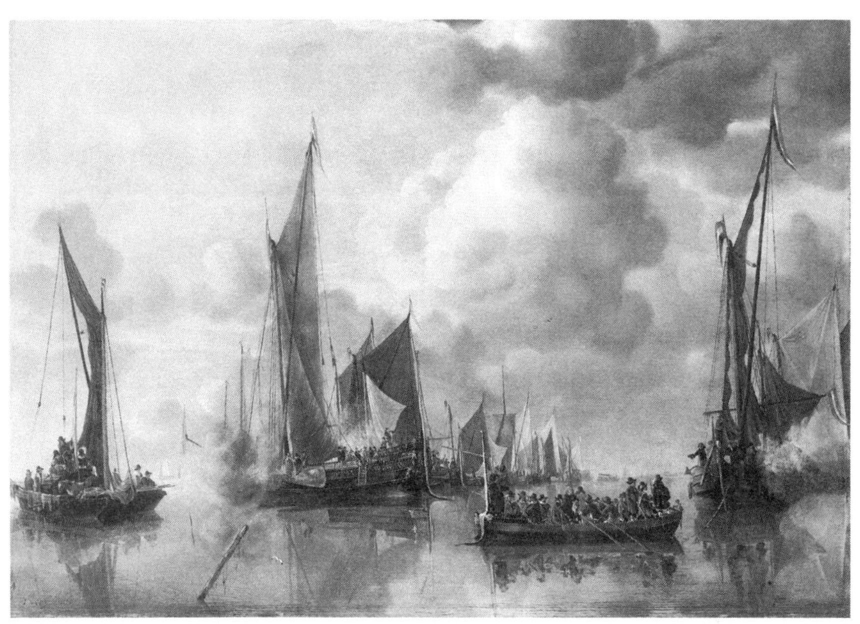

3.3 Jan van de Cappelle, *The Home Fleet Saluting the State Barge*, 1650. Oil on panel (Rijksmuseum, Amsterdam).

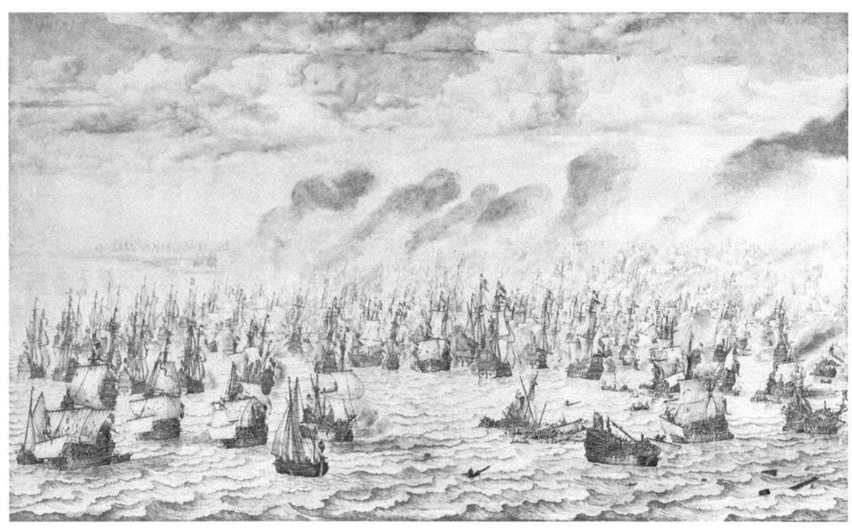

3.4 Willem van de Velde I, *The Battle of Terheide*, 1657. Ink on canvas (Rijksmuseum, Amsterdam).

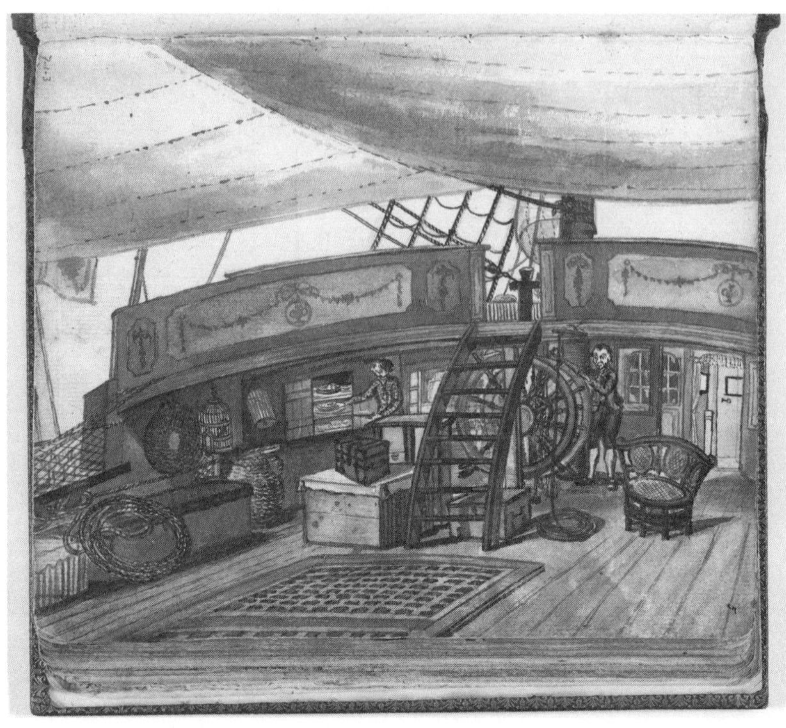

3.5 Jan Brandes, *View of the Deck on a VOC-Ship*, 1787. Watercolor on paper (Rijksmuseum, Amsterdam).

national allegiances. In turn, the interiors are rarely depicted; for example, Jan Brandes's documentation of a ship deck in the eighteenth century remains rare in the genre of maritime drawings and paintings (figure 3.5). One of the first images to show the interior of a ship, *Description of a Slave Ship* (1789), became an abolitionist "icon" when it was printed, as it made visually legible a trade that had been obscured in maritime pictures for over two centuries (figure 3.6).[20] The formal rhetoric and impact of *Description of a Slave Ship* also comes into focus when read against the earlier tradition of ship imagery, as in the drawing *Portrait of the Ship of the Seven Provinces* (figure 3.7). Light gray wash renders the lions of the United Provinces and barely discernible figureheads, the watery wash suggesting their erosion in salt water and ocean winds. The drawing documents the flagship of Michiel de Ruyter (1607–76), who was pivotal in gaining control over West Africa, as he reconquered the slave fortresses of Elmina and Gorée, taking the fortresses back from the English and thereby sustaining the role

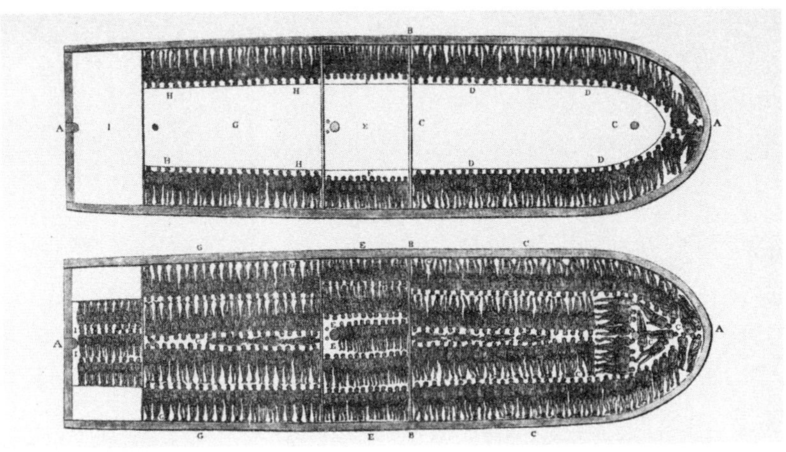

3.6 *Plan af slafskeppet Brooks*, 1896 (Schomburg Center for Research in Black Culture, Jean Blackwell Hutson Research and Reference Division, New York Public Library Digital Collections).

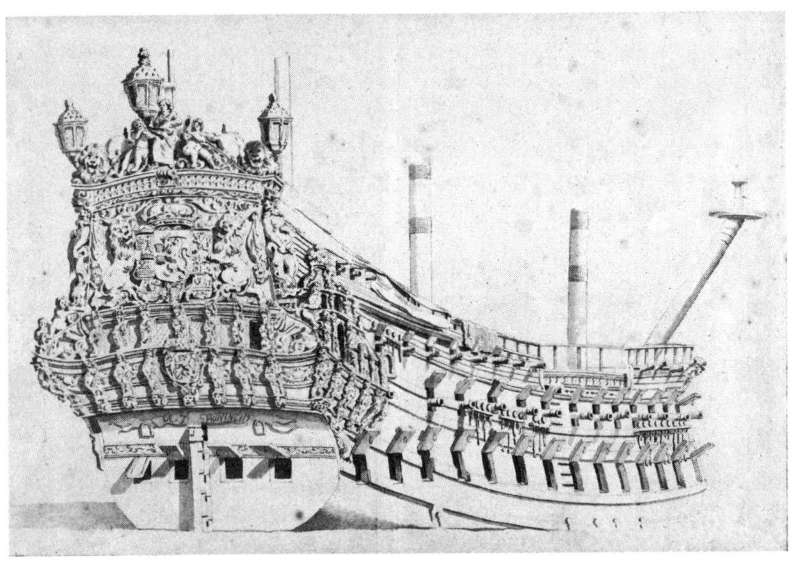

3.7 Willem van de Velde I (or copied after), *Portrait of the Ship of the Seven Provinces*, ca. 1665–1707. Brush drawing on paper (Rijksmuseum, Amsterdam).

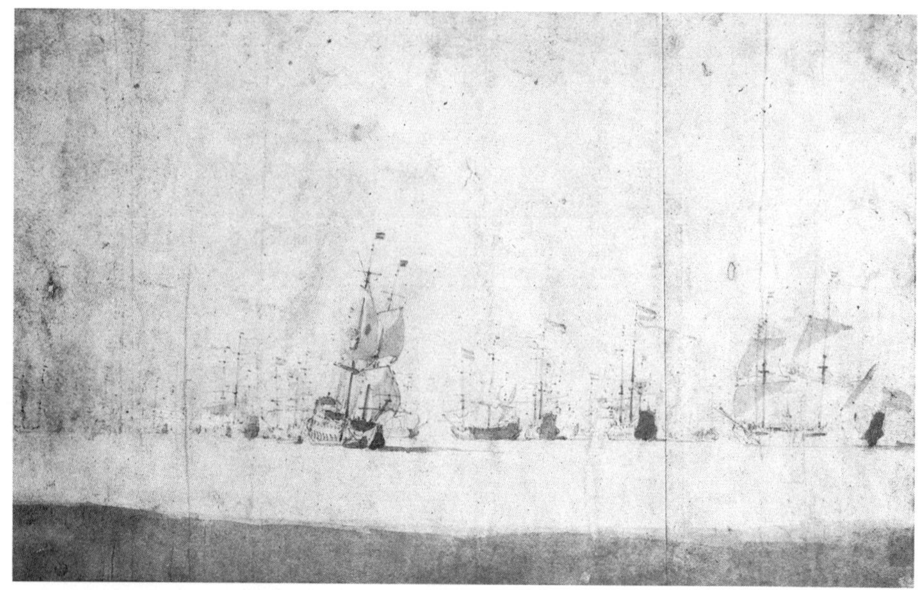

3.8 Willem van de Velde I and Willem van de Velde II, *Seaview with the Netherlandish Fleet*, ca. 1665–1707. Ink on paper (Rijksmuseum, Amsterdam).

of the Dutch in the transatlantic slave trade. This drawing captures only the figureheads eroding on the exterior, an ornamental program obscuring the cost of human life and the practices of containment held within and by the ship's structure.

Representations of maritime space in painting, from ships idling in coastal inlets to panoramic views of warships, share a perspective in which the crews are anonymous, minuscule, and often absent. The ships bear flags of various nationalities to dominate a zone that by the definition of early modern European legal code defied occupation. While these works formed a visual rhetoric for an emergent Dutch national consciousness, they also contributed to a larger Western image around the pictorialization of oceans. For Allan Sekula, Dutch marine painting was the starting point for his work on capitalism and maritime space. Sekula argues that this novel visual vocabulary emerged in tandem with the legal work of Dutch scholar Hugo Grotius (1583–1645), often described as the founder of to-day's international law.[21] Panoramic views, such as Van de Velde's brush drawings of ships at anchor, put "war machines" on display, with a hori-zon formed through atomistic vessels lolling in a blank open space (figure 3.8). The empty sheet of paper suggests an ocean devoid of character or place, a field distinguished only by the nationality of the ships temporarily at anchor.[22] For Sekula, the idling warships on parade depict the containment of the enemy at the point of the horizon, which creates a viewpoint that is determined as much by limits as by the promise of infinite expansion.[23] The capital promise of infinite expansion is precisely dependent on the ability to contain, both the economic expansion of other nations and also the ships as literal containers that bear goods across oceanic space. More detailed renderings of the ships focus on the architecture and artillery that perform the act of containment, such as Van de Velde's drawing *An English Frigate*, which studies the geometry of cannons projecting from gridded rows of windows (figure 3.9). The watery scrolls of ornament on the wooden hatch doors are barely indistinguishable from the short puffs of cannon smoke, weapons of war divorced from bodies and loss of life.

In the Van de Veldes' presentation of ships as vessels for goods and machines for limiting the enemy's international expansion, their works are early harbingers of the containerization that would embody the movement of capital across oceans. The act of containment at war becomes translated into the physical containers that carry goods, metal boxes that make possible the global transport of commodities. In Sekula's panorama of shipping containers, he creates a similar horizon dominated by the procedure of containment in an effort to achieve infinite expansion (plate 10). Sekula points out that the "concrete movement of goods" can be realized only through an abstraction equivalent to the flux in capital on the stock market: "If the stock market is the site in which the abstract character of money rules, the harbor is the site in which material goods appear in bulk, in the very flux of exchange."[24] The phenomenological experience of goods "guano, gypsum, steamed tuna, hemp, molasses" becomes abstracted into the vast metal crates that dominate harbors in the modern industrial world.

The dominance of the sea and ship as surface translates the wealth and movement of goods into a generalization of marine painting focused on meteorological conditions, flags in the breeze, pictorial conceits that obscure conditions of labor, and "the phenomenological quality of the goods." For the seventeenth century, these would include herring, whale blubber, beaver pelts, porcelain, salt, sugar, tobacco, and human beings. In turn, the laborers employed by the Dutch Admiralty, merchant ships, dockyards, roperies, and fishing vessels were often an international labor force, more so than in many other European countries.[25] For example, in 1635 about 20 percent of sailors recorded on Dutch ship manifests were born abroad,

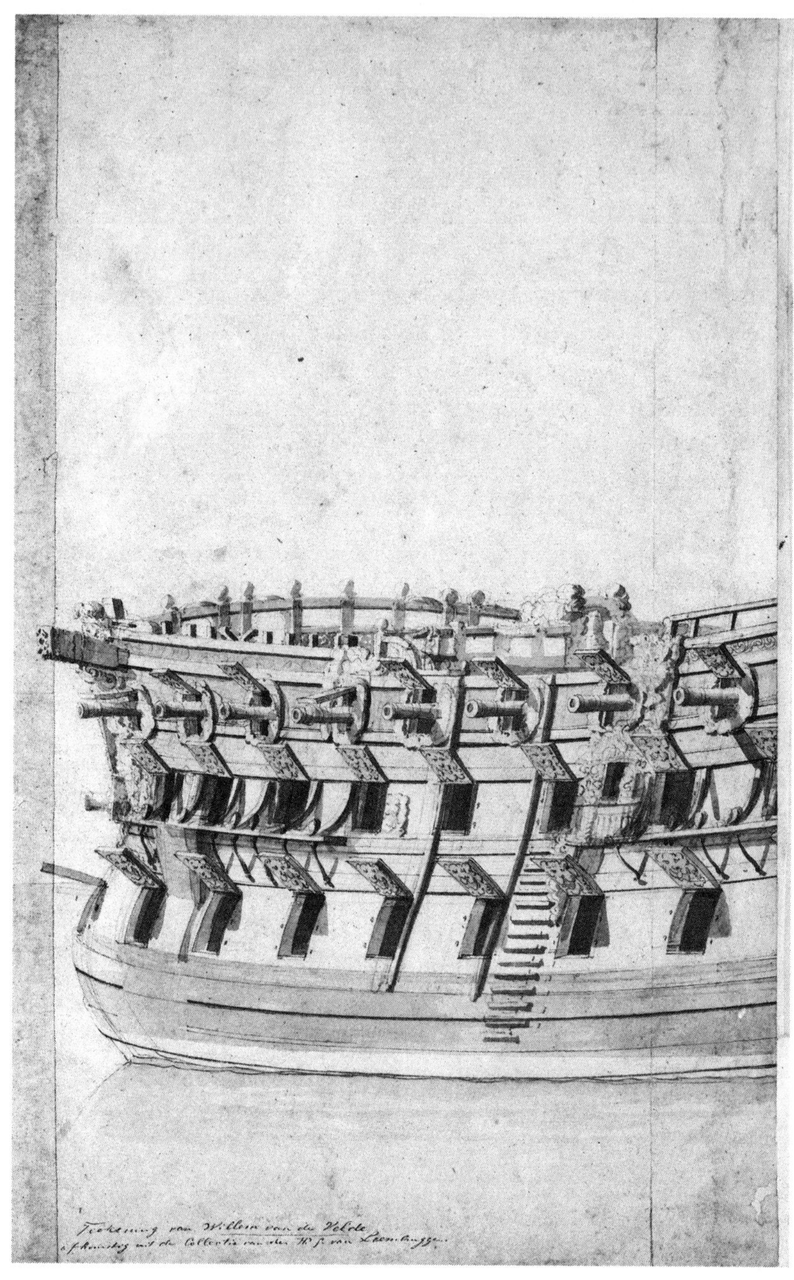

3.9 Willem van de Velde I, *An English Frigate*, ca. 1665–1707. Ink and pencil
on paper (Rijksmuseum, Amsterdam).

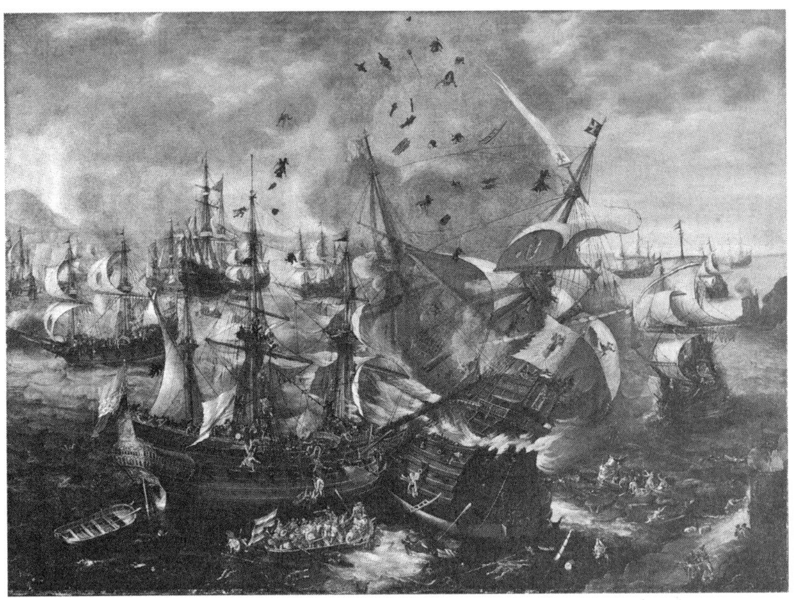

3.10 Cornelis Claesz. van Wieringen, *Battle of Gibraltar in 1607*, ca. 1665–1707. Oil on canvas (Rijksmuseum, Amsterdam).

whereas in 1638, Spain legally limited a ship to six foreigners.[26] Amsterdam was home to an international marine recruitment market, where Baltic, Spanish, French, German, English, and African crews were hired.[27] For the most part, the lives of these men employed by the Admiralty, the voc, the wic, or the fishing and whaling boats remain absent in Dutch painting, which presents the sea as a mirrorlike surface for reflection of sky and clouds, a place incapable of dominion. Nevertheless, one painting testifies to the expendability of this labor force, a *memoria* painted for Prince Maurits on an anniversary of the Battle of Gibraltar. The painter Cornelis Claesz. van Wieringen (1577–1633) captured the Battle of Gibraltar with small Brueghelian figures catapulting into the air through the force of the cannon fire, depicting its ability to fragment, splinter, and destroy the human body (figure 3.10). The Dutch ship is distinguished by its red, white, and blue flag, while the Spanish stands out through the divine image, threatened by the flames engulfing the ship. Gunpowder flings bodies into the air, like inanimate debris, suspended in flight, defying the qualities of the human body to become air bound.[28] Anonymous men somersault and plunge toward the water, suspended in their final moments, before being sent to their unnamed graves, open to the sky.

Central to defining a new vocabulary by which to conceive of the ocean as an uninhabitable surface for trade was Grotius's treatise *Mare Liberum: On the Freedom of the Sea* (1609), a pamphlet that was part of a larger work written in response to the actions of a Dutch admiral, Jacob van Heemskerck (1567–1607). The admiral had seized a Portuguese ship, the *Santa Catarina*, in the Singapore Strait. The piratical act yielded a profit of over three million Dutch guilders, although its legality remained uncertain.[29] Grotius defended Van Heemskerck's actions against accusations of unjust war, arguing that Van Heemskerck was forced to claim the Portuguese ship to break the monopolization of trade in the East Indies by the Spanish and Portuguese. In the absence of a legal authority, Van Heemskerck had the rights of a private citizen to claim the sovereign powers of the Dutch Republic and to punish transgressors of natural law, defined as rights to navigation and freedom of trade.

To legitimize Van Heemskerck's actions, Grotius defined the qualities of oceanic space that would support a natural law determined by free trade. He argued that the fluid nature of the sea and its propensity to erasure made it impossible to seize as a territory by any one nation. Whereas the earth could be cultivated and claimed as property through both labor and fences, the sea refused the plow: "The sea is incomprehensible, no less than air, it cannot be added to the goods of any nation."[30] For Grotius, "a ship sailing over the sea no more leaves behind itself a legal right than it leaves a permanent track."[31] While a property owner on land may demarcate his territory through borders, fences, marked pathways, and signs, the ability to claim ownership on the nearly formless waves remained impossible, according to Grotius.

Grotius's pamphlet would form the basis for a debate called the Battle of the Books, considered the foundation of today's international law. Attending to the language of Grotius and his interlocutors reveals an interchange about the nature of the ocean itself. As one English jurist, Sir Philip Meadows (1626–1718), maintained, the ocean is "a way, 'tis common to the peaceable traders of all nations."[32] Unlike a road on land, the sea could not be damaged by constant traffic: "A path over a field is of some damage to the Soil, though compensated with a greater utility, but a way over the sea is of no damage to the water." He concluded that the sea is "a common highway from one nation to another."[33] In the work of Grotius and the language of his fellow jurists, the sea is a field of oblivion, without history. The qualities of water and a perceived infinitude made both its resources and its surface appear inexhaustible. Incapable of holding stakes, flags, and monuments to demarcate borders and property lines, the sea must be common to all and provide a pathway of trade. Flowing water offered the ideal surface on which to obliterate the tracks of the ships crisscrossing the oceans, bringing textiles from the ports of the Dutch Republic to West Africa, enslaved individuals from West Africa to the Americas, and tobacco, sugar, and salt back to the Dutch Republic from the Americas.

It is perhaps not surprising that the protagonist in Grotius's pamphlet would also become the first Dutch naval hero, marking a turn toward a secular cult of maritime celebrity. He is historically celebrated as a hero for the Dutch naval win at the Battle of Gibraltar, where he was killed by a cannonball in 1607. Yet Van Heemskerck played a far more pivotal role in Dutch colonial expansion with his controversial seizing of the *Santa Catarina*, offering the impetus for constructing a novel maritime law that would form the basis of free trade in the early modern period. Therefore, while his role as the first *zeehelden* is typically traced to the Battle of Gibraltar, he stands out in Dutch maritime history for forming an oceanic space incapable of occupation, turning piracy into profit and trade. In his honor, the States-General and Admiralty erected a monument in Amsterdam's Oude Kerk, built the same year that *Mare Liberum* was published: 1609.

Van Heemskerck's monument marks where his body is buried within his home parish, testifying to the power of the Dutch Republic to carry its citizens home. The sculptor Hendrick de Keyser employed antique precedent for his memorial to the Dutch admiral, a large rectangular tablet engraved with a Latin epigraph and Dutch elegy (figure 3.11).[34] In the apron below the text, de Keyser depicted the Battle of Gibraltar in a low-relief panorama. Van Heemskerck's armor in which he was killed hung from a stone column across from the marble text. The armor is marked, to this day, by the absence of the left cuisse, shattered by the cannon fire (figure 3.12).[35] In hanging the armor with the epitaph, De Keyser also recalled the antique tradition of the *tropaeum*, in which armor was taken from an enemy and displayed on the battlefield. As one scholar points out, the antique battle trophy "symbolized the victor's claim to occupy the specific and highly contested space of the battlefield."[36] The contestation over geography and borders through the battle monument was also disseminated in print and coin. In both antiquity and the seventeenth century, printed replications of the monuments circulated across the empire. In antiquity,

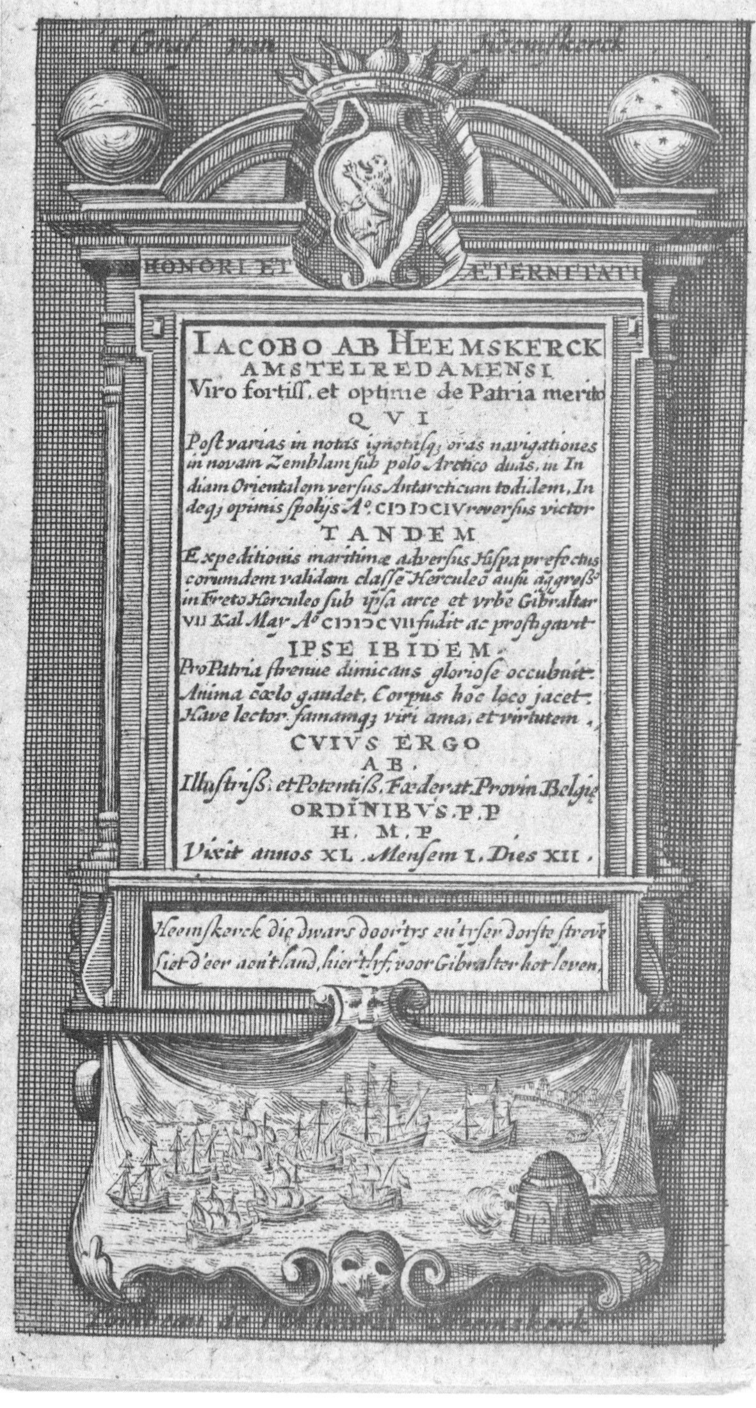
HONORI ET ÆTERNITATI
IACOBO AB HEEMSKERCK
AMSTELREDAMENSI
Viro fortiss. et optime de Patria merito
QVI
Post varias in notis ignotisq; oras navigationes
in novam Zemblam sub polo Arctico duas, in In
diam Orientalem versus Antarcticum todilem, In
deq; opimis spolijs Aº CIƆIƆCIV reversus victor
TANDEM
Expeditionis maritimæ adversus Hispa prefectus
corundem validam classe Herculeo ausu aggress
in Freto Herculeo sub ipsa arce et vrbe Gibraltar
VII Kal May Aº CIƆIƆCVII fudit ac profligavit
IPSE IBIDEM
Pro Patria strenue dimicans gloriose occubuit
Anima cælo gaudet, Corpus hoc loco jacet
Have lector famamq; viri ama, et virtutem
CVIVS ERGO
A B.
Illustriss. et Potentiss. Fœderat. Provin Belgic
ORDINIBVS. P. P.
H. M. P.
Vixit annos XL. Mensem I. Dies XII.
Heemskerck die dwars door'trs en'tyser dorste strev
liet d'eer aen't land, hier thyf, voor Gibralter het leven.

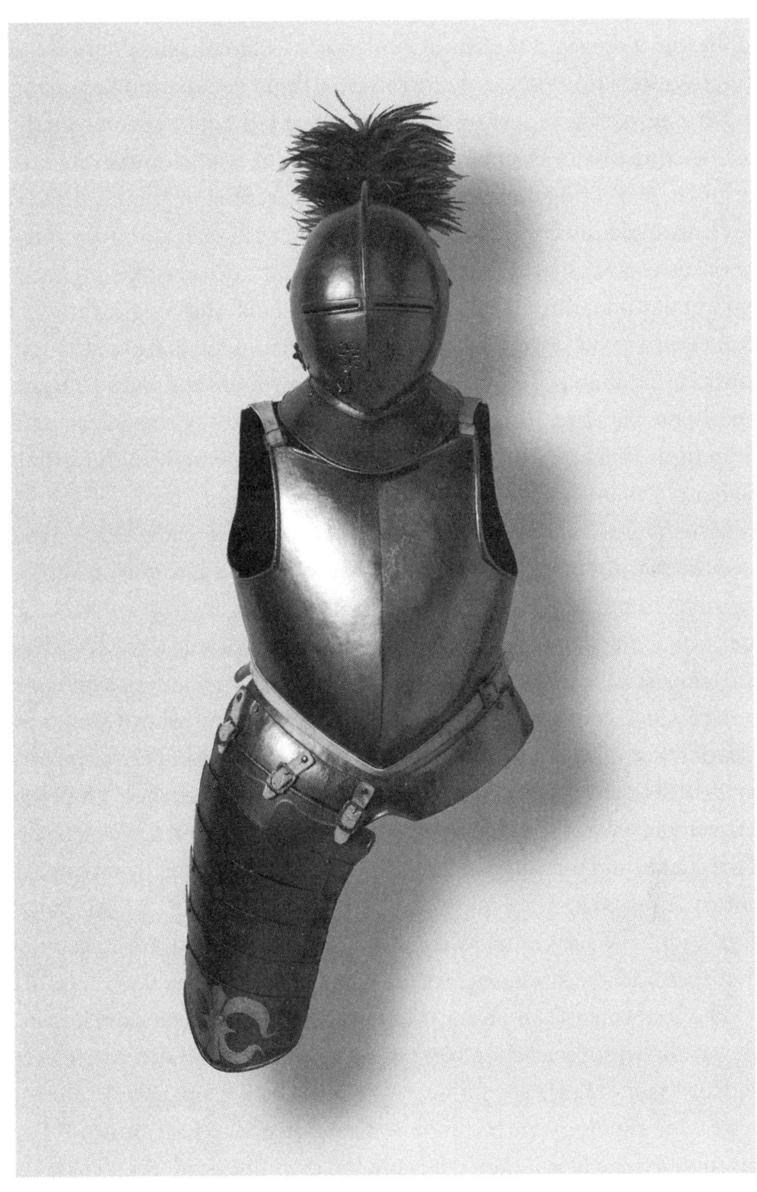

3.11 (*opposite*) Anonymous, *Monument for Jacob van Heemskerck*, ca. 1607–9. Etching after the marble epitaph (Rijksmuseum, Amsterdam).

3.12 (*above*) Anonymous, *Armor and Helmet of Jacob van Heemskerck*, ca. 1580–1607 (on loan from the Koninklijk Oudheidkundig Genootschap, Rijksmuseum, Amsterdam).

the Romans in particular reproduced their battle monuments in currency to claim the periphery and borderlands of their empire. In the Dutch Republic, prints enacted the same circulation of victory. These reproductive objects unified the contested territories and emergent nations, as exemplified in a newsprint reporting on the Battle of Gibraltar, which contains a small picture of Van Heemskerck's tomb with his armor, cantilevered from the pillar, projecting out toward his stone casket below (figure 3.13). The movement and dissemination of the monument in coin and print spreads the occupation of space from the battlefield of the ocean to the sites of currency and print culture, marking control over land, shipping pathways, resources, and knowledge. The print, coin, and monument also testify to the power of the Dutch Republic to carry a body home and bury its dead in their home parishes. Instead of displaying the armor of the defeated as in the antique *tropaeum*, the Dutch Republic monumentalized the armor of the hero to claim contested space.

In building the victory monument in the church, the States-General translated the maritime field of war from fluid waters to stone graves. Whereas according to the legal scholarship of Grotius, emerging nation-states could not occupy maritime space (as victors could a battlefield), the Dutch created a memorial cult around the maritime field of war and, through print-in-circulation, conveyed their power to, paradoxically, control and occupy oceanic space. The site of occupation moved from the formless waves to the empty walls, columns, and interiors of the Reformed churches. This elision between the nave of the church and the battleship, between the stone floor of the church and the salty sand of the ocean, is remarked on by seventeenth-century Amsterdam poet Joost van den Vondel, who states in "In Praise of Navigation": "What company conducts this bride to church—that church whose pews are reefs, whose grave unnamed lie open to the sky?"[37]

The Reformed Oude Kerk that housed the Van Heemskerck memorial was also the official church of the Amsterdam Admiralty, where Petrus Plancius (1552–1622), a prominent Calvinist theologian, gave sermons interweaving theology with travelers' accounts of the East Indies.[38] Plancius supplied the first Dutch fleet going to the Indies with their charts and navigational instruments, and he was fundamental to the founding of the voc.[39] His interest in voyage and trade in the East Indies was accompanied by his desire for missionizing, as he sent Calvinist theologians on some of the earliest merchant voyages. The church was also once home to paintings by sixteenth-century masters, such as Jan van Scorel (1495–1562) and Maarten van Heemskerck (1498–1574), works that were destroyed in the *beeldenstorm* (iconoclastic riots) of the 1560s. In the wake of this iconoclasm, seventeenth-century churches became the focus of a new genre of painting that documented the interiors and their bare walls.

Paintings such as Emanuel de Witte's *The Interior of the Oude Kerk, Amsterdam* reinforce the Reformed space as a place of burial and community (figure 3.14). While a dog lifts its leg to pee on a column next to an open grave, men in tall black hats — likely made of beaver pelts from North America — congregate over matters that appear mundane, suggested by the absence of clergy and the empty pulpit. Whereas formally the Christian community came together around the Eucharist, De Witte's work depicts a new form of civitas, a community founded on urbanity. The church becomes a site similar to the Amsterdam Bourse, a site by which to share information and knowledge, the basis of the stock exchange and wealth. Whereas once the community gathered around the absent body of Christ present in the communion of the Eucharist, the citizens in De Witte's painting now gather around an empty pulpit. The church commemorates no longer the body of Christ but instead the body of Van Heemskerck, buried in the church and marked by the relic of his armor. One scholar notes that Van Heemskerck's monument marks "the transition from the conventional church-based tomb to the modern secular memorial."[40] Van Heemskerck's tomb became a model for later *zeehelden*, as large marble memorials to naval heroes proliferated in Reformed Church spaces across the Dutch Republic.[41] In one of De Witte's many paintings of the Nieuwe Kerk in Amsterdam, he captures the tomb created for naval hero Michiel de Ruyter, fatally wounded by a cannon off the coast of Sicily (figure 3.15). His body was embalmed and shipped back to Holland, memorialized in the Nieuwe Kerk of Amsterdam in place of the main altar. Where once were paintings mediating the relationship between the congregants and Christ, there now rested the tomb and corpse of a naval admiral who was directly responsible for Dutch dominance in the slave trade.

In Angela Vanhaelen's consideration of architectural painting and the Reformed Church interior as a site of burial, she remarks that "paintings and tomb markers allowed citizens to distinguish themselves," creating "a public realm by relating people to one another." As she states, "In death, all are equal before an omnipotent God."[42] Vanhaelen's recognition of the church as a site to define citizenship in the Dutch Republic is crucial. Yet as Bosman's discussion of death on the West African coast makes clear, death was not equal across the seventeenth-century Dutch territories, during which a new sense of citizenship emerged that was tied to the loose conglomeration of urban

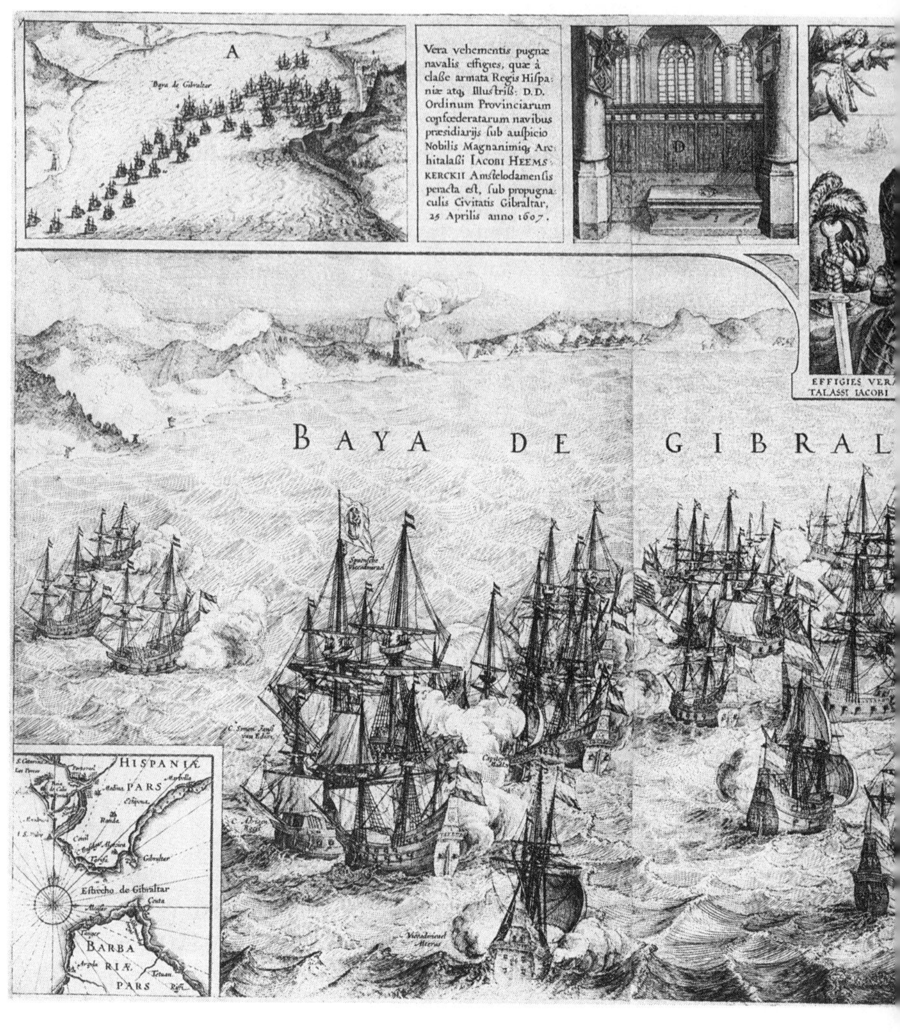

3.13 Claes Jansz. Visscher II, after David Vinckboons, *The Battle of Gibraltar*, 1607. Etching (Rijksmuseum, Amsterdam).

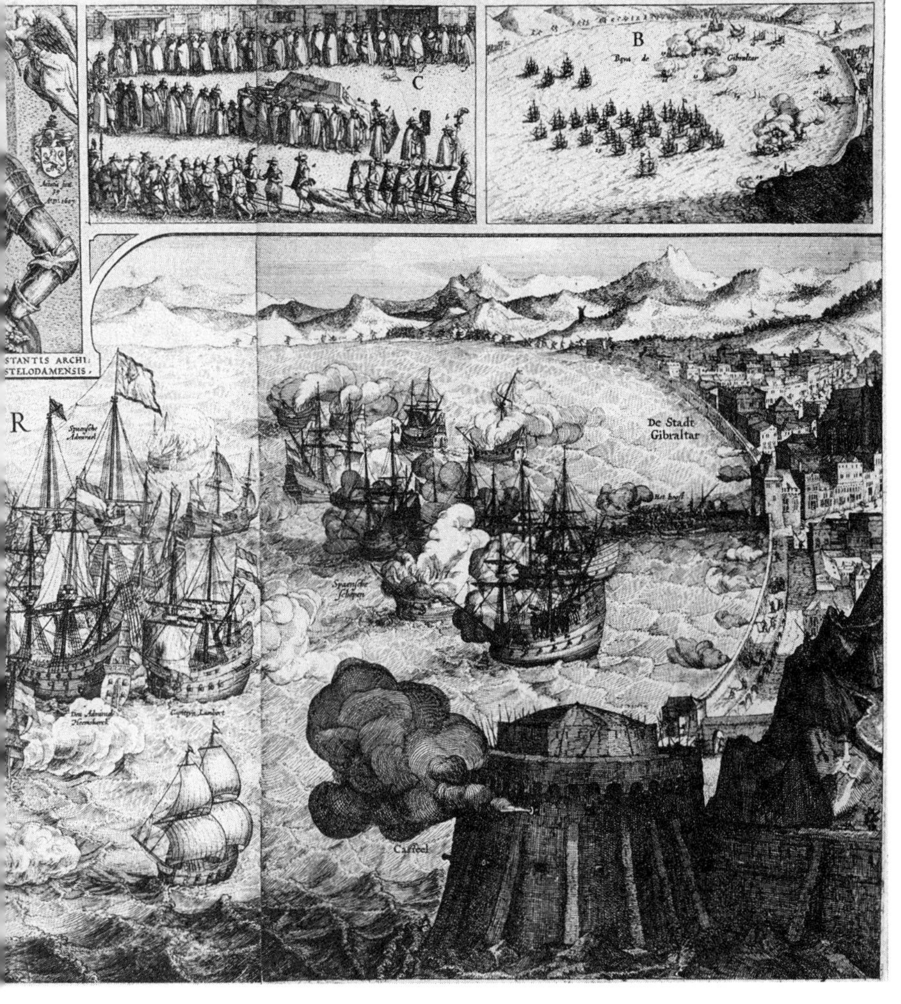
STANTIS ARCHI
STELODAMENSIS.
Actum sint
p Maii 1607
C
B
Baya de Gibraltar
De Stadt
Gibraltar
Het hooft
R
Spaensche
Admirael
Spaensche
Schepen
Den Admirael
Heemskerck
Capiteyn Lambert
Casteel

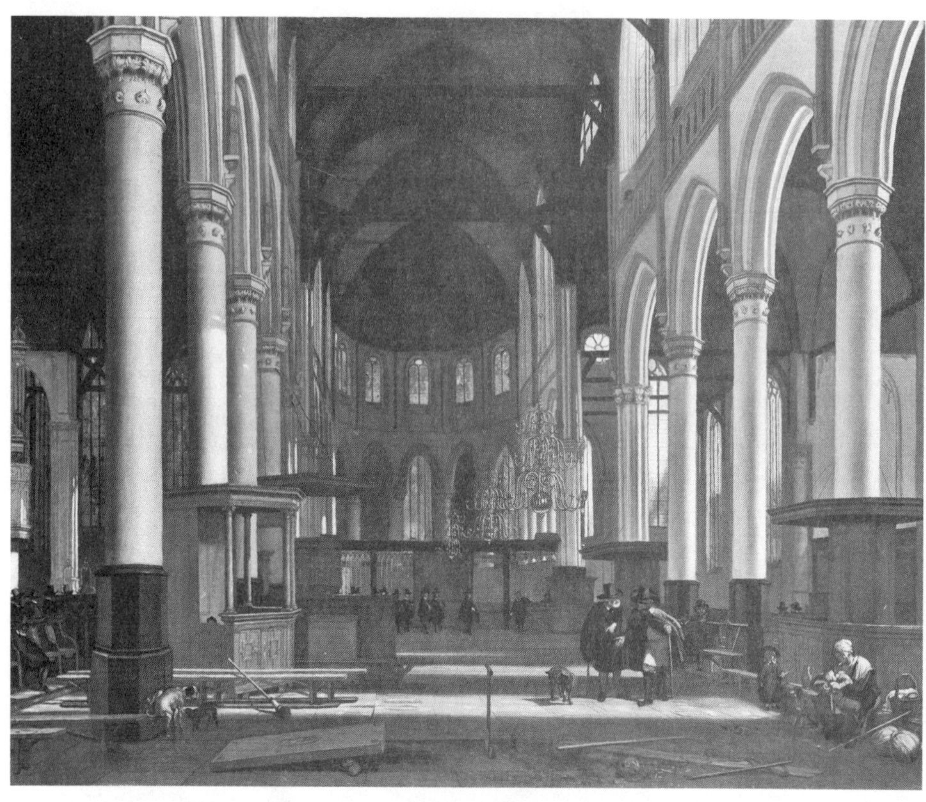

3.14 Emanuel de Witte, *The Interior of the Oude Kerk, Amsterdam*, 1660. Oil on canvas (Patrons' Permanent Fund, National Gallery of Art, Washington, DC).

centers, defined by an ability to carry their dead home and build maritime monuments in the contested space of the Reformed Church.[43]

The articulation of dead martial heroes as integral to nationhood and land also emerged in more private realms of representation. The artist Gesina ter Borch (discussed in the introduction) dedicated several works to depicting her brother Moses ter Borch, who died in a battle off the coast of England. The Ter Borches were unable to bring Moses's body home, and he therefore remained buried off the coast of England. Yet Ter Borch dedicated several drawings and a final painting to her brother-in-death, imagining him both within the landscape of their local municipality of Zwolle and off the English coastline. In one watercolor, Moses stands on the coast, alive and dressed in finery while a naval battle plays out in the background, ships sinking as skeletons claim more lives, including one that

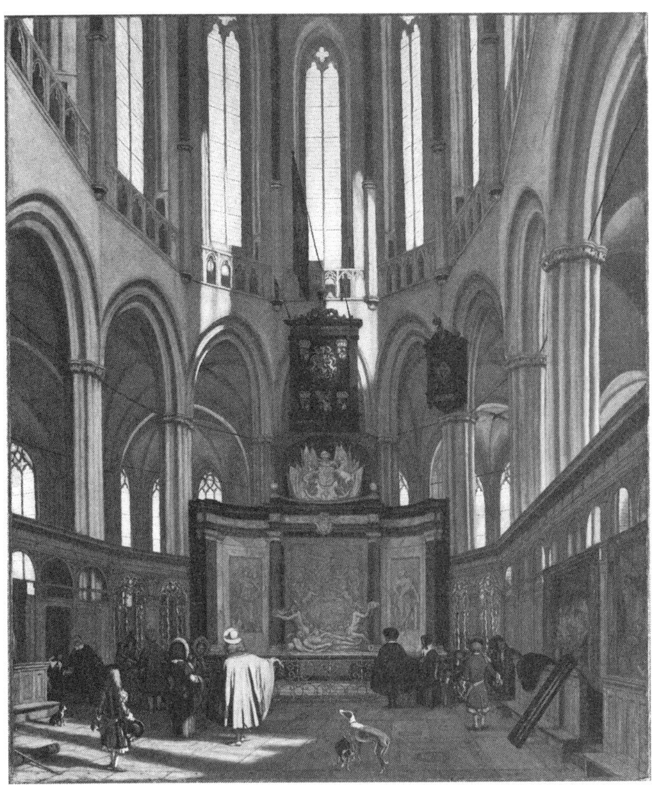

3.15 Emanuel de Witte, *The Tomb of Michiel de Ruyter in the Nieuwe Kerk, Amsterdam*, 1683. Oil on canvas (Rijksmuseum, Amsterdam).

emerges from behind a tree with an arrow aimed at Moses (figure 3.16). In another drawing, Ter Borch imagines her brother standing with a faithful hunting dog and the cityscape of Zwolle behind him (figure 3.17). These (and other) drawings were made in relation to a memorial portrait by Gesina and her brother, Gerard ter Borch (plate 11), in which a much younger Moses stands on a rocky coastline surrounded by allegorical symbols of death while the sea, which would be the site of his undoing, is pictured distantly in the background.

In all these works, Gesina ter Borch imagines her dead brother within certain landscapes, the places in which he lived and where he died. The works on paper visually intimate a representational process of bringing him home, as well as coming to terms with the physical loss of both his life and his body. Although his body was not carried home, Ter Borch actively

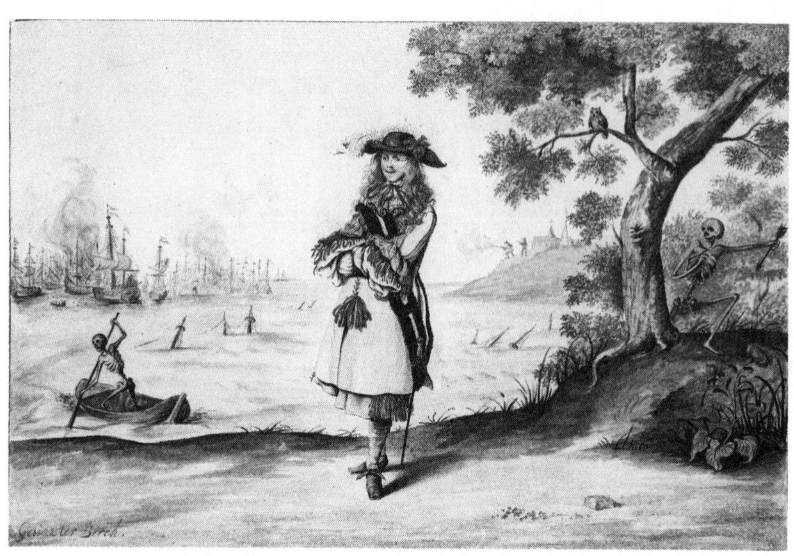

3.16 Gesina ter Borch, *Moses ter Borch on the English Coast*, ca. 1667–70. Watercolor on paper (Rijksmuseum, Amsterdam).

imagined his presence within her local landscape. These works are representations of mourning not only the absence of her brother, but also the physical absence of his buried body within their local parish. They speak to the particular grief of not bringing her brother home for burial, an acute pain that she counters with the watercolor of her brother standing against the Zwolle skyline, asserting his citizenship and belonging within their local townscape.

Private accounts such as Gesina ter Borch's and the more public monuments contextualize the violent dismissal by Willem Bosman that began this chapter, when he remarked that West Africans on the Gold Coast are "strangely fond of being buried in their own country." In the seventeenth century, Dutch concepts of citizenship, emerging nationhood, and landscape were inseparable from representing the ability (or inability) to bring home and bury those who died during wars of territorial expansion. Tracing the journeys of corpses—from the sea to the church—represents the emergence of a new relic around which identities formed to create the nation. Van Heemskerck in particular, while a maritime hero, was also important to Grotius, as his actions defined the parameters of international law. Yet unlike the Christological body created by miracle and transubstantiation, Van Heemskerck's body remains resolutely imperfect, material,

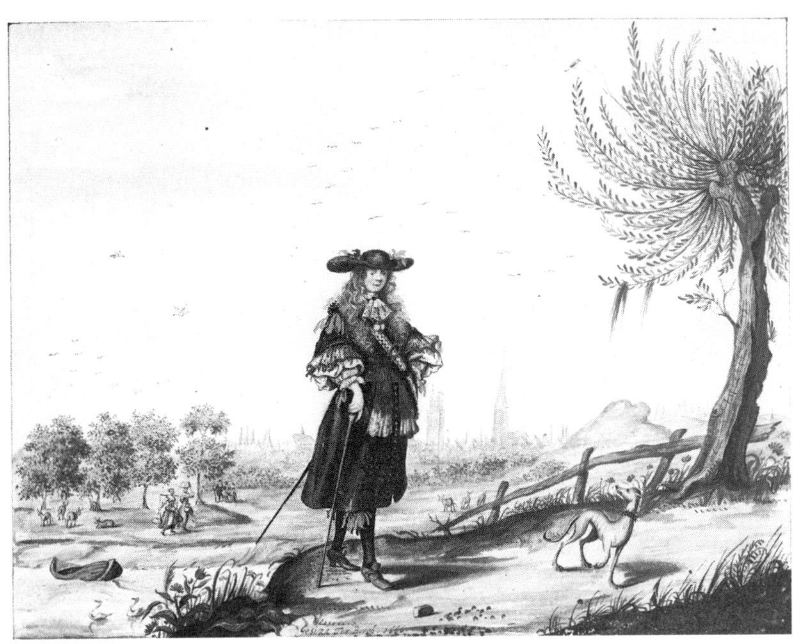

3.17 Gesina ter Borch, *Moses ter Borch in the Countryside Outside of Zwolle*, ca. 1667–70. Watercolor on paper (Rijksmuseum, Amsterdam).

bound to this terrestrial world—an imperfection realized in the partial armor, making visible that his physical corpse was fragmented. The portent of swallowing and disappearing was made evident in Van Heemskerck's missing cuisse, suggesting that not everything could be claimed and returned from the sea. Yet the armor nevertheless asserted the power of the Dutch state against this portending abyss of the ahistorical ocean by bringing Van Heemskerck home.

Grotius, in turn, was wrong. Ships do leave tracks across both the surface and floor of the ocean, penetrating dense ecosystems. The mythology that ships could cross oceans and leave not a trace—that the fluid waters could exist as borderless surfaces for trade—allowed the ocean to emerge as an imaginary space devoid of history, where shipwrecks and corpses, wealth and lives could disappear to the floor of the ocean. Yet as Walcott recognized, the "sea is History." The fluid body of the ocean—which allowed for the mythology of ships crossing water that left no tracks—was the site against which the borders of nations were defined. Grotius's proposition that a ship could cross the sea and leave not a trace implied that not only a ship but also a life could cross the sea and leave not a trace. Therefore, citizenship was founded in relation to the right to bury one's kin, demanding visibility to the trace that this life left on the earth. When Bosman remarked that West Africans were strangely fond of being buried in their own country, it is an offhand remark that betrays a new world order in which citizenship and rights would emerge in direct relationship with international law, trade, maritime space, and debates about who does and does not have the right to burial. Citizenship would emerge in direct relationship to making visible the trace that life left on this earth.

CHAPTER FOUR

Domestic Interiors and Natural History

An Index to the Indian Closset (1688) begins: "A Male child seven months old." The inventory continues: "an Indian Snake; a Pearl Oyster with a little Pearl in it; a sort of River Fish called Almanack; Priapus Vegetabilis the less; and a little Indian Adder that Feeds on Ants."[1] The list of 271 vertebrate and invertebrate animals, reptiles, insects, flora, and fauna ends on "an American squirrel; the shell of a large oyster from Ternata; and a Malabar shrub without leaf or flower." The commencement of this inventory with an infant is chilling in its comportment, placing the child in relation to branches devoid of leaves and jarred reptiles (figure 4.1). Printed outside the context of a catalog, the single line—a male child seven months old—would suggest multiple possible lives and futures. But in relation to the other items within the catalog, this single life takes shape as one forged by the exploitation of European colonialism.

The briefness of the description also occludes. The child would have been suspended in a solution as an anatomical specimen, although this is not mentioned, as no doubt the author presumed this fact obvious to any reader. Moreover, the child is placed among lizards, snakes, squirrels, plants—all in a state of suspended preservation. The description of the Malabar shrub—without leaves or flower—suggests that it is beyond its lifespan of reproduction. Yet this collection of the natural world remains conserved for display, refused the rhythm and cycles of cell degeneration,

4.1 Anonymous, page from *An Index to the Indian Closset which contains several Foreign Creatures, and Plants swimming in Balsalmick liquors as if now alive; to be seen in the Garden of the Academy of Leyden*, 1688 (Houghton Library, Harvard University, Cambridge, Massachusetts).

coming undone, disintegrating. The state of the child is not made evident, although implied, and this refusal to acknowledge the child as no longer holding a beating heart places the young life perpetually caught between life and death. The child's body is not granted the cycle bestowed on all living things to visually disappear and become integrated with other living creatures on a microscopic scale. It is perhaps not so much that the child is contextualized within the natural world, as humans are creatures of the natural world, but that this child is refused the syncopated rhythms of birth and death.

That the inventory commences with the male child attends to a hierarchy of being—placing the human infant at the beginning, perhaps the most significant place on the inventory. The placement of the child at the beginning reproduces the chain of being, a belief that the organic and inorganic world is ordered according to a rational hierarchy, with humanity occupying one of the uppermost rungs, below angelic creatures and God. By listing the child first, the writer reproduces this structure, suggesting a degree of humanity accorded to the young life. Yet as Zakiyyah Iman Jackson demonstrates, the chain of being "stratified humanity," so that "human recognition" might be granted "but only to serve further objectification."[2] The child must be recognized as existing within the human so as to serve the role that it was meant to hold within the collection, an objectification of human life to examine the limits of selfhood, personality, and intellectual consciousness. When a consciousness, an intellect, and a self enter a fetus remains a mystery and a continuing debate of political consequence. The male child at seven months old presented for its audience a point of fascination, as he grants the viewer a life—a human life, the life of a child—at the thresholds of consciousness. To examine the limits of selfhood, it is necessary to allow the child an inkling of belonging within the category of the human while also denying full membership so that the practice of placing young infants into jars for study does not reflect on the barbarity at the center of early modern natural philosophy.

The suspended state of the child within the fluid to preserve its body presents a mirror to the viewer, so that both death and birth are in an infinite suspension. Although deemed a child, the infant floated in a fluid like the amniotic sac of its earliest origins, and the young life is denied the rite of leaving the womb to be born, the loss of bodily form in death, and burial and mourning. The child offers to the viewer a glimpse at the possibility of life perpetually resting between birth and death, pointing toward a fantasy of overcoming the limits of the human coil, a promise of infinite preservation. This child is therefore granted by the writer of the inventory and the maker of the collection a sense of belonging so that they can provide the viewer a mirror by which to reflect on their own limits of self and body. Organized within the context of the larger collection, the child takes on aspects of the human while also pointing toward vegetative and animal modes of consciousness. This young life—at the limits of selfhood—becomes an objectified being by which to consider the temporal scale when the human disarticulates its being from the animal and the vegetative, and transitions from the seed implanted in the womb to a living being capable of language, memory, and creative articulations of thought and selfhood.

Within the inventory, its author refuses any physical or sensorial engagement with the collection, rendering it as a lifeless amalgam of biota. We do not know whether the Malabar shrub was prickly to the fingers or the American squirrel carried a faint smell. We do not know the smoothness of the pearls across the fingertips, or the sensation of a sharp intake of breath on beholding the child. These sensory data are stripped away, as the author presents specimens carefully disentangled from not only the particularity of touch, smell, and breath but also the cycles of creation, destruction, and faith. The inventory is a descriptive exercise, briefly enumerating the contents of a collection based on surface observations, and scholars have demonstrated how the rise of these particular descriptive practices was intimately bound with commerce, capital, and exploitation.[3]

In terms of the descriptions' brevity, Lorraine Daston argues that from about 1660 to 1730, modes of scientific description shifted from "long accounts bristling with particulars" to "concise reports made deliberately bland."[4] For the most part, Daston tracks this shift to the first half of the eighteenth century and within texts outside inventories, which already have a tendency toward the concise. Yet *An Index to the Indian Closset* also presents a natural world founded on naming universal types—often defined by geographic place—instead of rare and wonderful monsters or creatures. Though most inventories evacuate detail, this index demonstrates a move toward "type specimens" rather than individuals.[5] Daston connects this trend to the rise of "inalienable and immutable property rights." As she writes, the wars of religion destroyed the universal church. In its place, the universality of nature was invented: "First reform, then revolution, and finally conquest were all justified by recourse to *universal* nature, which superseded all local tradition and authority."[6] This evacuation of the specificity of local customs, cultures, and creation stories established the groundwork for Europeans to declare land as a commodity that could be acquired through "universal laws." For example, Europeans claimed that America was a wilderness, which Europeans tilled and transformed into an agricultural generator of revenue through their labor, thereby claiming the land as property while denying the rights of Indigenous nations.[7] The evacuation of specificity allowed a concept of land and resources that could fall under the jurisdiction of universal rights penned by European jurists, such as Hugo Grotius, who created legal terms that allowed for expansionist and colonial policies between the emerging European nation-states. Even the term *Indian closset* gestures toward both the East and West Indies—erasing geographic distinction between the two distinct areas, as plants from India are placed beside rodents from the Americas. They are all contained within a single collection that presents a concept of nature to be captured, preserved, and put on display to generate revenue. Within the Indian closset, the child is left without origin or place. Instead, this child, conceived somewhere between the East and West Indies, might remind the European beholder of an understanding of the human condition popular in the seventeenth century, often referred to as *homo bulla*, or "man is a bubble"—a momentary form, a reflection of light and color that will disappear into the ether. Yet within the Indian closset, this opportunity to reflect on mortality was created through the negation of death. The catalog marks a presence that haunts early modern natural history, the creation of ghosts by denying the cyclical logic of reproduction and death for those deemed just human enough to be categorized as a child yet not quite human enough to be granted rites of burial and mourning.

The word *child* also clarifies this infant's place as human within the chain of being, as often inventories and collections in this period employed the term *fetus*, suggesting that the lives were still in the womb, negating any violent disruption of abortion, still birth, or infanticide. The liminal state of these young lives and the difficulty of assigning the right terminology to their brief existence address the inability to assign a certain moment in which personhood is born.[8] In turn, the term *fetus* denies the possible breath and cry by which the infant came into (and left) the world, or the grief and loss experienced by the mother in the absence of her infant's cry, refusing the violence families, kin, and societies underwent as their infants were transported to European collections, as though they were a piece of exotic coral or a rare species of reptile. These children are suspended, as though still alive, and floating in the amniotic fluid of their mother's womb. The longer title for the inventory supports this amniotic suspension, as we are told that the list contains *Foreign Creatures, and Plants swimming in Balsalmick liquors as if now alive*, the emphasis on *as if now alive*, again refusing the necessity of death.[9] We are also informed that we can visit this collection in the garden of the Leiden Academy, presumably the Hortus Botanicus, the oldest botanical garden in the Netherlands, founded in 1590, which also contained the Ambulacrum, considered one of the first museums in the Netherlands, with its collection of "curious objects."[10] This presentation of a collection *as if alive* takes place within a long tradition of bottling and preserving that was integral to the rise of dissection and anatomy studies in the Netherlands, and its association with one of the first museums demonstrates the relationship between the formation of art as an aesthetic discourse and the "scientific" exploitation of life to examine the limits of self. Famous seventeenth-century anatomists such as Frederik Ruysch made a living through the display and commodification of anatomical specimens, employing new techniques to prevent decay and to make them appear "full of color."[11] The Hortus Botanicus, as part of the University of Leiden, was adjacent to an anatomical theater, where public dissections were held each winter. In the summer months, the anatomy theater transformed into an exhibition space, displaying "the brevity of human existence and the vanity of human desire."[12]

There was a culture of preserving and displaying the human body in jars for money. And while some of the infants were born in Europe, many collections, such as Ruysch's, held infants from Africa, the Americas, and Asia.[13] In the eighteenth century, infants from Africa and Asia were wrapped in beads around their ankles, wrists, bellies, and necks (often those used for trade and currency on the West African coast) before being exhibited.[14] One scholar connects the beads wrapped around the infants to a passage in the Dutch slave trader Willem Bosman's writing, in which he described local birth customs on the West African coast—a priest, known as "Fetischeer," would encircle the limbs of the child with beads as a measure of protection.[15] The children wore beads that served both as markers of protection within local ritual and currency that furthered exploitation and commodification. When the display of infants encircled by beads is understood beside the passage from Bosman's text, the exhibition becomes an ethnographic presentation of birth custom, preserving the children for the temporal status of the museum, in which lives and objects exist in suspended states of atemporality. The children become illus-

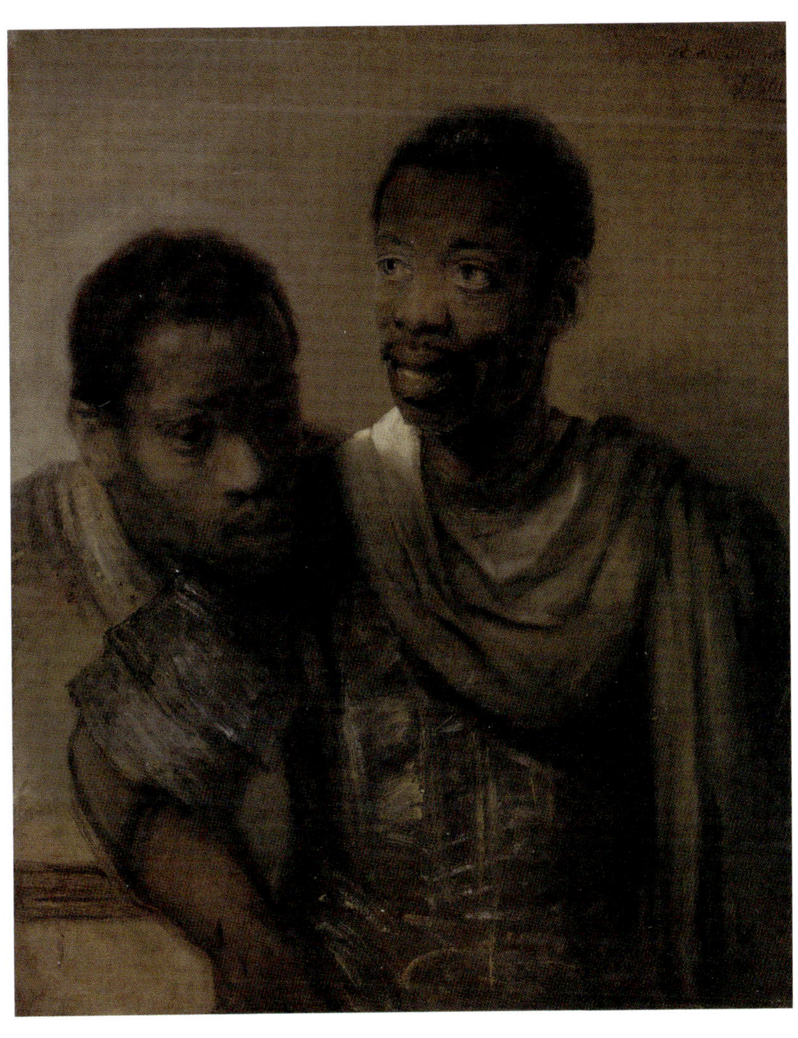

P1

Rembrandt van Rijn, *Two Men of African Descent*, 1661.
Oil on canvas (Mauritshuis, The Hague).

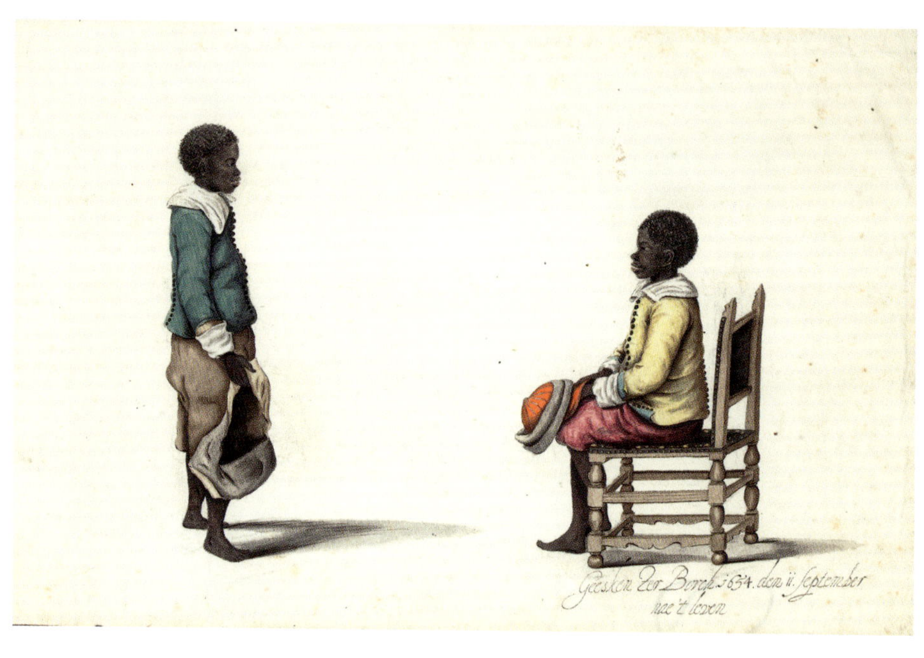

P2

Gesina ter Borch, *Two Young African Children*, in the
Familie-plakboek van Gesina ter Borch, ca. 1660–87. Watercolor
on paper (Rijksmuseum, Amsterdam).

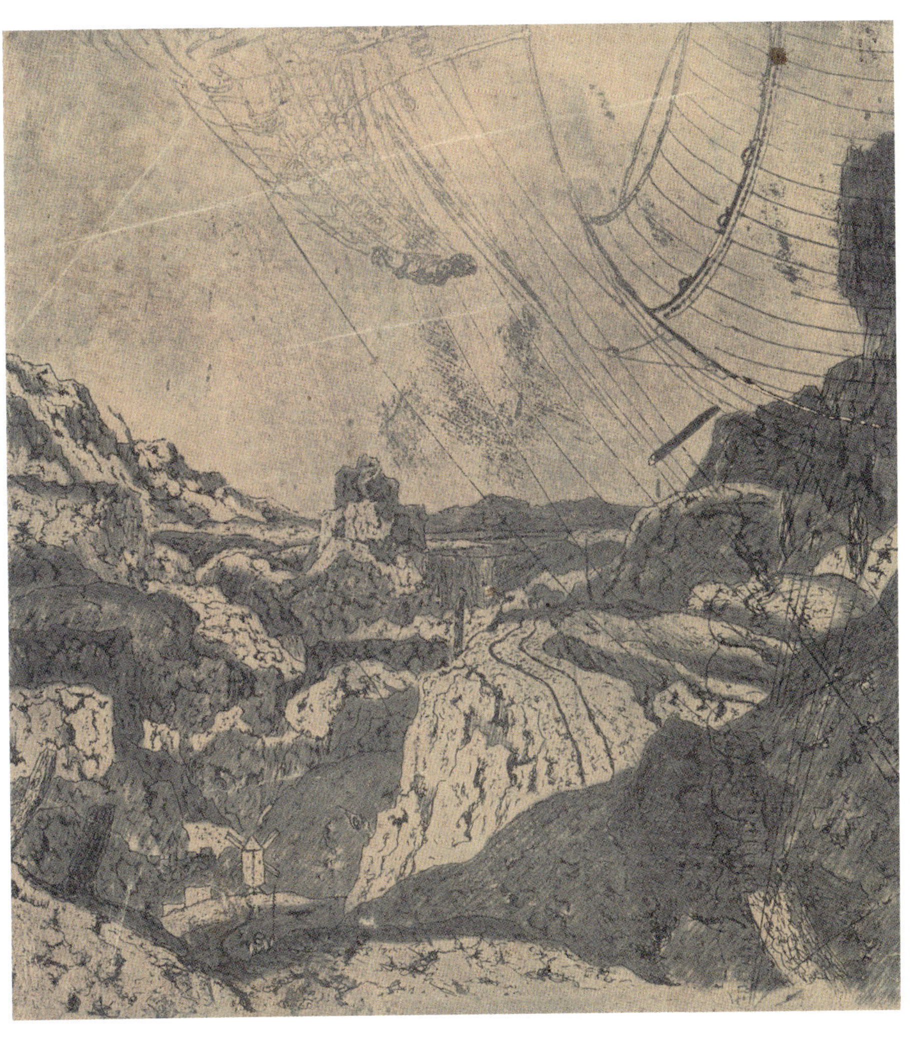

P3

Hercules Segers, *Rocky Landscape with a Gorge, First Version*,
ca. 1625–30. Line etching printed in blue on paper with a pink
prepared ground (Rijksmuseum, Amsterdam).

P4

Hercules Segers, *Mountain Valley with the Remains of a Ship*,
ca. 1623–25. Line etching and drypoint printed in black on
paper and colored with paint (Rijksmuseum, Amsterdam).

P5

Hercules Segers, *Landscape with a Waterfall, First Version*,
ca. 1625–27. Line etching and drypoint printed on blue paper
(Rijksmuseum, Amsterdam).

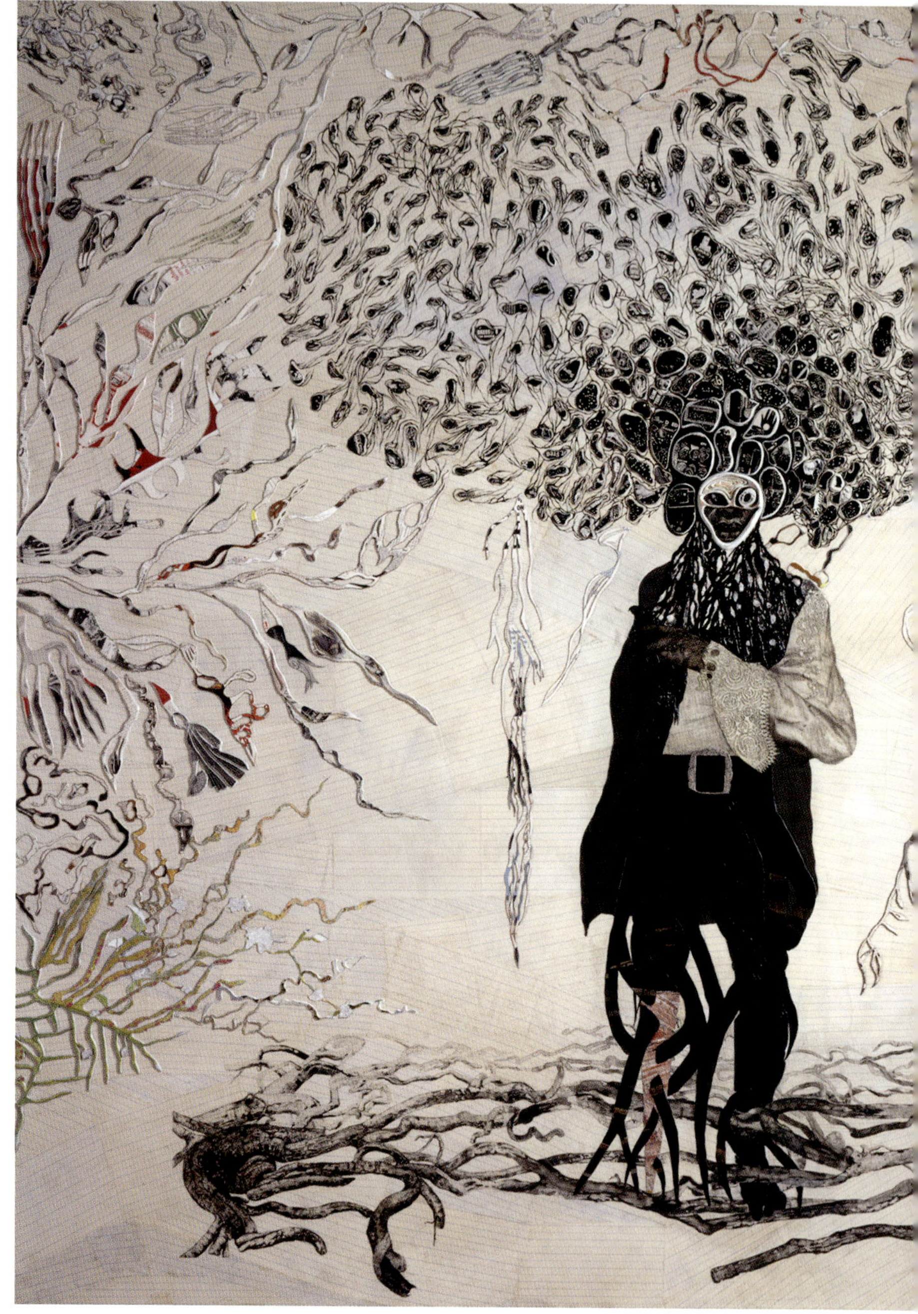

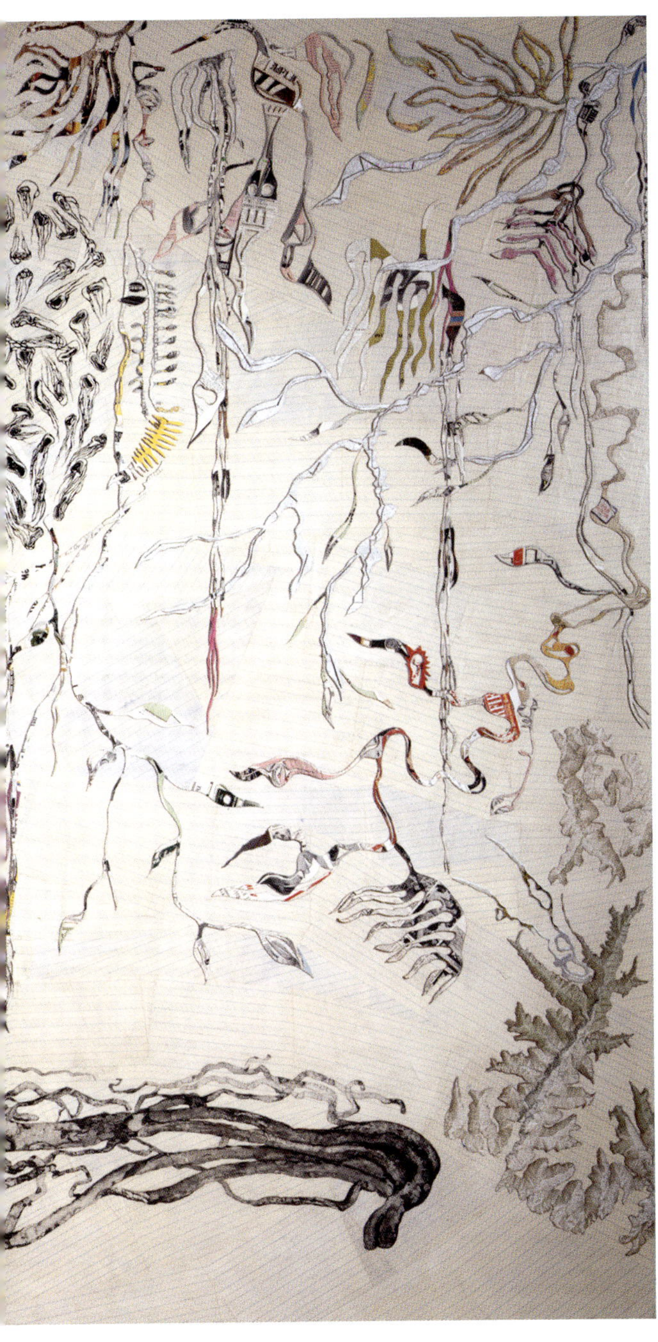

P6

Ellen Gallagher, *Bird in Hand*, 2006. Oil paint, ink, paper, polymer, salt, and gold leaf on canvas, 238.3 × 307.2 cm (© Ellen Gallagher. Courtesy of the artist and Hauser and Wirth. Photo: Mike Bruce).

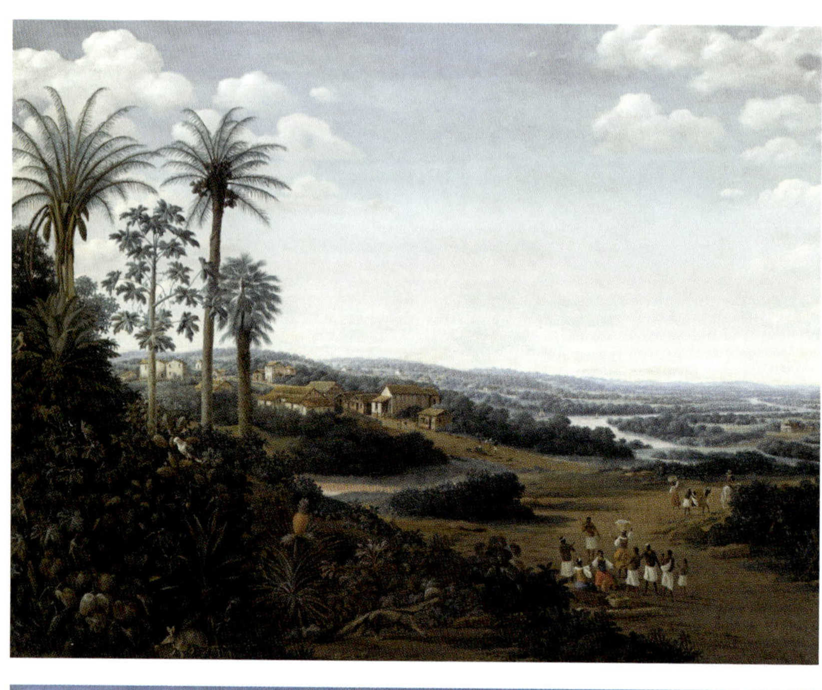

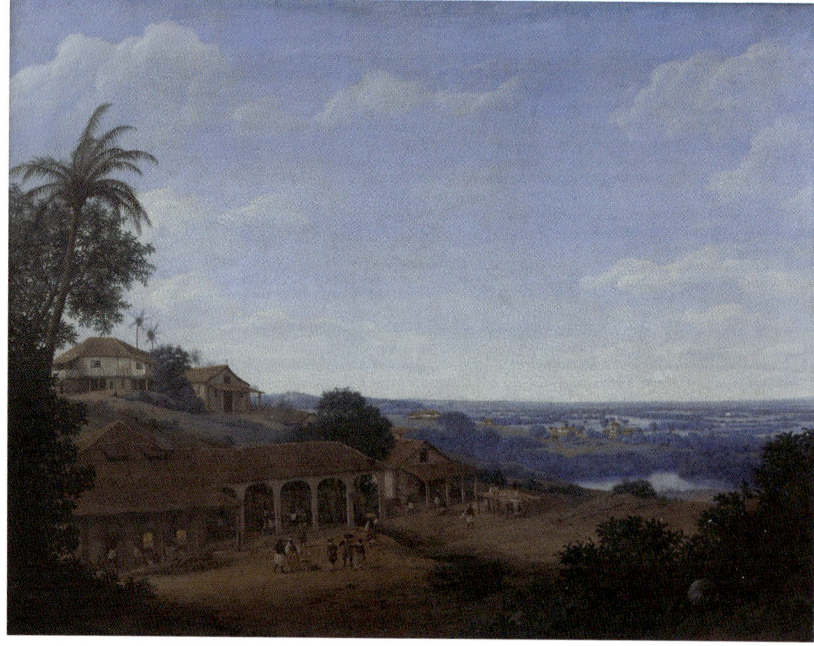

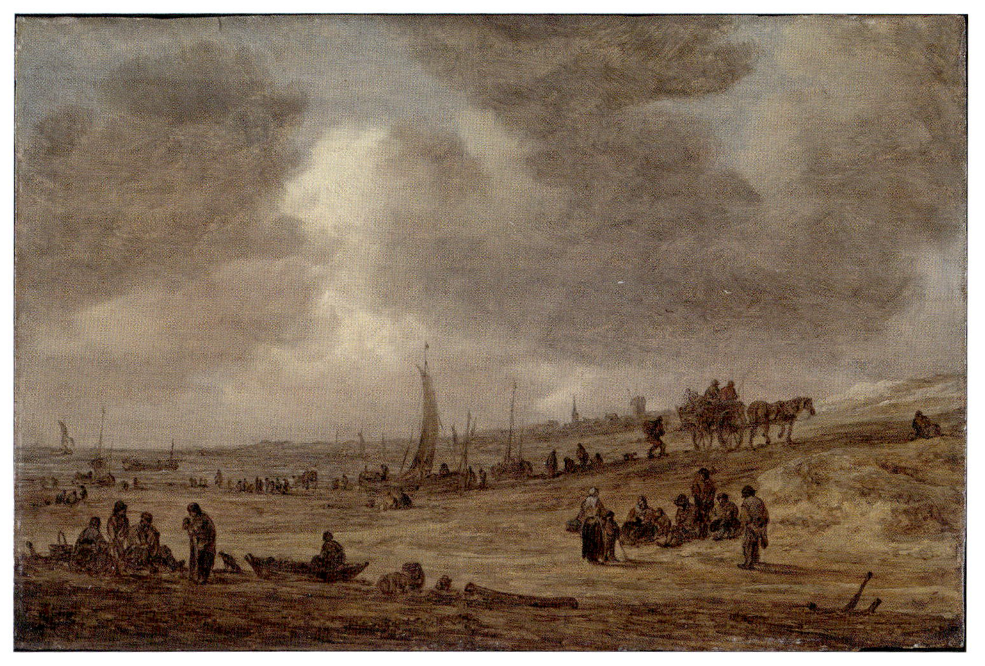

P7

(*opposite, top*) Frans Post, *Planter's House and Village*, 1644.
Oil on canvas (Musée du Louvre, Paris).

P8

(*opposite, bottom*) Frans Post, *Sugar Mill*, 1668. Oil on pane
(Statens Museum for Kunst, Copenhagen).

P9

(*above*) Jan van Goyen, *Beach with Fishing Boats*, 1653. Oil on
panel (collection of Rita and Frits Markus, bequest of Rita Markus,
2005, Metropolitan Museum of Art, New York).

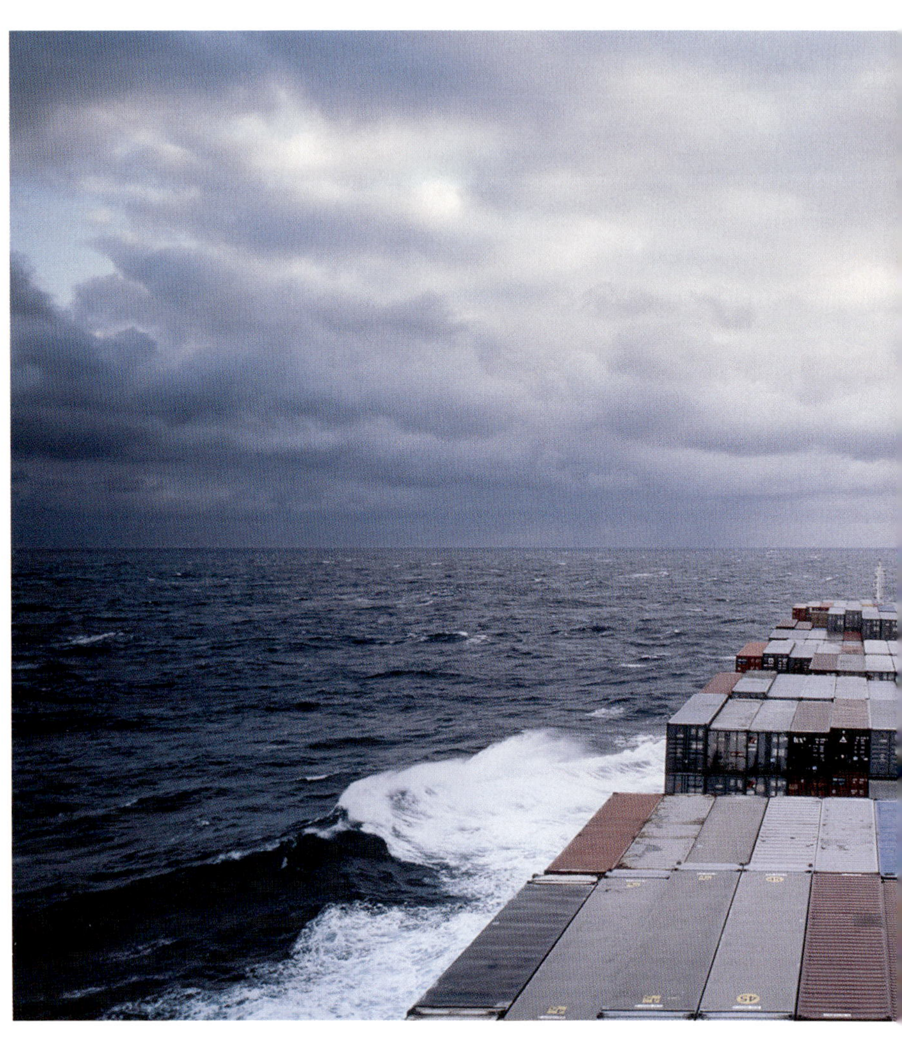

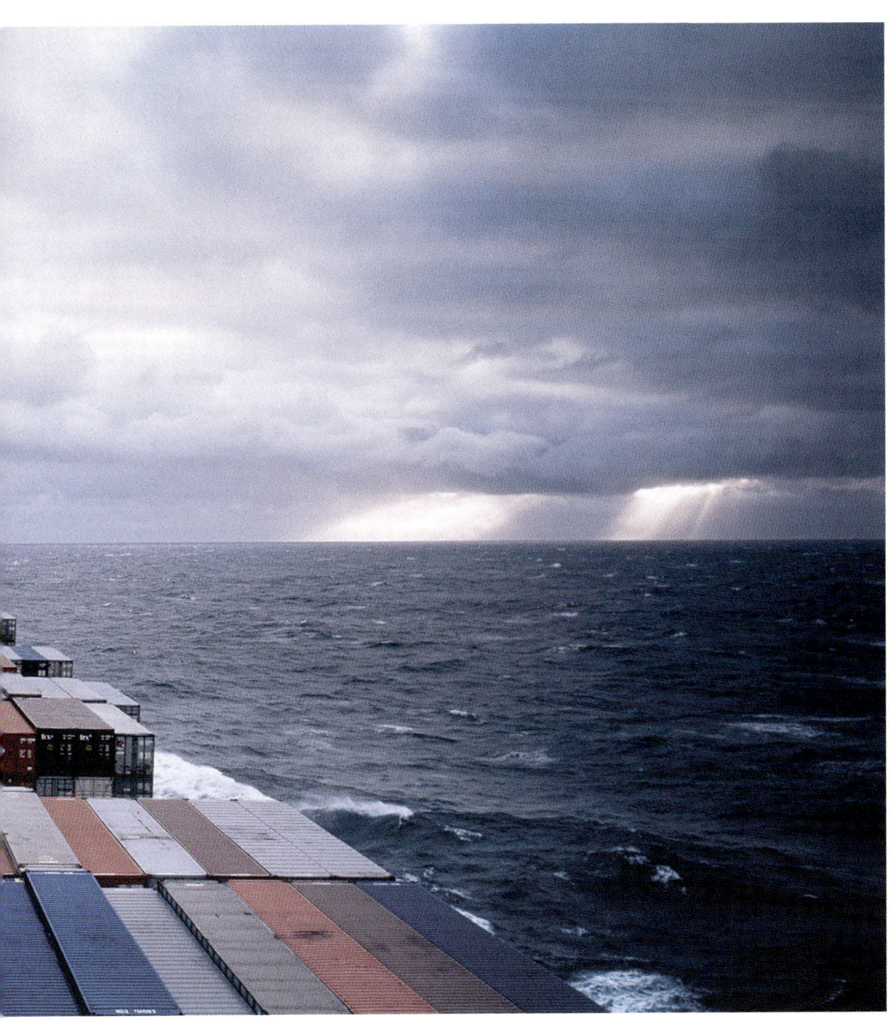

Allan Sekula, *Panorama: Mid-Atlantic,* November
1993, from the series *Fish Story,* 1989–95
(courtesy of Allan Sekula Studio).

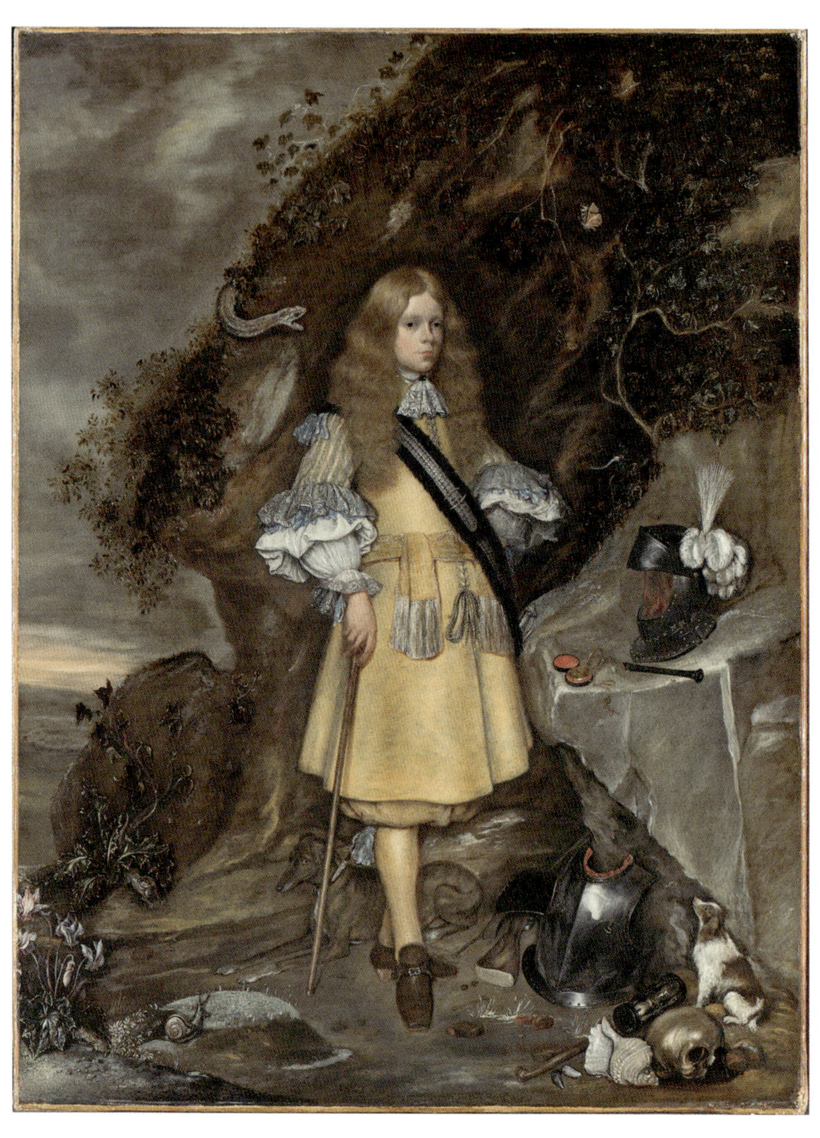

P11

Gesina and Gerard ter Borch, *Memorial Portrait of Moses ter Borch*,
ca. 1667–79. Oil on canvas (Rijksmuseum, Amsterdam).

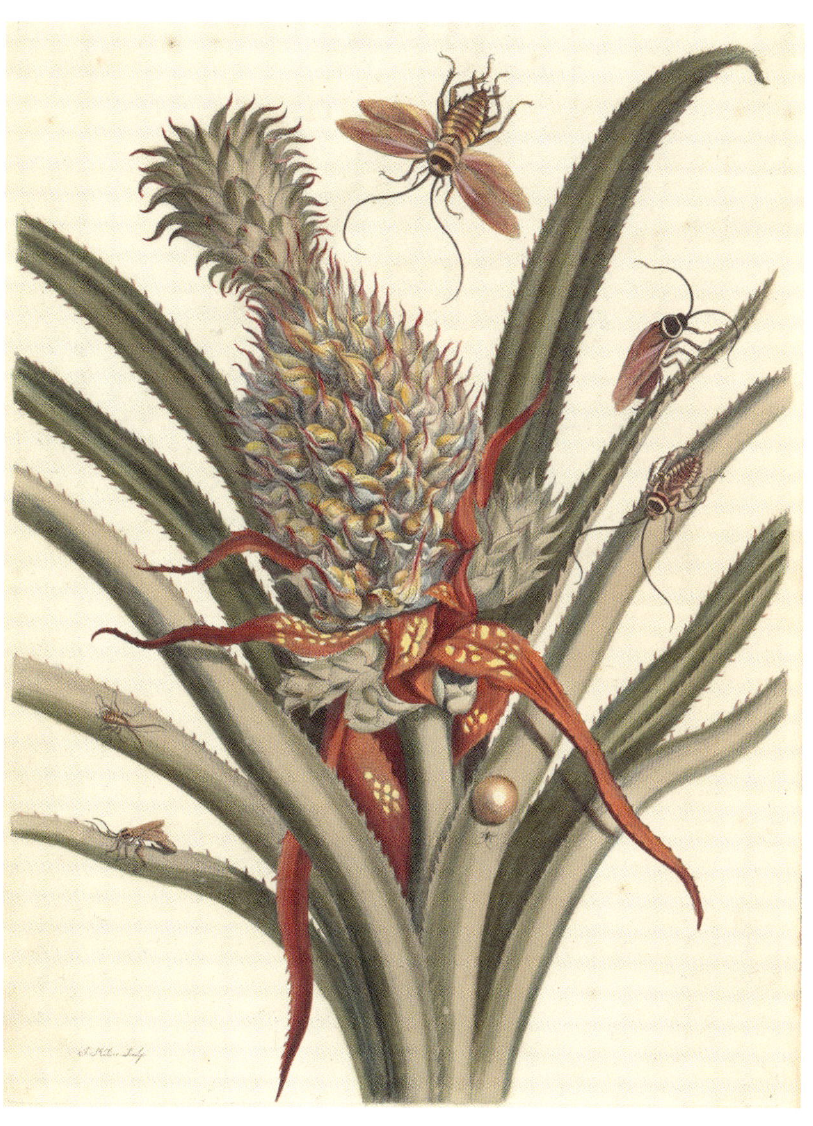

P12

Maria Sibylla Merian, *Pineapple with Cockroaches*, watercolor and
body color over lightly etched outlines, from *Dissertation sur la generation et
les transformation des insects de Surinam*, 1726, the French translation
of *Metamorphosis insectorum Surinamensium*, 1705 (Rare Book
Division, New York Public Library).

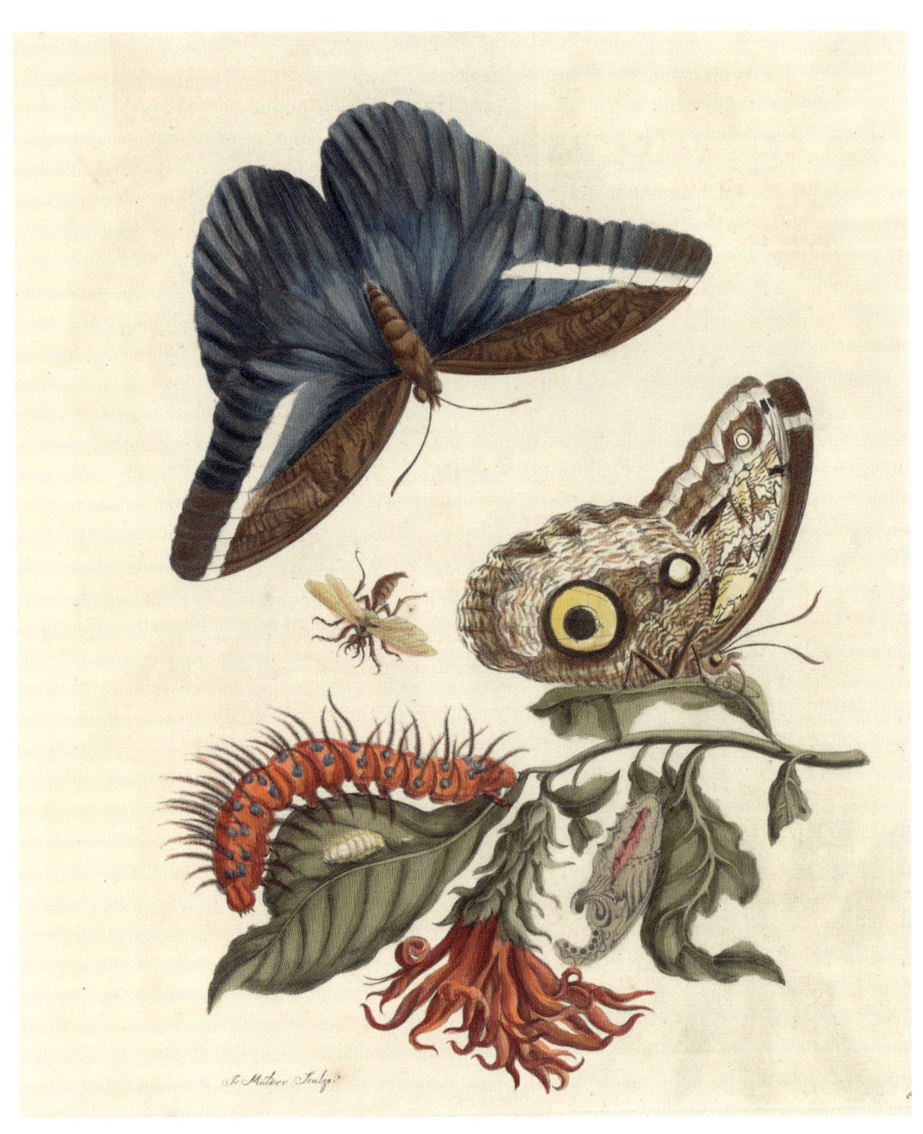

P13

Maria Sibylla Merian, *Groote Atlas and Paper Wasp* [identified by RCT as
Idomeneus Giant Owl Butterfly], watercolor and body color over lightly etched
outlines, *Dissertation sur la generation et les transformation des insects de Surinam*,
1726, the French translation of *Metamorphosis insectorum Surinamensium*, 1705
(Rare Book Division, New York Public Library).

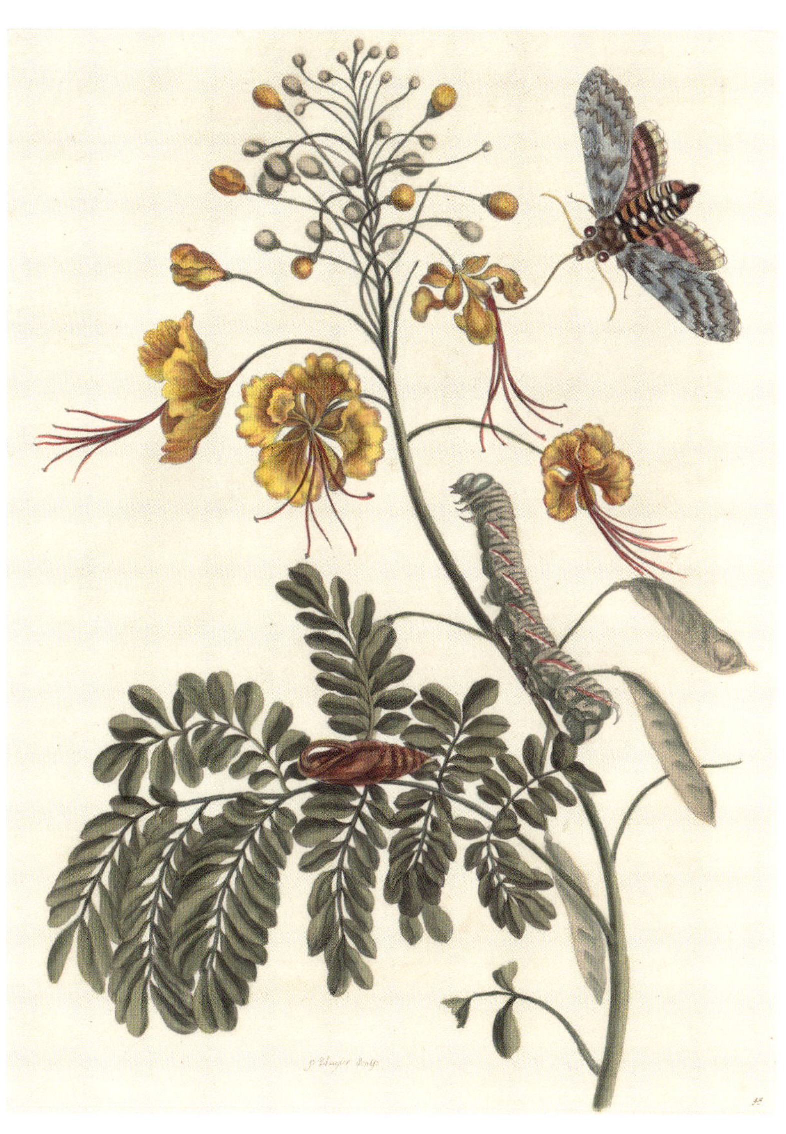

Maria Sibylla Merian, *Peacock Flower with Moth*, watercolor and body color over lightly etched outlines, from *Dissertation sur la generation et les transformation des insects de Surinam*, 1726, the French translation of *Metamorphosis insectorum Surinamensium*, 1705 (Rare Book Division, New York Public Library).

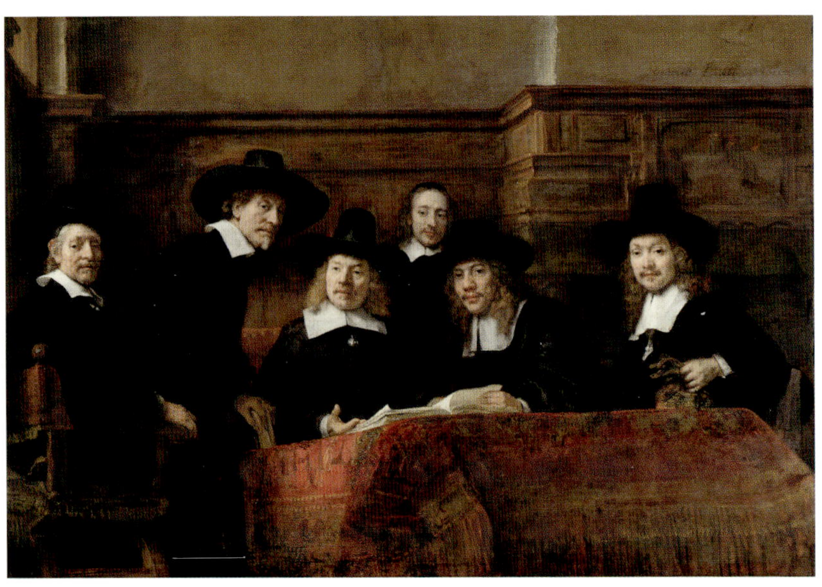

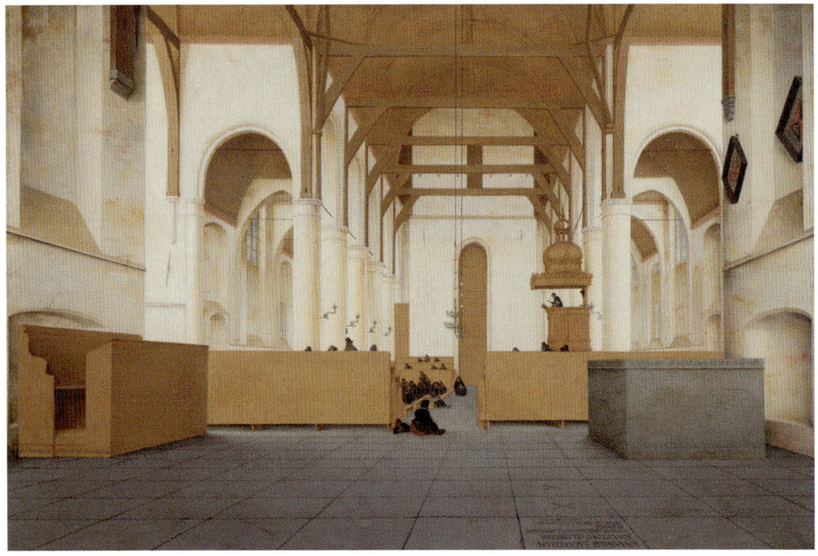

P15

Rembrandt van Rijn, *Syndics of the Drapers' Guild*, 1662.
Oil on canvas (Rijksmuseum, Amsterdam).

P16

Pieter Jansz Saenredam, *The Interior of the Cunerakerk in Rhenen*,
1655. Oil on oak (Mauritshuis, The Hague).

trations of ornament and fetish, and the protection granted by the strings of beads becomes perversely realized by their state of preservation. *As if alive* marks the act of preservation as inherently violent, a refusal to return the human body to the earth. The value of the beads encircling the child as both sacred objects and currency used along the African coast for trade binds the young life to a European culture that aimed to exploit and profit from non-Western religious practices, as a means to better understand the European self. As a commodity, these young lives occupy the center of an economy dedicated to extraction so as to order, support, and allow for the liberal realization of "self" at the center of the Enlightenment project. The children are presented as case studies in development, personhood, and individuation, while also being transformed into fungible commodities wrapped in local currencies of trade. A degree of humanity is granted to these young lives so that they can become objects of study for men such as Ruysch to articulate and understand the limits of their own personhood and its temporal coming into being from development in the fetus to death. Existing simultaneously in states of birth and death, the display of the children asks when the self enters and leaves the body. These lives and their "lightning presences" are not a macabre aberration in the history of art and science in the Netherlands, the cabinet of curiosity, or the early history of collections.[16] These children and their display in a culture that commodified both knowledge and human flesh are intrinsic to any history of art and knowledge in Dutch pictorial production.[17] While metaphysics and an exploration of God as creator have been ascribed to seventeenth-century Dutch art and science, these children perform in a perpetual state, uprooted from place and kin.[18] Refused burial and mourning, the child is exiled from sociality while paradoxically placed within God's creation, "a male child seven months old."

This tradition is routinely repeated in the most famous cabinets of curiosities in the Netherlands, from the anatomical collection of Frederik Ruysch to the cabinet of curiosity curated by textile merchant Levinus Vincent, whose collection was famous throughout Europe.[19] Vincent charged an entrance fee to his cabinet of curiosities (two guilders), and he published an inventory of his collection (three guilders). In his catalog, an engraving displays the fashionable elite examining the specimens in a space that is grandiose to the point of fantasy (figure 4.2). While most viewers are dressed in European robes, two men are in Turkish dress, perhaps alluding to the importance of the Ottoman Empire and its trade networks in establishing such a collection.[20] In the foreground, one wigged and pow-

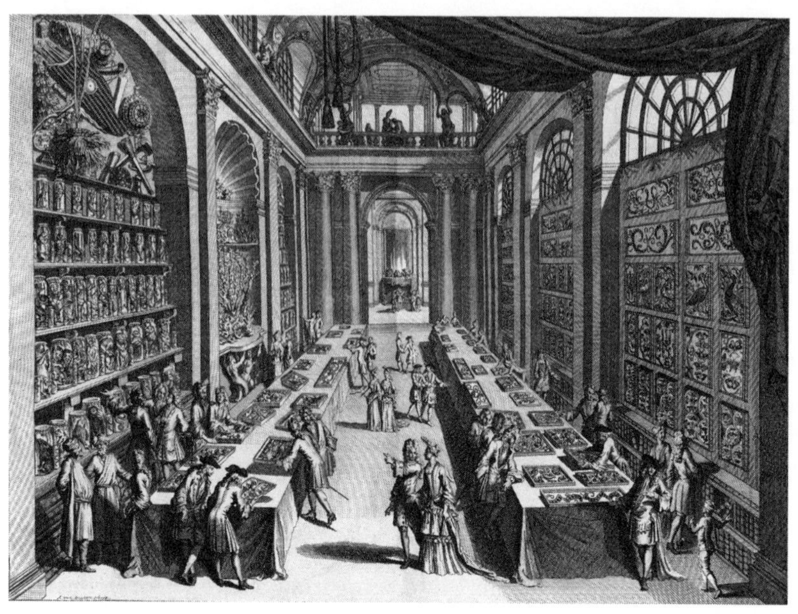

4.2 Levinus Vincent, frontispiece, *Wondertooneel der Nature*, 1706 and 1715 editions (University of Strasbourg, France).

dered man picks up a tray of butterfly specimens for inspection, reminding the viewer that the works on display could be handled, examined, turned around in the hand, studied closely, much like the print itself.

Glass jars in which specimens are placed for preservation within liquids line the walls of the halls. The order of the jars is tenuous, predominantly guided by aesthetics and size. While the uppermost jars are occupied by small reptiles, the shelves closer to the gazes and hands of the visitors clearly display infants. In this engraved representation, one of the infants expands and presses against the confines of the glass, his eyes closed and compressed against the transparent wall, his midsection swollen, while his small feet float off the bottom of the jar. He remains suspended in time and place, removed from burial, from ancestors, from land, from place, and contextualized violently within a collection of birds and reptiles. Moreover, the dressing of his body with beads specifically aligns him with a tradition of children removed from their kinship, families, and rites of birth and death to be placed within European collections, signaling a foreign continent on display.[21]

From Levinus to the Indian closset, the traces of these lives make absolutely apparent the interrelationship between the pursuit of natural history in early modern Europe and the simultaneous degradation and commoditization of life. Although many of the classic histories of early modern collections attend to the integral role of the Dutch East and West India Companies in garnering objects, while also attending to the often brutal and exploitative relationship between colonialism and botany, the stories implied by the children haunting these collections remain unexamined.[22] "A male child seven months old" in an inventory of botanica, insects, and reptiles demonstrates the role of reproduction and its study in early modern Europe as interwoven with the rise of the plantation economy in the Americas. Human reproduction and the development of a life from seed to breathing, crying, speaking being—the creation of this self—as both a biological and a metaphysical project was a developing science, and the plantation was one site where the limits of human reproduction and personhood were pushed in relation to one another. As *An Index to the Indian Closet* clarifies, this emerging "science" of selfhood and reproduction was not contained to the human, as often cycles of human reproduction were understood only in relation to biological and insect cycles of development. The rest of this chapter focuses on a collector of butterflies and other insects, Maria Sibylla Merian, who studied reproduction, generation, and metamorphosis within the insect and plant kingdoms. While living on a plantation in Suriname, Merian used the world of insects and plants to reflect and obliquely picture the failure of domestic spaces of reproduction and household economy within the interior of the plantation.

Maria Sibylla Merian

Maria Sibylla Merian, one of the most famous naturalists of the early eighteenth century, traveled to Suriname to observe the metamorphosis of South American insects from caterpillar to chrysalis to butterfly.[23] Throughout the many accounts of her life, she is celebrated, although scholars are increasingly acknowledging her complicity within a colonial system of enslavement and extraction.[24] The fact that insect societies are described as colonies is not merely a coincidence. As Eric Brown articulates, insect colonies and their propensity toward either harmonious sociality or parasitic destruction—and the perception of their internal governance by Europeans—was inseparable from the colonial project.[25]

While insects might have occupied the lower rungs in the great chain of being, the sociality of insects and their ability to organize and reproduce have been understood since the Roman poet Virgil as a mirror of human society and government. For Virgil, bees embodied Roman ideas of state and citizen: "The bees have common cities of their own, / And common sons; beneath one law they live, / And with one common stock their traffic stall; / All is the state's, the state provides for all."[26] Historically insects, particularly bees, were models of governance, both public and private; insect communities embodied "perfect governance and efficiency."[27] This sociality of insects reflects human interaction and government, a trope that continued into the seventeenth and eighteenth centuries, in which the word *colony*—derived from the Latin *colere* (to cultivate)—was first used to describe insect populations. The Roman *colonus* "was as likely to be a farmer, bringing physical order to the land, as a settler reordering the population."[28] This trope reappears in images such as George Cruikshank's *British Bee Hive* (1840), in which industries and professions, from magistrate and chemist to chimney sweep and coal miner, are ordered in a pyramidal hierarchy, contained within the colony of the hive (figure 4.3). Agriculture and free trade occupy one of the uppermost tiers, centered in the hierarchy of economic order.

From Roman poetry to nineteenth-century allegorical prints, the governance of insect colonies served as an analogy for human social orders. For Merian and her contemporaries, insects offered fertile ground by which to study not only nature's propensity for order and self-governance but also the capability of social colonies to thrive, populate, and survive through reproduction. As Merian realized, both humans and insects transform the populations where they choose to colonize, and this propensity for insects to challenge and reorder population through both generation and destruction forms the crux of Merian's fascination with lepidoptera in Suriname—their ability to populate and generate colonies.

According to Merian, she traveled to Suriname to observe insect reproduction. As specimens from South America, Asia, and elsewhere entered European collections, insects arrived dead in European ports after the oceanic journeys. In the introduction to her magnum opus *Metamorphosis insectorum Surinamensium*, Merian expresses a desire to see the environments that nourished the South American moths and butterflies. While acknowledging the importance of Ruysch's and Levinus's collections (she specifically names both men), she remarks on their absences as well. In particular, Merian focuses on information about the original environment in which the specimens lived, laid their eggs, and transformed from pupae into insects in flight. To make these observations, Merian un-

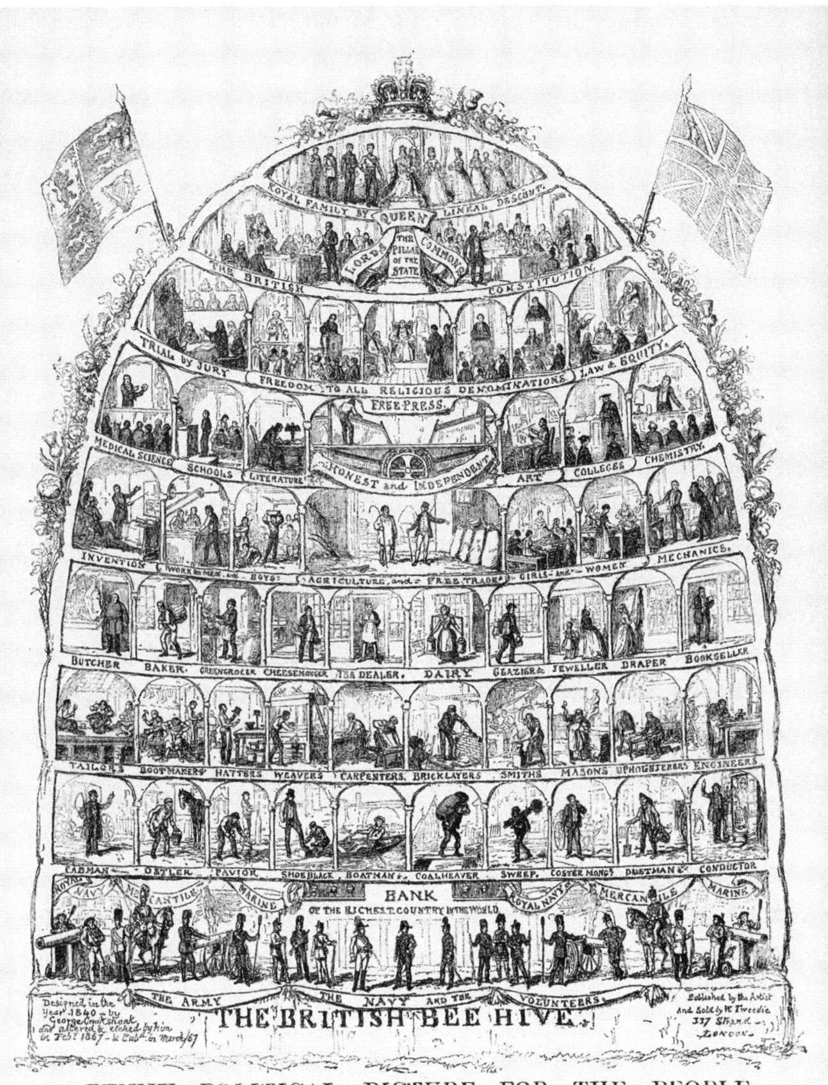

4.3 George Cruikshank, *The British Bee Hive*, designed 1840 and printed 1867. Etching (Victoria and Albert Museum, London).

dertook a journey that was dangerous. Members of a religious community, with whom Merian lived for a period, who had traveled to Suriname years earlier, were attacked by pirates and left marooned in the middle of the ocean.[29] Although they arrived in Suriname, their reports were grim accounts of heat and death. Unlike the previous trips of artists such as Frans Post, Merian's journey was not financed by the government, a trading company, or a patron, and she took on debt and sold her work to meet the financial demands of traveling to Suriname.

When she returned to Amsterdam in 1705, she published *Metamorphosis insectorum Surinamensium*, a lavish sixty-plate study of butterflies, moths, reptiles, and plants from Suriname.[30] The illustrations have been celebrated as a revolution in natural history, as they attend to the microecosystems in which the insects lived and thrived. Although she focused on insects (as elaborated in the title of the work), her engravings give equal space to the botanical world that supported Suriname's insects. In her luscious illustrations of plants, Merian depicted the domestic spaces for insects, which provided them through their brief lives with the branching and flowering structures on which to protect eggs and pupae and nourish themselves. In turn, she attends to nibbled leaves, presenting the importance of the plants for nourishment once the eggs hatch into caterpillars. And finally, she pictures cocoons and the transformation of caterpillars into moths and butterflies, who will ultimately serve as pollinators for the plants on which they depended for sustenance and growth. While she would not have been familiar with the concept of pollination, which was not fully developed until Christian Konrad Sprengel published in 1793 *Das entdeckte Geheimnis der Naturi im Bau und in der Befruchtung der Blumen*, Merian directly pictures the symbiotic and sometimes destructive relationship between insects and plants. For these reasons, her work is largely considered a revolution in natural history illustration, as she did not represent insects as isolated creatures in collectors' cabinets. Instead, she captured the sociality among plants and insects within the space of the plantation, the garden, and the forest.

Nevertheless, the articulation of these relationships was often willful, and the juxtapositions that she formed narrate a history of the plantation economy in Suriname as much as the relationships among insects and plants.[31] As mentioned, Merian drafted ecosystems in miniature, focusing on isolated interactions between a single plant and the insects it houses and feeds. The artistry of Merian's illustrative craft contributed to a long tradition of studying the sociality of reproduction among plants, insects, and animals in the eighteenth century, a project that would culminate in Charles Darwin's *On the Origin of Species*. Yet her work was also informed by the domestic sphere of women's labor and consumption in the home. Merian's fascination with insects began in childhood with breeding silkworms, an insect prized for its ability to create the precious raw material for the silk industry. And her earlier printed work, such as *Neues blumenbuch* (1680), was explicitly intended for embroidery and lacemaking patterns and designs to be translated with thread and linen into objects for domestic interiors. While Merian's Suriname work would be important for entomologists, botanists, and natural historians throughout the eighteenth century, the context of domesticity and the home is also central for contextualizing her work produced in Suriname, which pivots around crises in domesticity and conflicts between the domestic space of the plantation and its counterpart in Amsterdam.

Domestic Interiors

In *Metamorphosis*, Merian placed the minute scale of the insect colony in relation to the human, forcing an attention to details that might be easily overlooked during a stroll through a plantation garden, or a walk into the forest. The illustrations never allude to a border between the plantation and the forest, between the space of agriculture and the demarcated areas of dense growth and mountainous forests, which were also home to the maroon communities, composed predominantly of African and Indigenous individuals fleeing the conditions of the plantation to build their own society in the dense Surinamese forests. The large expanse of paper provides the neutral background for all images, so that there is little differentiation of varying ecologies from which the examples derive. The illustrations instead focus on the micro-interactions between insect and plant while often the larger context for the specimen (forest or garden) is provided by Merian's text. The pupae and larvae, which might be easily overlooked in a forest, or even in a garden, often become the size of a thumb, while spiders and butterflies dwarf pineapples and grapefruits. There is no relative scale within the illustrations. Through the monumental size of the folio prints, Merian brings the insect into scale with the human body. She draws the viewer into the micro-ecosystems, so that the beholder may study the certain pattern of the butterfly's wing, or the coloring of a caterpillar, suggesting that the metamorphosis of a butterfly belongs on the same scale as a history painting. The size supports these ecosystems as monuments in print, small ecosystems that otherwise might be overlooked as they are constantly in cycles of generation and death. The illustrations do not portray a single moment in the life of an insect. Instead, like a history painting, her scenes narrate a series of events across the paper, portraying the life of an insect from its development as an egg to its birth and later stages of life. The life of an insect is transformed into the scale of history and monument, so that the insect world comes into relation with the space of the human body. Instead of existing as creatures that one can ignore, swat away, or briefly admire, the insects in the book draw the gaze of the human to their sensors, prickles, and antennae.

The natural world depicted in Merian's work is one of parasitic destruction, and like the specimens in *Indian Closset*, she presents her insects as if alive, although she almost certainly captured their likeness in death, preserved in drawers and jars that she brought back with her from Suriname to Amsterdam. As one scholar notes, "Merian generally drew the wing position as adopted at the moment of death."[32] Her narratives often begin with the caterpillar and its devouring of the plant's leaves, a process captured in illustrations constantly marked by nibbled and yellowing leaves, no doubt expressing the plant's precarious state in response to hosting the insect. Merian was fascinated with "'bloodless creatures' that cause damage to plants. She never drew a plant with leaves that did not have holes or nibbled edges."[33]

Merian commences her book with the pineapple and a cockroach with curving antennae extending out from its body, two whiplash lines nearly touching the sharp talons of the fruit's petals (plate 12). Hummingbirds, honeybees, and bats are the main pollinators of this fruit, so Merian creates an incongruous pairing. Yet she states that cockroaches prefer sweet foods, "which is why they are very fond of this fruit."[34] While the engraving attends to the nestling of the fruit within its stalk, the prickles of its waxy leaves, and the pointed texture of its flowers, the pestilent cockroach and its probing antennae evoke the sweet and sticky inside of the pineapple. The size of the cockroach in flight, with its flowing lines of antennae, endows the creature with a sensate form. With the exaggeration of the antennae, Merian accentuates the sensorial tickle of these creatures, "the best known of all insects in America," as they destroy costly goods, including "wool, linen, food, and drink."[35] Merian's interest in the cockroach is not confined to its propensity for property damage but extends to its reproductive cycle, which thrives within the context of the plantation house, so that the young hatch and then invade boxes and cupboards, "where they spoil everything."[36] Merian draws her reader and viewer into Suriname through the cockroach and its ability to permeate and invade domestic spaces, particularly the closeted interiors of cupboards and chests that hold foodstuffs and costly family linens. While the cockroach is pictured on the pineapple's exterior, her text evokes an insect that penetrates into the innermost corners of domestic space.

Merian was likely unaware of its origins, but the cockroach is not indigenous to the Americas. Its presence has been traced to the increased traffic of ships from Africa, a history fossilized in the survival of a mummified cockroach on the pages of an eighteenth-century slave ledger (figure 4.4). Yet even without being aware that she was discussing a creature that had arrived in tandem with the rise of the transatlantic slave trade, Merian begins her work with an invasive species that had a propensity for ruin and destruction. In turn, the pineapple evokes the rise of exotic horticulture in Europe and the dinner tables of wealthy elite merchants and aristocrats, who served pineapple—the king of fruits—as a luxury item. The role of the pineapple in forming ideas of aesthetic taste appears most explicitly in a passage in John Locke, in which he articulates his concepts around experience and knowledge through the ability (or inability) to imagine the taste of this rare, exotic, and expensive fruit.[37] By placing the cockroach in direct proximity to the pineapple, Merian collapses the distinction between interior and exterior within the plantation. Using an insect renowned for its ability to crawl through floorboards and between walls, to penetrate into the interior of cupboards and chests, Merian places the reader within an interior domestic space that is under attack, and the sharp quills and points of the pineapple flower become the metonymic site by which she visually represents the domestic interior of the plantation. By drawing the pineapple and the cockroach next to each other, Merian illustrates the coexistence of the elite fruit and the pestilent insect, an invader of domestic spaces that arrived with the ships bringing kidnapped men, women, and children from the west coast of Africa. The cockroach traveled from the hold of the ship to the folds of the linen cabinet, and its portrayal on the waxy, prickly leaves of the pineapple's exterior articulates a pervasive absence that informs, haunts, and structures Merian's natural history: the inability to visualize and picture the economy of the domestic interior within the plantation. Instead, the interior domestic spaces of the plantation are pictured obliquely in Merian's text, through the sensors of the insects that she portrays, remarking on their ability to invade, encroach, destroy, and penetrate the plantation home.

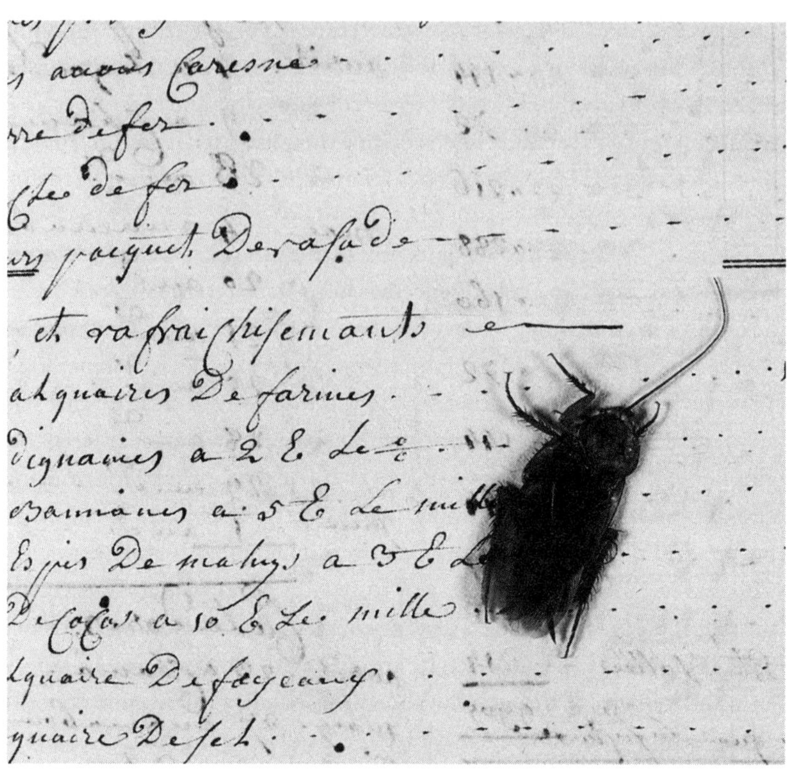

4.4 Logbook from the ship *La Société of Nantes* and an eighteenth-century mummified cockroach (reference: HCA32/153/18/1; National Archives, London).

The Absence of the Plantation Interior

Beginning with Frans Post, a pictorial history of plantations and colonization in the Americas commenced, although this visual history was exclusively dedicated to landscape and the structures of the plantation—sugar mills, churches, plantation houses—from the exterior. This tradition continued into the later seventeenth and eighteenth century, so that the interior spaces of the Dutch plantations in the Americas remain predominantly absent from the pictorial record.[38] This stands in marked contrast to the proliferation and steady accumulation of paintings depicting the Dutch home interior, which were popular on the market in seventeenth- and eighteenth-century Holland. The rise of domestic Dutch interior scenes in the seventeenth century is often explicitly read as emblematic of the larger governance and order of the Dutch Republic.[39] This is a genre of painting produced by artists such as Gerard ter Borch, Nicolaes Maes, Frans van Mieris, Gabriël Metsu (among others), and, perhaps most famously, Johannes Vermeer.[40] While the genre varies according to painter and period, during the seventeenth century in the Dutch Republic, a type of painting developed in which elite and wealthy women were portrayed within their homes, playing instruments, entertaining male visitors, receiving letters, making lace, or engaging in various activities more leisure than labor. Allusions to the Dutch colonies are frequent within these scenes, whether a seascape or map pictured on the wall, or costly goods, such as pearls and porcelain, obtained through trade and overseas commerce. These veristic displays of domesticity are often viewed by scholars as emblems of Dutch prosperity and as societal markers of not only economic wealth but also moral citizenship. As Martha Hollander notes, the house in seventeenth-century Holland was understood as a place to raise and cultivate moral and spiritual citizens who also participated in the social and financial economy. This display of material wealth was complemented by the privacy of interior conscience, as the house and its domestic interior were "a vehicle for asserting one's individual and civic identity."[41]

This visual articulation of civic identity in the home emerged through picturing the interior lives of women engaged in private thoughts as they wrote and received letters, planned out gridded lace designs, and practiced musical scales. Yet as Powell pointedly notes, "almost always occupied by women, these interiors belong to houses that are by all indications the property of men."[42] The paintings of private home interiors reflecting the inner lives of women became a commodity to be bought and sold on the art market, pointing toward not only the domestic interior as a site of consumption but also women as consumers necessary for the rise of the Dutch economy in the seventeenth century. Many of the goods that surround these women, as markers of wealth and taste, were dependent on Dutch markets and settlements in the colonies, from pearls obtained from Indian and Atlantic waters to beavers harvested along the Hudson and silver, sugar, and salt arriving from the Americas. The dominance of this genre painted in patria stands in marked contrast to the near-complete absence of scenes of domestic interiority from the colonies.[43] One might argue that Vermeer never traveled to Suriname, although this simplistic reduction overlooks how the conditions of interracial marriage, concubinage, sex, and enslaved labor created an interior that would have ruptured the image of civic virtue and identity that coalesced in Ter Borch's satin gowns and Vermeer's light-filled rooms. Yet despite the near-complete absence of interior scenes of the plantation house, Merian directly brings the domestic space of the plantation into her work as descriptions of the interior—and its parasitic invasion by insects—exists beside and in relation to her natural history illustrations, as instantiated with her cockroach and pineapple.

In her closing passage to the *Metamorphosis*, Merian writes: "In January 1701 I entered the forest of Suriname to see if I could discover anything."[44] Here, she found a red caterpillar that she brought home (plate 13). Under her watchful gaze, it transformed into a butterfly, and Merian illustrates the creature both in flight—with exterior blue wings of deep variant hues—and at rest, capturing its outer wings of black, yellow, and brown patterning. As she remarks, in Holland the butterfly is known as the *groote Atlas* (large Atlas). Bearing the name Atlas, this final butterfly gestures to the tradition of Dutch mapmaking, geography, and exploration that undergirded Merian's project. In turn, she places the Atlas in relation to the wild wasp, a domestic species known for its ability to build paper houses. Merian focuses on the impact of paper wasps on plantations, "found everywhere in Suriname, even in the houses and in the fields." The wild wasp crosses effortlessly between interior and exterior spaces, although it is perhaps most famous for its own paper houses. She remarks that such houses "show signs of care, how they have been built against rain and wind, to put the eggs in a safe place." The protection of the wild wasp eggs in their paper houses creates a plague, however, as "eggs first develop into a white worm, like the one lying under the caterpillar. It gradually changes into this sort of wild bee, which is a plague of this land [*die een plage des zelven Lands zyn*]."[45] This line concludes Merian's text, a brief meditation on the wild wasp and its pestilent blight. The functionality of the domestic space of the wasp—a virulent contrast to the industrious honeybee—contrasts to the plantation homes and crops ravaged by the insect and its stinger. Yet as with the honeybee, Merian alludes to the wasp's strong household economy as it builds a domicile that protects its eggs from the outer elements. Also, unlike the other insects, which she clearly pictures in relation to botanic life—using leaves, petals, stalks, and floral anatomy as structures for protection and growth—the wild wasp constructs its own home.

Merian's framing of her work through the pestilence of the cockroach and the wild wasp articulates a natural world distinct from that of many of her colleagues. Natural historians, such as her contemporary Johannes Swammerdam, asserted that for all created beings, "the agreement between them is most surprisingly regular and harmonious; everything conspiring equally to fill us with sentiments or admiration and reverence for the great Author of nature."[46] Often the butterfly was central to grasping both the economy of nature and the processes of reproduction and metamorphosis, from the insect across the chain of being to the human. Swammerdam's expression of the harmony of nature reflecting the beneficence of its creator forms the foundation of the *economy* of nature that would be most famously articulated by Carl Linnaeus in the middle of the eighteenth century, when he wrote about "the all-wise disposition of the Creator in relation to natural things, by which they are fitted to produce general ends and reciprocal uses."[47] The butterfly was emblematic of nature's economy as seen through its life cycle, for it was not two distinct creatures—the caterpillar and the butterfly—but a single creature.

The economic transformation of the butterfly was appreciated not only on its own merit but also as a means to better understand human reproduction. Both Swammerdam and Merian's work takes part in a series of debates in the late seventeenth and eighteenth centuries about the genesis of form: Is it predetermined before birth or developed in utero? Is it contingent, or imprinted before the egg is even released? There were debates about whether an individual's form was determined before fetal development and already extant, a theory known as preexisting germs (or preformation), or whether the form gradually developed in the womb (epigenesis).[48] As the work of early eighteenth-century entomologists exists in the universe of pre-Darwinian natural history, insect reproduction offered a window onto human reproduction and the formation of life from an egg to a human. Swammerdam, for example, wrote: "It is clearer than the light at noon, that man is, like insects, produced from a visible egg [and that] man, that rational animal, finds his first nourishment and represents, as it were, a Vermicle or Worm, or to use Harvey's words, a Maggot lying in the egg."[49] In this passage, Swammerdam draws on his observations to argue against the Aristotelian concept of spontaneous generation out of feces or mud. Instead, he maintains that insects (like humans) grow from eggs. Swammerdam argued that the caterpillar did not die and resurrect as a butterfly; it was not an entirely different creature reborn. This particular understanding informed Swammerdam's belief in a harmonious nature overseen by a creator, an understanding of reproduction and being central ultimately to Linnaeus's economy of nature, in which nothing goes to waste in the various transformations of matter.

While Merian looked to the insect world as a system of reproduction to better understand human generation, the nature that she writes about is not one of economy produced by a beneficent creator. Instead, the natural world in her text is structured in terms of invasion, survival, and destruction. The breakthrough in her illustrations—depicting micro-ecosystems—understands plants as the locus for insect domesticity. They are the structures that provide the conditions for the reproduction and generation of insects, and they are also sometimes ravaged by their inhabitants. Merian discusses, for example, a certain caterpillar known to destroy cassava crops, causing starvation and hunger.[50] For insects, the plants serve as home, a site that in Merian's text also remains porous, constantly under siege by invading ants, cockroaches, and wasps. Unlike odes to the industry of honeybees, the insects that parallel the human in Merian's text possess the capacity for ruination as much as industry.

While her work focuses on insects, Merian thinks with the insect to comprehend the human, particularly its place within the economy of the plantation. In bringing her illustrations to the scale of the human body, and endowing the insects with gross antennae increasing attention to their sensate abilities, Merian draws on the intelligent characteristics of the insect to draw likeness between the insect and the human. In creating this likeness, she displaces the violence of the plantation system onto the natural world, so that it mirrors the struggle of sociality and kin that is at the center of the plantation economy. Within this context, one of the most frequently cited passages in Merian's text must be read in relation to her fascination with the domesticity of insects and their plant worlds. For just as her work is concerned with the physical spaces and social relationships that allow for the reproduction and metamorphosis of insects, she also recognizes the plantation as a site that is its own micro-ecosystem, creating certain conditions for human reproduction. In particular, Merian describes the peacock flower, a known abortifacient, and its usage by enslaved and Indigenous women so that their children would not be born into the state of enslavement.

In her illustration of the peacock flower, one seed ruptures the skin of the pod, recalling illustrations of female fetuses, punctured across the surface of the skin to reveal the inner seed (P14). This analogy was already encoded in early modern natural history in the work of Giambattista della Porta, who pictured a seed pod in contrast to a child floating in a womb with the skin flayed (figure 4.5). The process of human reproduction enters into scale with plant generation. The botanical matter becomes animated, while the fetus becomes vegetative. Merian's ruptured seed pod therefore belongs in a history of illustration in which the seed of the plant is brought into likeness with human reproduction. The caterpillar takes refuge on the

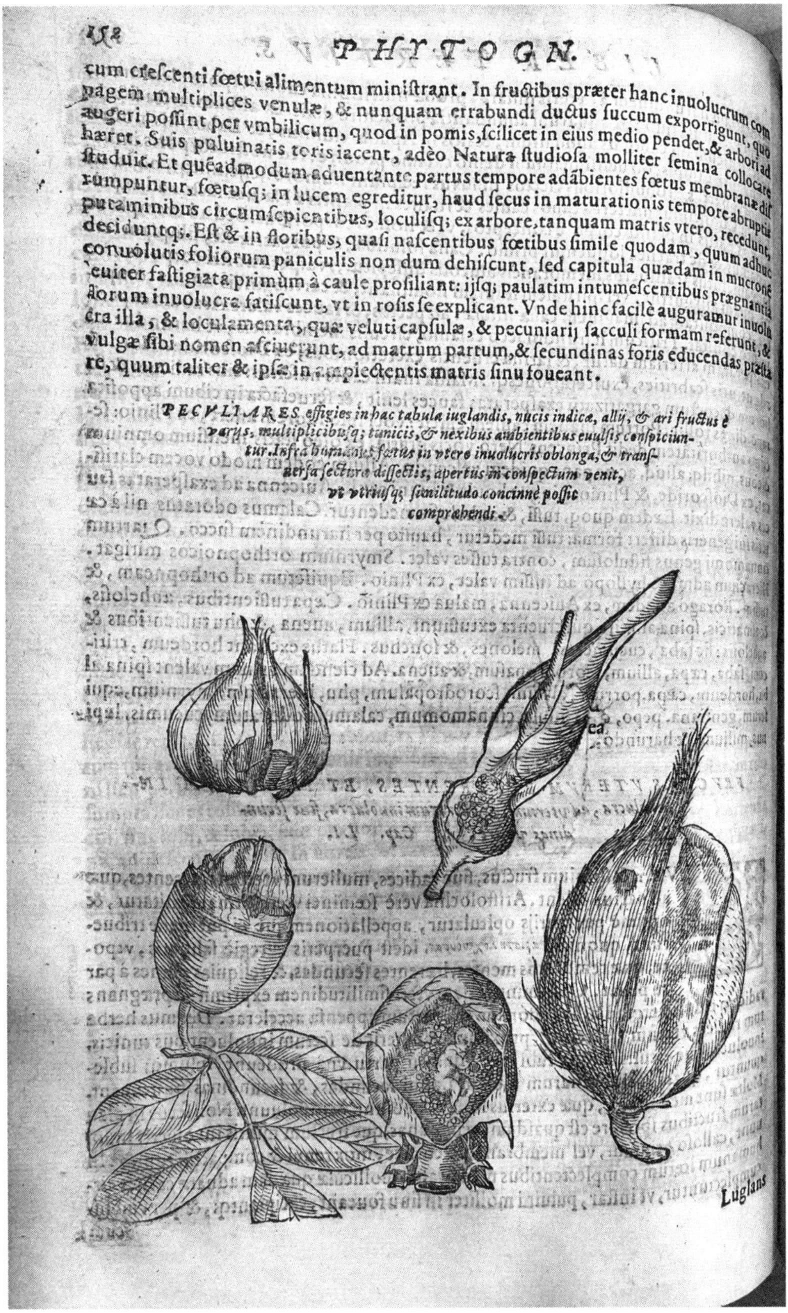

cum crescenti fœtui alimentum ministrant. In fructibus præter hanc inuolucrum com
pagem multiplices venulæ, & nunquam errabundi ductus succum exporrigunt, quo
augeri possint per vmbilicum, quod in pomis, scilicet in eius medio pendet, & arbori ad
hæret. Suis puluinatis toris iacent, adèo Natura studiosa molliter semina collocare
studuit. Et quéadmodum aduentante partus tempore adābientes fœtus membranæ dif
rumpuntur, fœtusq; in lucem egreditur, haud secus in maturationis tempore abruptis
putaminibus circumsepicantibus, loculisq; ex arbore, tanquam matris vtero, recedunt,
deciduntq;. Est & in floribus, quasi nascentibus fœtibus simile quodam, quum adhuc
conuolutis foliorum paniculis non dum dehiscunt, sed capitula quædam in mucroné
euiter fastigiata primùm à caule prosiliant: ijsq; paulatim intumescentibus prægnantia
florum inuolucra satiscunt, vt in rosis se explicant. Vnde hinc facilè auguramur inuolu
cra illa, & loculamenta, quæ veluti capsulæ, & pecuniarij sacculi formam referunt, &
vulgæ sibi nomen asciuerunt, ad matrum partum, & secundinas foris educendas præta
re, quum taliter & ipsæ in amplectentis matris sinu foueant.

PECVLIARES effigies in hac tabula iuglandis, nucis indicæ, allij, & ari fructus è
varijs, multiplicibusq; tunicis, & nexibus ambientibus euulsis conspiciun-
tur. Infra humanus fœtus in vtere inuolucris oblonga, & trans-
uersa sectura dissectis, apertus in conspectum venit,
vt vtriusq; similitudo concinnè possit
comprahendi.

4.5 Giambattista della Porta, *Doctrine of Signatures*, in *Phytognomonica*,
1588. Woodblock print on paper (Chapin Library, Williams College,
Williamstown, Massachusetts).

plant, its cocoon in the shape of a conch shell, and once the multipedal creature transforms into a moth, it extends a long curving black line of tongue to drink the nectar, while red stamens flow from the center, prominent lines demarcating the filaments and anthers that compose the anatomy of the flower and dominate the illustration. The moth takes on an anthropomorphic quality, splayed flat with two of its legs like arms, while the round black eyes protrude from its head, the movement of its antennae and tongue mirroring the undulating flows of the flower's red sex organs. The captured moth prominently drinks from the nectar of the flower, which issues down, mirroring the flowing of menses. Merian's peacock flower with its prominent lines of red issuing forth points toward the inchoate matter that flows from women's bodies to cyclically demarcate the temporality of reproduction but also the viability of birth and generation.

Beside this illustration, Merian writes about the Indigenous populations (*de Indianen*), who are treated so terribly by the Dutch that they are driven to abort their children so that the they do not "become slaves like them." She also discusses the enslaved women from Guinea and Angola who not only refuse to have children but also "take their own lives because they are treated so badly," and in hopes that "they will be born again, free [*in een vreijen staat*] and in their own land."[51] As Merian's work is dedicated to recording processes of reproduction, it is not surprising that she attends to this particular instance of human reproduction, in which women aborted their pregnancies in reaction to the conditions of the plantation system. This has no parallel in Merian's work on insects, reptiles, and plants, revealing the particular ability of human nature to produce a set of conditions that defy the logic and order of nature. Merian's inclusion of the peacock flower and its accompanying text speaks about the violence enacted on the Indigenous and African-diasporic populations in Suriname, a brutality that otherwise remains barely visible. Yet instead of directly representing the conditions of forced labor on the impossible spaces of the interior, Merian touches on the unsustainable structure of the plantation through its impact on human reproduction, employing the peacock flower as the figuration of this violence. On the one hand, Merian's text violates the intimate conversations held among African and Indigenous women, placing them into the public sphere for analysis, furthering perception of non-European bodies as delimited for labor and reproduction. On the other hand, her text also offers a glimpse of what Jennifer Morgan terms "strategic assessments of, and responses to, the violent structures of value and commerce in which they [enslaved women] were embedded."[52]

Within this brief paragraph, the peacock flower becomes a tool by which to deny the logic of the plantation system. Merian's text demonstrates a critical period in the plantation economy, in which women and their reproductive capacity became means to accumulate "capital," as their children were born into the state of enslavement, and her brief paragraph illustrates the strategic response to refuse the commerce of enslavement and the transubstantiation of life into another man's property. In this act of refusal, the women referenced in Merian's text stand as direct counterparts to the complicity of the women pictured within Dutch interior paintings, women who partake in, profit from, and drive the logic of a global economy that the women in Merian's text challenge by taking control over their reproduction. The peacock flower and the attendant description of domestic space within the plantation challenges the locus of home and domesticity that defined the rise of Dutch genre painting back in the Netherlands. Whereas the women in Merian's text longed to be born free in their own land, the women populating the interiors of genre scenes embodied the Dutch homeland in their domestic space.

Vermeer in particular is famous for his paintings of silence, interiority, and women. As Perry Chapman remarks, in Vermeer's women is "a striking articulation of an emerging valuing of privacy and individuality."[53] In one of the most iconic paintings, often described with the term *interiority*, Vermeer painted a woman holding a letter between her hands (figure 4.6). The folded sheet retains her attention, her gaze fixed on its surface. Although we do not see the window, light falls across the canvas so that the whitewashed wall behind her glows a bright white before falling into shadow. A map hangs on the wall, and she is clothed in a blue overcoat from which her stomach protrudes, a profile that has generated speculation on whether she is pregnant. The painting pictures the unfolding of thought through the act of reading. Sequestered in the home, mediated by servants bearing letters, and light falling through windows, standing in relationship to maps of the outside world, the unknown interior lives of the woman become a point of reflection for the viewer. The process of interior reflection itself—alluded to through a letter that cannot be seen, a map, and a suggestive silhouette—becomes a point of fantasy and fascination. Yet the delineation of privacy here is a performance, produced for a consumer to hang on their wall, so that "privacy exists as a creation of the market."[54]

Vermeer's works have been considered as emblems of the modern self: contained and reflective, a visualization of privacy as central to modern no-

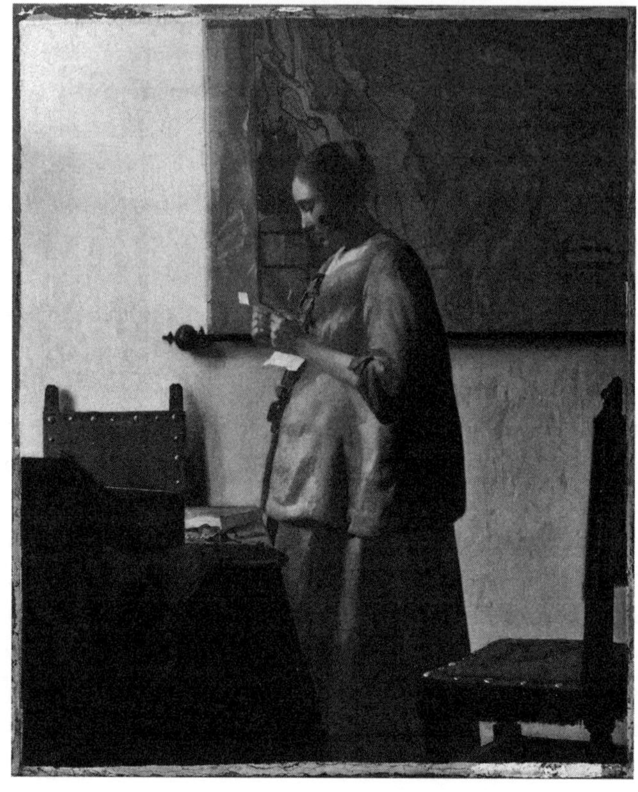

4.6 Johannes Vermeer, *Woman in Blue Reading a Letter*, 1663. Oil on canvas (Rijksmuseum, Amsterdam).

tions of liberty. Within Vermeer's work, this articulation of inwardness is figured through the body of the woman to picture a meditation on Dutch citizenship and nascent nationhood. The construction of privacy within Vermeer's world is always constructed in relation to an absent other, intimated by a letter, a momentary interruption, allusions to love, and maps suggesting husbands holding colonial posts in overseas territories. In turn, these paintings were meant to be bought and sold, so the production of making an interior world becomes a commodity. The inner life of thought is also an intangible reality reified and translated into wealth. The women and their interior worlds become personifications of an economically successful republic, as they finger pearls, receive letters, and take part in a nation extending itself from the beaches of Scheveningen across the Atlantic and Pacific Oceans.

These interior worlds—both physical and mental—are impossible without the production of wealth forged in the plantations of the Atlantic, the Pacific, and the Indian Oceans, alluded to in their furs and pearls, their porcelain ware, and again, in the maps painted and hung on walls. These women become commoditized visions of private interior lives, contained within the borders of the Dutch home, and its opening to the outside world. Historically, scholars have read the plantation economy within the goods that populate these scenes, the opaque surface of pearls (obtained by pearl divers in Caribbean or Indian waters), or porcelain sugar bowls, silver ewers, still lifes of trade and commerce. Yet the absent presence of the plantation economy extends beyond performing an iconography of goods and materials, telling micro-histories of their trade routes and the enslaved labor that was necessary to harvest, produce, and ship the goods to the Netherlands. Instead, this visualization of the Dutch interior home within the United Provinces must be read beside the visual absence of the Dutch interior in the colonies, within the space of the plantation, an interior world that is glimpsed only in works such as Merian's, where cockroaches and wasps dominate.

The domestic interior within Dutch genre painting read beside Merian's domestic world on the plantation elucidates the fragility of privacy as a freedom within a global economy, particularly when transformed into a commodity. In particular, Merian's attention to the role of reproduction and generation and its failure within the space of the plantation positions the Dutch homeland as a site where moral Dutch citizens are reproduced and raised. Yet these two scenes of physical interiors and mental interiority— one visible and pictured (Dutch genre painting), the other invisible and extant as an allusion (the absent plantation interior)—became interdependent in the seventeenth and eighteenth centuries. Jennifer L. Morgan describes the cessation of privacy to people of African descent while Dutch genre paintings developed a vocabulary for privilege and privacy. Morgan remarks that "African women's sexual and reproductive behavior was positioned in such a way as to signal the erasure of boundaries, as writers alleged that black women engaged in unregulated sexual congress, gave birth in public places, might easily bury or abandon live children who encumbered them, and, in any event, barely interrupted their work lives to attend to nurslings."[55] This violation of reproductive interiority and space is embodied in the display of infants within anatomical collections, cabinets of curiosity, and early museums. One of the most private and unimaginable griefs endured—the loss of a child, whether in miscarriage, in birth, or after—becomes denied. Refusing a right to hold and bury the body, the acquisition of fetuses and children, as though coral specimens or foreign butterflies, violated the most private space of grief and loss. In separating children from their geographic origin, the display of children within jars also disconnected reproduction from the womb, the breast, and the stages of development that the child takes in relation to the heart, mind, and body of its caretaker(s). Separating children into singular anatomical displays suggests that birth and reproduction is solely a process of individuation instead of also a process of socialization within a community.

The visible rise of *privacy* as a thematization within painting emerges during a period in which the space of reproduction—menstruating, birth, childcare, the formation of kin, and generational wealth—became redefined by plantation economies and enslaved labor, a shift captured in Merian's text and her enfolding of this history into natural history. Yet her work also introduces a reflection on a state of bodily privacy that remains alluded to, yet never pictured, within Vermeer's work: the intertwined worlds of bodily function (menstruating, pregnancy, postpartum) and thought. Vermeer's painting unequivocally pictures privacy as an intellectual act, as women's bodies become abstract ciphers for Dutch citizenship. Yet from Vermeer's *Woman in Blue Reading a Letter* to Merian's peacock flower, privacy emerges as a right that is either commodified or negated. There emerges in Vermeer and his fellow genre painters a tangible visualization of privacy as an ideal that forms a new citizen, as some are granted the right to picturing an interior life, and some are denied this right in the most unequivocable manner. Vermeer and his fellow artists created a visual language in the seventeenth century to imagine the interior world of a woman that in turn personifies the order of the state in public and domestic spheres. The articulation of privacy from Vermeer takes part in a world that wants to delimit a private interior self as central to modern notions of liberty and freedom while refusing the most fundamental rights of privacy and liberty to others: not only the choice of whether to bear children, but also the right to hold, care for, and bury one's children.

Merian's work on the peacock flower alludes to the fragility of privacy as a conceit in our modern world, a precarity made evident by the overturning of *Roe v. Wade*, which was established on the right to privacy. Merian's investigation into reproduction and domestic spaces within Surinamese plantations exposes the interior pleasure (both physical and psychological) of Vermeer's women as itself a fallacy, constructed to provide a reflective surface for a market, and to further mythologies about

Dutch economic prosperity. Judgments formed by the corporate body of Dutch merchants, bureaucrats, and politicians in Amsterdam influenced decisions around reproduction, lovemaking, sex, and kin by women in the Americas. These two scenes of the interior—the merchant house in Amsterdam and the plantation house in the colony—exist in relation to each other. Understanding the private and silent Dutch interiors in relation to the impossible-to-figure yet present interiors of the Dutch plantation make palpable the fragility of privacy and interiority in this modern construction of self. Merian's text obliquely demonstrates that reproduction is not only about giving birth; it is the world into which life is brought, the resources and care that it is granted, the way in which caretakers are valued, and an awareness of disparities among rights, access, and healthcare across geographic, racial, and class lines. It is the micro-ecosystems that support reproduction and metamorphosis, and the sociality of reproduction that guides her text. The natural history of the eighteenth century—from the children placed in jars for exhibition to Merian's focus on generation on the Surinamese plantation—demonstrates that our modern ideas around reproduction, individuation, and privacy were established within a world in which personhood and inwardness became the visible means by which to contain and erase the moral erosion and failure of a Dutch global *oeconomia*, a society more akin to the paper wasp than to the honeybee.

Historiography and Race

<hr>

This book has attended to sites of abstracted figuration: coastlines devoid of laborers and yellow flames in sugarcane kilns; Reformed church interiors and smooth ocean surfaces absent of depth; palimpsestic prints of ghostly ships and botanical studies of tropical plants and insects. In the language of transubstantiation, all these pictures employ the representation of one thing to embody another—from the flame of the kiln to articulate the violence of the plantation economy to the sociality of insects on the plantation to depict the failure of the domestic interior. To elucidate the visual transfigurations of form, I have drawn on an extant archive of texts that traveled *beside* these works, always in tension with the visual field, whether it is an inventory pasted to the back of a canvas; narrative accounts of oceanic exploration and law; a biography of an artist's life; or the descriptions of a natural historian such as Maria Sibylla Merian.

On the one hand, it is standard to consider a painting in relation to its inventory, an artist's work in tension with their biography, a new genre such as maritime painting in conjunction with maritime law. Yet Sedgwick's concept of *besideness* enables a more incisive consideration of how these works have coexisted in friction, as historians have practiced varying modes of allowing these texts to be included in scholarship, revealing the constant negotiation with visibility in the historiography of Dutch art around the rise of the plantation economy. In seventeenth-century Dutch painting is a disjunction between the written and visual records that has been difficult for art historians to untangle, as the written record in many instances blatantly counters the visual, and this is fraught for a historiography that often engages with the seeming quality of direct observation. Moreover, the seventeenth-century Dutch Republic is often viewed as an antecedent to aspects of the modern world that are celebrated: individualism, privacy, a middle class; art markets freed from church and state; a profound investigation of the quotidian. Therefore, a strain emerges when considering the textual archive in relation to the visual, as in an inventory that describes the violence of sugarcane plantations traveling beside a corpus of paintings depicting those plantations. Despite being published in the central monograph on Post, the relation between a paragraph of descriptive brutality alongside landscape scenes often described as "beautiful" has never been examined.

Consideration of the written material in conjunction with the visual demonstrates the impact of the transatlantic slave trade on seventeenth-century Dutch visual culture as a crisis in figuration that resonated with the iconoclastic crises of the previous century, which persisted into the seventeenth. The erasure of images, bodies, and figures from the walls of Reformed churches, which would become home to maritime monuments, to create spaces of citizenship and exclusion mirrored a similar trajectory on the oceans traveled by maritime heroes. Whereas the whitewashed walls of the Reformed Church created a space devoid of palimpsestic histories of devotion, the fantasy of a smooth ocean surface devoid of history and monuments made the ocean a space of erasure on which citizenship and otherness could be defined according to the rise of nation-states fighting for dominance over open waters, fluid bodies that both resisted possession while making possible territorial gains. In attending to the spaces of nonfiguration, I examine the ongoing struggle in the seventeenth century to depict the transubstantiation of the individual into a commodity. The visualization of a plantation economy and its economic impact cannot be studied only in images of the human figure. The process of transubstantiation is an impossible image, and for artists emerging from a period of iconoclasm and debates about the limits of representation, the rise of new genres such as landscape and seascape painting provided a set of visual tools by which to imagine and picture the transformation of lives into commodities in visual sites that resisted bodily figuration.

In this conclusion, however, I focus on the human figure to consider the limits of working within a historiography that is in the process of confronting the implicit structuring principle of race within some of its most pervasively cited texts. In many ways, this examination of historiography engages with a tendency in fiction already articulated by Toni Morrison, in *Playing in the Dark: Whiteness in the Literary Imagination*, as Morrison confronts the "Africanist properties" that structure American fiction from Willa Cather to Mark Twain, a presence that most critics refuse to engage.[1] Morrison demonstrates that the presence of African Americans in the United States, "which shaped the body politic, the Constitution, and the entire history of the Culture," was also integral to its literature, although in ways that remain overlooked.[2] The historiography of Dutch art in the twentieth century has similar pervasive "Africanist presences," often by art historians writing from distinctly different national traditions yet nevertheless engaged with an "Africanist presence." Attending to formative readings of Rembrandt's *Syndics of the Drapers' Guild* particularly demonstrates that concerns around race and personhood are embedded within writing about Dutch art since at least the early part of the twentieth century. Like all the texts discussed in this book, these historiographic essays are well-known works, in which the implied structuring principles of race have remained overlooked. Nevertheless, a body of writing emerged in the twentieth and twenty-first centuries in relation to this Rembrandt painting that demonstrates the ongoing influence of seventeenth-century Dutch visual culture in formulating a visual vocabulary around defining citizenship and otherness, belonging and denial, recognition of life and refusal of burial.

Syndics of the Drapers' Guild

Rembrandt's monumental group portrait *Syndics of the Drapers' Guild* is a painting about interruption. The man at the center of the composition gestures toward the book on the table, as his colleagues turn toward the beholder. The work portrays textile merchants, who are in the process of examining fabric samples to compare the density of weave, variations in color, and relative smooth or rough finish to establish value and price for the market (plate 15). Before the viewer's entrance disturbed their concentration, they were calculating quality to determine cost. The guild members move from their assessment of textiles to address the viewer. They shift a gaze devoid of passion from a set of commodities to the unexpected guest. In the words of Roland Barthes, who briefly discusses the work in a short essay on Dutch painting, "You become a matter of capital." As Barthes recognized, "There is no sadness and no cruelty in that gaze; it is a gaze without adjectives, it is only, completely, a gaze which neither judges you nor appeals to you; it posits you, implicates you, makes you exist."[3]

Forcing a confrontation between the viewer and the merchants, Rembrandt produces the acute awareness of the beholder's own existence through the artifice of the interruption. One man stands—as though to greet the viewer—and yet another takes up his gloves, gathering his things. This is not the eternal stillness of a portrait. The creation of interruption produces an acute awareness of time, both historical and as an economic unit. The viewer takes the merchants away from their work, demands a moment of their time. In turn, the address between the merchants and the viewer creates an awareness of the beholder's presence, standing before historical figures who continue to assert their physical selves beyond the limits of their temporal lives. The economics of time and the ontology of historical presence become inseparable, as the acute temporality of the painting is realized through physical disruption of concentrated work, a disturbance that punctures the divide between past and present as the guild members turn their gaze toward the viewer. Rembrandt fashions this encounter through neither the representation of divine realms nor the rendering of history—biblical, mythological, or other. Instead, the unexpected happenstance with a group of merchants—middlemen—has caused this rupturing of time and space. The viewer is brought to consider their own precarity by meeting a group of merchants who mediate between producers and consumers, their historical present and ours. It is a radical repositioning of the individual, not in relation to God—nor even to another person—but instead to a corporate body that represents financial markets from which the beholder cannot be extricated, any more than they can be removed from the acuteness of their own historical moment.

Barthes describes the faces in portraits of this genre—group portraits of the Dutch patrician class—as "a kind of hothouse flower, brought to perfection by careful forcing."[4] He repeatedly refers to taxonomic histories to articulate class within Dutch painting, once likening Adriaen van Ostade's images of peasants to "unfinished creatures, rough drafts of men, arrested at an earlier stage of human development. . . . As the ape is separated from man, here the peasant is separated from the burgher precisely insofar as he is deprived of the ultimate characteristics of humanity, those of the *person*."[5] To define the specificity of Van Ostade's rendering of faces (figure

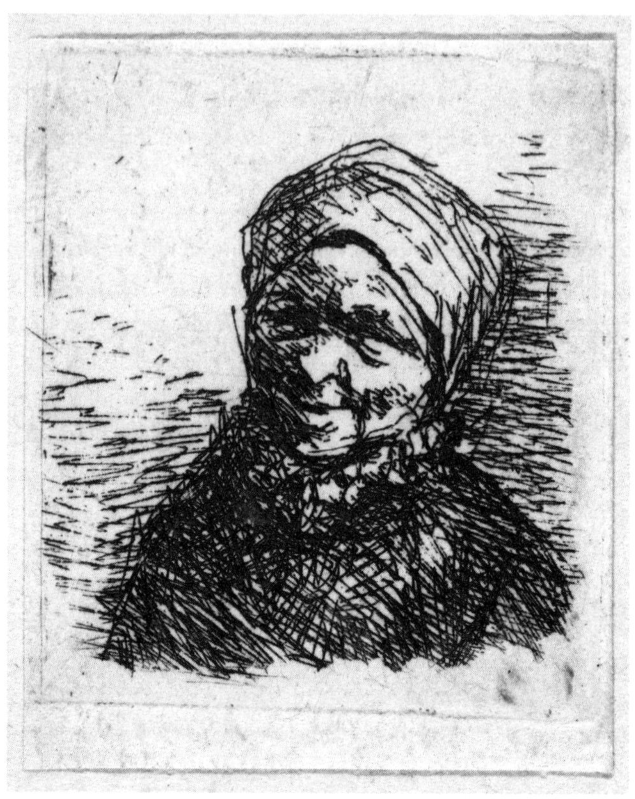

C.1 Adriaen van Ostade, *Peasant Woman*, ca. 1610–85. Etching
(Elisha Whittelsey Collection, Elisha Whittelsey Fund, 1951,
Metropolitan Museum of Art, New York).

C.1), Barthes turns to a language rooted in Darwinian ideas of evolution and divisions between species—particularly human and simian—
ideas that are inseparable from histories of race in the twentieth century.
In turn, the guild portraits also present a species produced through careful
breeding under prime conditions. As he writes, "All these faces are treated
as units of one and the same horticultural species, combining genetic resemblance and individual identity."[6]

In his writing on Dutch patrician portraiture—of which the apogee
is Rembrandt's *Syndics of the Drapers' Guild*—Barthes evokes a language
of biological difference. It is through the logic of sexual reproduction that
these men become signifiers of the patrician class: "It is formed after a long
sedimentation which has accumulated all the characteristics of a social par-

ticularity within a class: age, size, morphology, wrinkles, veins, the very order of biology separates the patrician caste from the functional substance (objects, peasants, landscapes), and imprisons it within its own authority."[7] In his deployment of indirect and direct references to Darwin, primates, genetics, and species, Barthes activates a vocabulary that was central to demarcating racial difference and inequality in the nineteenth and twentieth centuries. He attempts to restrict its usage to class, thereby obscuring the history of this language within modern "sciences" of race. Barthes's reading of Rembrandt's painting through a language of description often deployed to ascribe racial difference in the twentieth century obliquely positions his reading of the painting as an emergent visual vocabulary of the breeding of species according to genetic resemblance. Produced through careful genetic reproduction—like hothouse flowers—these men are not created through an intermixing of "species," Barthes specifies, but are "pure" examples of the Dutch patrician class. In drawing on the language of biology and sexual reproduction, Barthes clearly places the all-encompassing gaze that these men possess as particular to their economic station in life as merchants, which is inseparable from their breeding, their birthright, their genes, the color of their skin.

Although race remains obscured yet evoked through language in his brief meditation on Dutch painting, Barthes's writings on photography in *Camera Lucida* are more explicitly determined by his engagement with racialized bodies. As many scholars note, Barthes depends on photographic examples of enslavement to elucidate his theories of photography while he simultaneously denies agency to the individual pictured and the role of race in his construction of photography. In *Camera Lucida*, Barthes repeatedly references the history of slavery, citing works such as Richard Avedon's portrait of William Casby, *Born a Slave*, while negating its historical relevance to theorizations of the photographic medium. Instead, the history of slavery emerges as a presence that is unmediated by the photograph. In regard to a photograph of a slave market, Barthes argues that it offers direct evidence: "The historian was no longer the mediator, slavery was given without mediation, the fact was established *without method*."[8] In the case of the history of slavery, its photographic record is not composed, formulated, contrived, or structured into an image. It is present without any method that might determine, frame, or structure how future generations build institutions out of the juridical legacy of slavery on American soil and the ongoing legacy of its violence. Barthes does not pause to consider how the "photographic evidence" of slavery's history is an enduring con-

struction of how racialized bodies are imagined, discriminated against, categorized, and seen or not seen.

Barthes likens the photographic evidence to "the proof-according-
to-St.-Thomas-seeking-to-touch-the-resurrected-Christ."[9] As in the language around transubstantiation, the metaphor of Christological miracle
becomes central to grasping the transformation of life into a commodity.
For Barthes, it is the image of persons on the auction block for sale. Yet
unlike Philip's description of transubstantiation, in which the individual
undergoes an impossible transformation that defies sensory experience of
the world, Barthes relies on embodied sensory experience as central to the
history of slavery through photography. He is the doubting Thomas, the
apostle who required direct evidence (the touch of Christ's wounds) to
believe in his resurrection. Within this metaphor, the body on the auction block becomes the risen Christological body with its wounds. Instead
of recognizing the sensory impossibility of this transformation of life,
Barthes grounds the visualization of the history of enslavement within the
necessity of evidence, direct touch, and the *right* to reach out and feel the
wounds of the body in order to believe their history, their status, their racialization. Barthes also suggests that the history of race, violence, and enslavement demands photographic evidence to be believed. To be true, it
must exist as a picture. The legacy of this historiographic impulse infil-
trated beyond Barthes's writings on photography, so that similarly, the sites
of nonfiguration that I have discussed have resisted interpretation because
they refuse the evidential model of direct touch.

For Barthes, this analogy of photography to the doubting Thomas informs his understanding of it as a medium of touch that emanates from the
referent to his body, "an umbilical cord" that unites him with the individuals
depicted in the photograph, so that photography acts as a "carnal medium"
that allows him to "share a skin" with those who were photographed.[10] As
Shawn Michelle Smith writes, in this passage Barthes defines a "provocative
shared corporeality, Barthes's own position as a free, white, self-possessed
European viewer is unsettled, for his 'shared skin' metonymically links him
with slavery, blackness, and objectification under a white gaze."[11] As Smith
draws out, Barthes's use of the term *carnal* moves photography beyond the
realm of representation. Instead, it becomes a medium that realizes its own
limits in order to reproduce, join, copulate, and physically mingle with the
viewer through a language that merges the sexual (carnal) with the reproductive (umbilical cord). The photograph overcomes its material form by
physically reproducing within the body of the viewer.

The portraits in Rembrandt's *Syndics of the Drapers' Guild* are also of a "carnal order" for Barthes. He specifically writes, "Here the matrix of the human face is not of an ethical order, it is of a carnal order; it consists not of a community of intentions, but of an identity of blood and food."[12] His language around breeding, species, and carnality explicitly connects the portraits to a sexual reproduction that extends beyond the canvas. It is not only that the Dutch burghers "imprison" themselves within their genetics of whiteness but that they also draw the viewer into this carnal order through their address. The beholder becomes implicated within this scene of genetic reproduction, unsettled under the objectification of this white gaze, which assumes that the beholder's presence will only reaffirm and reproduce into the future their mastery of the world and its objects. The force of Barthes's language in describing the Dutch burghers as a particular species bred in hothouses to reproduce themselves genetically articulates a critical account of representing "whiteness" in the history of European portraiture, with its "morphology, wrinkles, veins, and very order of biology." These faces produced through "hothouse breeding" are accompanied by a gaze that replaces divinity (all-encompassing and transcendent), so that Rembrandt's *Syndics* are masters of their world: "In this perfectly content patrician world, absolute master of matter and evidently rid of God, the gaze produces a strictly human interrogation and proposes an infinite postponement of history."[13]

Barthes focuses on topologies of whiteness in this essay on Dutch painting, beginning with works by Pieter Jansz. Saenredam that depicted the white walls of Dutch Reformed churches. Saenredam famously painted church interiors after they were scrubbed of icons and religious paintings, dedicating himself to representing the whitewashed walls (plate 16). Barthes describes Saenredam's paintings as "sugary" white surfaces that produce an "esthetic of silence."[14] In this painting of "nothingness," Barthes finds a precursor to modernity, an emptying out of meaning to create a vacuum that will be filled by the desire for consumption, goods, and the fashioning of selves in relation to free markets as opposed to metaphysical faiths. The "whitewashed plaster" depicted by Saenredam—likened to sugar—is the image by which Barthes fashions the modernity of Dutch painting, a capacity of whiteness to erase and to create insidious silences.

Just as the whitewashed walls of the Dutch Reformed Church removed icons and altars to create an aesthetic ground for nothingness, so Rembrandt's patricians usurp God's iconic gaze with their own embodying merchants concerned with economic markets more than metaphysical doubts.

Like the erasure at the center of the Reformed Church interior, they falsely position themselves as the site of origin, the objective and empty ground devoid of history. The white walls of the Reformed Church deny the history of styles, artists, faith, and devotion, creating an imaginary space of silence to be punctured by the voice of the preacher from the pulpit. The voices and visions of previous ancestors, ministers, painters, parishioners, believers, and deniers are removed to create a phantasm of nothingness. In turn, the "infinite postponement" of history in the gaze of Rembrandt's patricians suggests that they have removed themselves from the contingency of their own historical time so that they forever defer their historical limits. Like the whitewashed walls of the church interior, their faces bear no traces of action and passion, the palimpsest of lives formed through losses and victories (minute and magnificent). Instead, they have paused as they turn to address the beholder, forever deferring their own conclusion. Although Barthes never explicitly recognizes race as a structuring principle within Dutch painting, the whitewashed walls of the church interiors echo throughout his essay until they resound in the language of genetics and breeding employed to describe Dutch portraiture.[15] Barthes was not the first, however, to depend on racial characterization to describe Rembrandt's *Syndics*. The spectral presence of racialized bodies evoked in Rembrandt's painting also appears in the writing of the art historian Alois Riegl, who draws an unexpected relationship between the gaze of a child, whom he describes as "Moorish," and the address of the burghers.

Riegl, like Barthes, was fascinated by the rise of corporate portraiture in the Dutch Republic. He argued that the formal qualities of group portraiture demanded that the individual members of the corporation (from charitable societies to guilds) sacrifice personal freedom to work toward a collective purpose. This sacrifice of the individual for the "collective good" was realized through formal subordination, which allowed for an internal coherence within the picture plane. Group portraits became successful once painters began to subordinate various members of the group to others instead of trying to place all the figures on a level plane. As Riegl remarked, it is an ability "to use subordination to establish unity."[16] The visual hierarchies of subservience among the figures—and between the sitters and the viewer—create a tension for Riegl that was both formal and psychological.

For Riegl, Rembrandt's *Syndics* was a masterpiece through subordination. It demonstrated a recognition that the group portrait could succeed only through hierarchy, so that certain figures existed in demotion to others. As Riegl writes: "Let me summarize Rembrandt's artistic volition in a sentence: Rembrandt exploited subordination in a painting as a means of coordinating the figures among themselves (on a psychological level) and with their surrounding space (in a physical sense)."[17] In Rembrandt's *Syndics*, subordination governs the movement of attention, as the central figure who gestures does not directly address the viewer. The refusal of his gaze subordinates the beholder, indicating that their presence has not justified a need for him to cease speaking. A servant stands in the background, the only other figure to also not address the viewer. Instead, his eyes shift toward the man caught in his elocution. The withholding of the gaze by these two men (one a servant, one a member of the guild), their continued attention to the matter at hand, sustains a tension both within the work and toward the beholder. The refusal of their address heightens the sense of interruption and the suspension of time, as the viewer is left to wait in perpetuity.

To expand on subordination and its culmination in Rembrandt's late masterpieces, Riegl turns to a small etching by Rembrandt, *The Beheading of John the Baptist* (figure C.2). For Riegl, this somewhat obscure print demonstrates a stage in the process toward Rembrandt's mastery of formal and psychological subordination in group portraiture, describing the composition as "the Baptist and his executioner united in their own subgroup, plus the young Moor on the right side, holding the platter and waiting for the execution to take place."[18] The man whom he describes as "the young Moor" expresses the quality of attention that he finds exemplified in the *Syndics*, a mode of observing action in the world absent of passion. As Riegl writes, "Of all the figures in the etching, the Moorish boy is obviously the one upon whom Rembrandt lavished his whole-hearted artistic attention. The expression of attentive waiting is caught perfectly in the boy's face and body, as well as in the way he is readying the platter."[19] Herodias, responsible for the execution, smiles while Herod's ambivalence is marked, his eyes askance. Yet as Riegl noticed, the servant neither looks away nor smiles. As the Baptist closes his eyes, and his sinuous neck and torso submit to the blow, the young man watches.

In Riegl's identification of the figure as "Moorish," he places the scene within the religious and racial climate of the Mediterranean, assuming that a Black servant would be born of Islamic faith and dark skin in North Africa. In using this vague terminology to define the young man, Riegl determines his status as an outsider based not only on the color of his skin but also on his faith. The mode of attention expressed by the young man is the same quality that Riegl finds mastered in the faces of *Syndics of the*

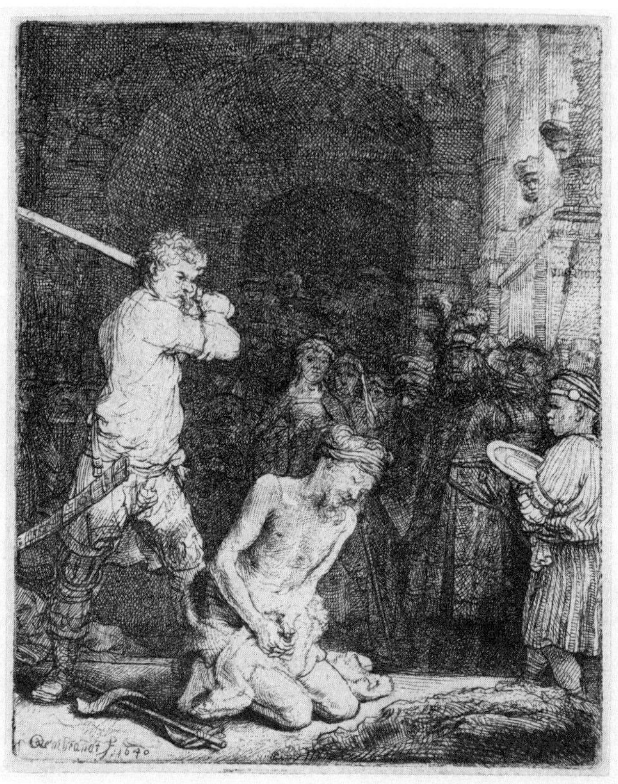

C.2 Rembrandt van Rijn, *The Beheading of John the Baptist*,
1640. Etching and drypoint (Rijksmuseum, Amsterdam).

Drapers' Guild. It is an articulation of an interior life not through the outer exposition of inner turmoil but instead through the quiet ability to observe. As Riegl writes: "The expression of attentive waiting is caught perfectly in the boy's face and body, as well as in the way he is readying the platter."[20] The servant recognizes the faith embodied in John's expression of prayer, eyes closed, hands grasped. Within the crowded scene, only the young man sees the Baptist. Through the young man's attention, the viewer is asked to comprehend the injustice, faith, and martyrdom that create the scene. Riegl recognized this aspect of Rembrandt's composition and made the young Black man central to his exposition of attention in group portraiture.

Nevertheless, Riegl expands on his understanding of attention without a consideration of the stark differences between the *Syndics* and the young man. In the case of the group portrait, the members are the governing structure of society: they determine its rules, policies, who lives and who dies. The Black man in the etching, however, is an outsider, both through faith and the color of his skin. He has no power to determine who lives and who dies. Yet he is also the only witness who recognizes the Baptist in his grace. Riegl's inclusion of this figure within his interpretation of attention places Blackness and its figuration at the center of Dutch group portraiture, as both Riegl and Rembrandt are interested in the inequality of power relations, investigating how individuality emerges in relation to others through processes of subordination, denial, and disregard.

In his examination of these two works, the monumental group portrait and the small etching, Riegl places them beside one another, forcing a relationship between the depiction of the young man and the Dutch patricians. John the Baptist is made visible through the gaze of the young Black man. In selecting a scene of the *Beheading of John the Baptist* to incorporate into his study of Dutch group portraiture, Riegl places the patricians and their staid portraits within a history of state violence and execution. In the seventeenth-century Dutch Republic, executions were common. Events such as the public flaying of politicians would become central to the political and visual landscape in the 1670s, as when Johan and Cornelis de Witt were executed and publicly flayed by a mob, an event captured in a painting by Jan de Baen. Riegl suggests that the same gaze granted to a visitor entering a room could also be turned to a scene of execution. The starkness of this comparison, and the inclusion of a direct figuration of Blackness in the writings of Riegl, have been almost completely overlooked, except by one reader: Derek Walcott. For the poet and painter, this incongruous pairing between the white patricians and the Black man placed into servitude becomes a central motif in one of his final poems, *The Prodigal*, in which he directly places a "blackamoor" at the scene of Rembrandt's *Syndics*.[21]

The poem, as the title suggests, is about wandering, inheritance, and the possibility of returning "home," which for Walcott remains a light on the horizon. Within the title, Walcott cites the biblical parable of the son who leaves home, spends his inheritance, and returns home to forgiveness (Luke 15:11–32). Yet as Walcott triangulates among North America, Europe, and the Caribbean, he queries the notion of inheritance itself in the wake of the violence of the plantation economies and the bloodlines forged between Europe and the Caribbean, a creation of prosperity generated through not only capital but also the construction of generational wealth across racial lines, often determined by who was legitimate and who was deemed illegitimate.

Throughout the stanzas, Walcott traverses the Atlantic and the Alps, moving through museums and public squares, journeying on trains and boats, constantly examining the Western canon and the natural landscapes of Europe and the Caribbean as his "inheritance." Many works of art feature prominently, but none as insistently as Rembrandt's *Syndics of the Drapers' Guild*, which is mentioned on three separate occasions.

Walcott situates the *Syndics* inside the "oily" canals of Amsterdam, referencing the Dutch Shell Oil Company, whose practices of mining in the Dutch Caribbean caused economic and racial tensions into the twentieth century, continuing the legacy of slavery beyond abolition. He first introduces Rembrandt's painting on observing a group of men at lunch in Lausanne: "Then the old gentlemen at lunch in Lausanne / with suits of flawless cut, impeccable manners / an update of Rembrandt's *Syndics of the Drapers' / Guild*."[22] This contemporary syndicate (one can imagine Swiss bankers) reincarnates for Walcott the wealth of seventeenth-century Dutch burghers, who created the first global economies through innovative financial institutions. Walcott traces their ancestry to "John the Baptist heads," as he "translated the pink, shaven faces of the Guild to their dark-panelled and polished ancestry / of John the Baptist heads each borne on a saucer / of white lace, the loaded eyes, the thinning hair / over the white streaks of the foreheads, a / syndicate / in which, far back, a negligible ancestor / might have been a member, greeting me / a product of his empire's miscegenation / in old Saint Martin."[23] In his evocation of a "negligible ancestor" intertwined with the *Syndics*, Walcott punctures the mythology of "hothouse flowers" bred to perfection intimated in Barthes and traces his own genealogy (a product of their empire's miscegenation) and inheritance to the *Syndics*.

As Walcott struggles to find what "things are ours" among the canons of Western art, he returns (for a second time) to Rembrandt's painting, picturing a scene in which "carried on a black charger of starched lace, / a young blackamoor brought in my ancestor's / head / to the orange-fleshed burghers of the Drapers' Guild / at that luncheon in Lausanne."[24] In this juxtaposition between the *Syndics* and a Black servant (using the racialized term *blackamoor*) bearing the head of Walcott's negligible ancestor, he unravels this cloth of the singular corporate body, making evident the underlying context of sex, generation, filiation, and violence that undergirds the intimate exchanges that reflect the larger economic exchanges at the Bourse. Moreover, in drawing lines of filiation between Amsterdam and Old Saint Martin that are both blood and administrative, Walcott creates a version of himself as the "product of his empire's miscegenation in Old Saint Martin" that resonates with the concept of the "creole pilgrim administrator," an idea coined by Benedict Anderson to explain the development of nationalism in the Americas.[25] Anderson argues that "administrative units" were the foundation for the nationalism that would ultimately coalesce into revolution. Colonial administrators in the periphery were central to garnering power and wealth within the metropole, and these bureaucrats held a shared language and set of documentary tools with their European counterparts. Yet they were also excluded from the metropole and advancement in their careers, forever consigned to the colony. Walcott evokes the transatlantic world of administrators and functionaries, for whom "there is no assured resting-place; every pause is provisional. The last thing the functionary wants is to return home; for he has no home with any intrinsic value."[26]

On this journey of administrative jobs, the functionary finds fellow companions with whom he shares "a single language-of-state." In his description of his wanderings in *The Prodigal*, Walcott evokes this pilgrimage, only the shared language is not that of the state but that of Western art. Yet the creole pilgrim administrator is resonant as he imagines a distant ancestor, a pilgrim like him, who shared a "single language" with the Dutch patricians, while also remaining forever consigned to the periphery. The concept of the creole administrator also draws Rembrandt's figure of the young Black man in the etching beyond the realm of "Black servant," an iconographic subject expounded on at length in art-historical scholarship. Instead, the history of this figure might be better contextualized by the world of colonial administrators, who were exploited by men such as the *Syndics* while also central to their economic success and stability. In turn, as Anderson argues, these colonial administrators were ultimately the source of revolution and sovereignty in the Americas. Introducing Rembrandt's monumental group portrait within a trajectory of bloodlines between Amsterdam and Old Saint Martin, Walcott makes evident that the celebration of personhood and interiority—often at the center of interpretations of Rembrandt's painting—cannot be disentangled from its indebtedness to genealogy, wealth, inheritance, and race. In his meditation on his "inheritance," Walcott struggles with the orange-faced burghers, their whiteness, and the racialization of bodies within the seventeenth-century Dutch empire. Moreover, there is also a more complex history for the figure of "the Black servant" within a trajectory of administrators who served European powers while also becoming the site of their undoing, the revolutionaries who could speak the language of the state as they demanded their own constitutions and democracies.

In this poem, which wrestles with the inheritance of the Western canon, the insidious figurative tradition, and wealth and bloodlines embodied in paintings such as Rembrandt's *Syndics of the Drapers' Guild*, Walcott completes this meditation on the pictorial tradition of the Western canon at sea—sailing with dolphins, swift moving creatures that can never be held, briefly glimpsed, "steadily, on the bright rim / of the world, getting no nearer or nearer, the / more."[27] Earlier in the poem, Walcott describes bronze dolphins at the pedestals of fountains across European cities, creating an image of exhaustion through the corrosion: "Time, that gnaws at bronze lions and dolphins / that shrivels fountains, had exhausted him."[28] As he crisscrosses European cities, revisiting the monuments of European art, he juxtaposes museums, statues, paintings, and monuments to the natural world, so that in the completing lines of his verse, the bronze dolphins transform from figures within his memory of European monuments:

> I saw their wet brown bodies gunning seaward,
> more brown than golden despite the name
> "dorado,"
> but I guess in the wet light their skins shone
> too raw, too quiet to be miraculous,
> too strange to quiet my fear, the skittering fish
> . . . .
> And yet elation drove the dolphins' course
> as if both from and to you, their joy was ours.[29]

For the poet who decried the absence of monuments on the sea, Walcott finds in these final lines a freedom akin to joy as dolphins—their rusting bronze carcasses—are free.

§

It is perhaps odd to end a book primarily about seventeenth-century Dutch painting here, with Walcott gathering, refusing, and challenging his inheritance while watching dolphins. Yet in these final lines, Walcott points to the brown bodies of the dolphins as lightning flashes that counter the graveyard that he has otherwise mourned at the bottom of the sea. As this book began with Clifton standing at the shore of the Chesapeake, it ends with Walcott in the middle of the ocean. Bookending these essays with two poets and their engagement with the legacy of the Middle Passage on our natural world demonstrates the importance of attending to the representational sites beyond the human figure—as the Middle Passage remains marked within both the land and the sea. Within coastlines and sugarcane fields, within seascapes and botanicals, the land and the sea were repeatedly evoked and revoked, recognizing that the transformation of life into a commodity was inseparable from claiming land as territory, and seas as characterless surfaces of fluid commerce.

As artists in the seventeenth-century Dutch Republic turned away from the figurative possibilities of divinity in the wake of iconoclasm, they turned toward the natural world, from enigmatic coastlines to dead butterflies, to consider the transformation of life into property. Yet this practice of representation—this obscuring of the human in favor of the view, the horizon, the butterfly wing—also transformed the natural world into a commodity to be abstracted, bought, and sold. The history of art in this short book is primarily one of violence—a narrative that has remained unspoken in histories of Dutch painting until recently. Yet there are many strange and skittering worlds held within these paintings, as negotiations of making the natural world, the human figure, and divinity visible and invisible. There is a lesson as Walcott ends his meditation on art, museums, painting, and sculpture—at sea. In watching brown-bodied dolphins gunning toward the horizon, Walcott suggests that this world bears the violence of transatlantic history and enslavement in its bodies, its institutions, its canons, its oceans—but that there also exists a world that is "too raw, too quiet to be miraculous, / too strange to quiet my fear," yet nevertheless capable of evoking joy. Both of these worlds are the inheritance of our present.

NOTES

Introduction. Transubstantiation across Atlantic Worlds

1   "Rolfe to Sandys, January 1619/20," in Kingsbury, *Records of the Virginia Company*, 243. Discussed in Sluiter, "New Light on the 20," 395–98. As the fundamental 1619 Project demarcates, this was the beginning of slavery in North America; Hannah-Jones, "Idea of America," 16.

2   Van der Valk, "De eerste Afrikaanse Amerikanen." The document granting the right to privateer (raid enemy ships) is in the Zeeuwse Admiraliteit in the National Archives, The Hague, and was issued to Johan de Moor, a merchant based in Zeeland who contracted with English ships. Archieven van der Admiraliteitscolleges (nr. Toegang 1.01.46) inv. nr. 2425, Dutch National Archives, The Hague. On the arrival of the *White Lion* and the start of enslaved labor in the Chesapeake, see also Walsh, *Motives of Honor*, 113–19; and Thornton, "African Experience of the '20 and Odd Negroes,'" 421–34.

3   For the best overview of the Dutch Atlantic historiography, see Rivera, "Whitewashing the Dutch Atlantic." See also Games, "Conclusion"; and Lyon and Fowler, "Revision and Reckoning."

4   Clifton, "surely i am able to write poems," in *Mercy*, 23.

5   Stephen Best articulates the precarity of race in this period and its relationship to slavery; see "On Failing." Jennifer L. Morgan also explores the uncertain development of race in the Atlantic world in the mid-seventeenth century; see *Reckoning with Slavery*. On the historicization of race in the early modern world, see Rubiés, "Were Early Modern Europeans Racist?" Blakely also attends to the complicated definitions of race across the various Dutch empires; Blakely, *Blacks in the Dutch World*, 31–38. In the context of the French Enlightenment and the relationship between the visual arts and race, see Lafont, *L'Art et la race*.

6   Kate Lowe also describes a "perceived invisibility" of the Black African presence in Renaissance art, arguing that it is a production of colonialism and nationalism instead of a material absence, also noting that "far from being genuinely invisible, the traces of these fifteenth- and sixteenth-

century black Africans can be found in almost every type of record: documentary, textual and visual; secular and ecclesiastical; Northern and Southern European, factual and fictional"; Lowe, "Black African Presence," 3.

7 Brienen, "Albert Eckhout's 'African Woman and Child'"; Van den Boogaart, "Black Slavery and the 'Mulatto Escape Hatch'"; Daum, "Das Privileg des Blicks"; Massing, "Albert Eckhout, Frans Post"; Massing, "From Dutch Brazil"; Massing, *Image of the Black*," 143–82; Sutton, "Bittersweet"; Brienen, "Embodying Race and Pleasure."

8 The literature is vast. Allison Blakely wrote one of the first sustained and ongoing influential works on the entanglements between seventeenth-century Dutch art and the slave trade; *Blacks in the Dutch World*. More recently, an explosion of literature has grappled with the visual legacy of the transatlantic slave trade in Dutch history and culture. In particular, the Rijksmuseum mounted an exhibition with an accompanying catalog; Sint Nicolaas et al., *Slavery*. See also Van der Ham, *Tarnished Gold*; and Daalder, Tang, and Balai, *Slaven en schepen*.

9 James, "What Will Blackness Be?"

10 Blakely, "Black Presence in the Dutch World," in *Blacks in the Dutch World*, 225–74. Rembrandt's portrait of the two young men plays a central role in Gikandi's introduction to *Slavery and the Culture*, 1–3, in which he contrasts the portrait study with the simultaneous dehumanization of Black lives through the rise of the slave trade. On the Afro-Dutch community in Amsterdam, see Ponte, "Black in Amsterdam around 1650"; and Hondius, "Black Africans in Seventeenth-Century Amsterdam."

11 In Titus Kaphar's TED Talk, "Can Art Amend History?," he discusses "shifting the gaze" to acknowledge the presence of Blackness in early modern painting, focusing on a Frans Hals family portrait.

12 Brathwaite, *Rediscovering Black Portraiture*, 10. Cheryl Finley also discusses work by contemporary artists engaging with this archive as "mnemonic aesthetics"; Finley, *Committed to Memory*; Finley, "Encore"; Peter Erickson, "Invisibility Speaks."

13 Nelson, *Slavery, Geography, and Empire*.

14 For reasons of scale, this book focuses on the transatlantic slave trade, although the slave trade was also formative and integral to the Vereenigde Oostindische Compagnie (Dutch East India Company) in Asia, a field that deserves much further study. Vink, "World's Oldest Trade."

15 For a broad overview, see Rubin, *Corpus Christi*; and Elwood, *Broken Body*.

16 Nadler, "Arnauld, Descartes, and Transubstantiation."

17 Rubin, *Corpus Christi*, 347. For an overview of various understandings of presence and absence in the sixteenth century, see Wandel, "Fragmentation and Presence."

18 Nimako and Willemsen, *Dutch Atlantic*, 14.

19 One of the best overviews of Dutch painting remains Westermann, *Worldly Art*. For an important series of essays engaging with the term *realism* and Dutch painting, see Franits, *Looking at Seventeenth-Century Dutch Art*.

20 Cedric Robinson cites the "Genoese Bourgeoisie" as the first to realize the economic value of the transatlantic trade; Robinson, *Black Marxism*, 103–9. See also Eric Eustace Williams on the intertangled histories of capitalism and slavery; *Capitalism and Slavery*. For an overview of a reception of Williams's work, see Robinson, "Capitalism, Slavery, and Bourgeois Historiography."

21 Marx, *Capital*, 70.

22 Philip, *Zong!*, 196.

23 Gilroy, *Black Britain*, 21. Also cited in Balkenhol, "Canonizing De Kom," 64.

24 Campt, *Listening to Images*, 50.

25 Gikandi, *Slavery and the Culture*, 1–3.

26 Baucom, *Specters of the Atlantic*.

27 On November 29, 1781, fifty-four individuals were killed; on December 1, forty-two were murdered, and later in December twenty-six were murdered. After these killings, ten individuals threw themselves overboard and committed suicide rather than be murdered. See Burnard, "New Look at the *Zong*."

28 Baucom, *Specters of the Atlantic*, 62.

29 The Westindische Compagnie (WIC, or Dutch West India Company) did not insure their enslaved, but the business was profitable for private corporations, such as the Middelburgsche Commercie Compagnie (MCC), and illegal traders. See Van Niekerk, *Development of the Principles*; da Silva, *Dutch and Portuguese*; and Go, *Marine Insurance in the Netherlands*.

30 Leo Balai, *Slavenschip Leusden*.

31 Lurvink, "Insurance of Mass Murder," 226.

32 Bradley and Marassa, "Awakening to the World," 126.

33 Hegel, *Aesthetics*, 1:169.

34 This quality of Dutch painting—its shine and surface, and its production during a period of defining political freedom—continues to influence art history outside the subdiscipline of seventeenth-century Dutch painting. For example, Krista Thompson discusses Dutch painting, its "surfacism" and translation of objects into commodities through an attention to surface, in her work on shine and surface aesthetics in hip-hop; Thompson, "Sound of Light."

35 Tavares, "Hegel, critique de l'Afrique"; Buck-Morss, *Hegel, Haiti, and Universal History*; Joseph, "'Haitian Turn.'"

36 Stedman, *Narrative*.

37 Fromentin, *Old Masters*, 131.

38 Fromentin, *Old Masters*, 132.

39 There is also an important body of scholarship on the ambiguity of Dutch

genre painting and the genre's role in the daily political life of the emerging republic. See Helgerson, "Soldiers and Enigmatic Girls," in *Adulterous Alliances*, 79–119.

40 Alpers, *Art of Describing*, 122. The complexity of Alpers's argument has often been simplified, although it is deeply indebted to narrative theories and the work of Ann Bancroft, as best explicated in Louis Marin's review, "In Praise of Appearance." Other important reviews include Grafton and Kaufmann, "Holland without Huizinga"; and Westermann, "Svetlana Alpers's 'The Art of Describing.'"

41 Marin, "In Praise of Appearance," 108.

42 Hochstrasser, *Still Life and Trade*, 200.

43 Quilley and Kriz, *Economy of Colour*, 2.

44 Massing, "Albert Eckhout, Frans Post," 171.

45 Philip, *Zong!*, 201.

46 Kettering, *Drawings from the Ter Borch*, 62.

47 Prak, "Burghers, Citizens, and Popular Politics."

48 For the best overview of the Dutch Atlantic historiography, see Rivera, "Whitewashing the Dutch Atlantic"; and Games, "Conclusion."

49 Van Lottum and Lucassen, "Six Cross Sections"; Van Lottum, "Labour Migration and Economic Performance"; Van Rossum et al., "National and International Labour Markets."

50 For an overview of the importance of martial ideas of virtue as central to Dutch artistic practice, see Brusati, "Pictura's Excellent Trophies."

Chapter 1. Art Markets and Futures Speculation

1 For a brief overview of this literature, see Falkenberg and Westermann, introduction. The work of John Michael Montias remains invaluable in this regard; see Montias, "Cost and Value"; Montias, *Artists and Artisans in Delft*; and De Marchi and Van Miegroet, "Art, Value, and Market Practices."

2 Prak, "Golden Age."

3 For the most recent estimates, see Fatah-Black and Van Rossum, "Beyond Profitability." For a consideration of the economic impact in terms of local trades in the Netherlands and the economy of fitting out the slave ships, see de Kok, "Cursed Capital." Scholars have studied, in particular, the impact of the marine insurance industry in Amsterdam. See Lurvink, "Insurance of Mass Murder."

4 M. 't Hart, "Merits of a Financial Revolution"; Barbour, *Capitalism in Amsterdam*; Lesger, *Rise of the Amsterdam Market*; Horst, "De peperhandel van de Vereenigde"; Prakash, *Dutch East India Company*; Steensgaard, *Asian Trade Revolution*.

5 Ufer, "Imagining Social Change."

6   For an overview of this thesis, see De Vries and Van der Woude, *First Modern Economy*. For a critique of their argument, see Van Zanden, "'Revolt of the Early Modernists.'"

7   Gelderblom and Jonker, "Completing a Financial Revolution"; G. Parker, "Emergence of Modern Finance"; Steensgaard, "Dutch East India Company."

8   Thank you to Margaret Graves for bringing these plates to my attention; Kerr, *Asian Ceramics in the Hallwyl Collection*, 163–68. The original Dutch titling: "Pardie al mÿn Actien Kwÿt / Schÿt Actien enwindhandel."

9   De Vries and Van der Woude, *First Modern Economy*, 150–52.

10 De la Vega, *Confusion of Confusions*, 4. See also Petram, *World's First Stock Exchange*.

11 De la Vega, *Confusion of Confusions*, 19–20.

12 Some scholars argue that the "profit margins" on the slave trade were relatively slim, while others have demonstrated the impact on the Dutch economy within other labor sectors, such as shipbuilding, and the rise of the marine insurance industry. For an overview of these debates, see Fatah-Black and Van Rossum, "Beyond Profitability"; Eltis, Emmer, and Lewis, "More than Profits?"; and Fatah-Black and Van Rossum, "Profitable Debate?" As discussed in the introduction of this book, Kwame Nimako and Glenn Willemsen argue that the Peace of Westphalia was inseparable from the transatlantic slave trade and the establishment of a new European economic order founded on collaboration and competition, and dependent on enslaved labor; Nimako and Willemsen, *Dutch Atlantic*.

13 On the intellectual justifications of this tension, see Weststeijn, "Republican Empire."

14 Leeflang and Roelofs, *Hercules Segers*, 187–88.

15 Leeflang and Roelofs, *Hercules Segers*, 175–76.

16 Leeflang and Roelofs, *Hercules Segers*, 189–90.

17 Van Hoogstraten, *Inleyding*, 312.

18 Jaap van der Veen, "'Hercules Segers, Disregarded and Yet a Great Artist': A Sketch of His Life," in Leeflang and Roelofs, *Hercules Segers*, 28.

19 Van der Veen, "'Hercules Segers,'" 29.

20 Montias, "Cost and Value."

21 Looking at a slightly later period in Dutch painting, Angela Ho demonstrates that knowledgeable collectors in the seventeenth and eighteenth centuries actually valued "creative repetition." Ho, *Creating Distinctions*.

22 Leeflang, "'For He also Printed Paintings': Hercules Segers's Painterly Prints," in Leeflang and Roelofs, *Hercules Segers*, 39–74. Leeflang builds on the work of Sluijter in "Over Brabantse vodden." See also Gifford, "Style and Technique."

23 Translation from Leeflang and Roelofs, *Hercules Segers*, 328; Van Hoogstraten, *Inleyding*, 240–41.

24 See Leeflang and Roelofs, *Hercules Segers*, 187.

25 The most famous collection is that of Michiel Hinloopen, whose fifty-two volumes were bequeathed to Amsterdam in 1708; see Van der Waals, *De Prentschat van Michiel Hinloopen*.

26 Leah Price points out that in the nineteenth century, food wrapping was a satirical tradition to dismiss literary works, a convention that began in the Reformation as Bibles and religious manuscripts were unbound and destroyed while the paper or parchment was recycled into other uses. Price, *How to Do Things*, 219.

27 Price, *How to Do Things*, 233.

28 Van Hoogstraten, *Introduction to the Academy*.

29 Kossmann and Mellink, *Texts concerning the Revolt*, 165.

30 Kossmann and Mellink, *Texts concerning the Revolt*, 109.

31 Quoted in Weststeijn, *Commercial Republicanism*, 495; Lipsius, *Epistolario de Justo Lipsio*, 373–374.

32 Weststeijn, *Commercial Republicanism*, 504–5; Barlaeus, *Rerum*, 185. On Barlaeus's view of slavery, see Phaf-Rheinberger, "Von Sklavenhandel und chrisüichen Vorbehalten," 1.

33 Alpers, *Rembrandt's Enterprise*, 107.

34 Alpers, *Rembrandt's Enterprise*, 115.

35 Montias, *Art at Auction*, 180–87.

36 As Stephen Best points out in his work on the emergence of personhood and slavery in nineteenth-century America, slavery "is not simply an antebellum institution that the United States has surpassed but a particular historical form of ongoing crisis involving the subjection of personhood to property"; *Fugitive's Properties*, 270.

Chapter 2. Seascapes and Landscapes

1 Oughtred, *Circles of Proportion*, 184.

2 Corrêa do Lago, *Frans Post*, 372–77. Although Post did not sign the drawings, they were completed on the voyage that he took to Brazil, and the handling of pen and wash is so similar to his work in Brazil that the drawings have been attributed to Post with little to no contention.

3 On Dutch Brazil, see Boxer, *Dutch in Brazil*; Van Groesen, *Legacy of Dutch Brazil*; Van Groesen, *Amsterdam's Atlantic*; and Schmidt, *Innocence Abroad*.

4 On the Dutch Gold Coast, see da Silva, *Dutch and Portuguese in Western Africa*; Klooster and Oostindie, "West Africa," in *Realm between Empires*, 98–120; Van Kessel, *Merchants, Missionaries, and Migrants*; Doortmont and Smit, *Sources for the Mutual History*; Blakeley, *Blacks in the Dutch World*, 1–38; Van der Ham, *Tarnished Gold*; and Ratelband and Basejou, *Nederlanders in West-Afrika*. On the international early modern sugar trade, see Ebert, *Between Empires*.

5 For the impact of the practice of coastal seafaring on the development of maritime painting, see Siegert, "'Chorein' of the Pirate."

6 Waters and Garcie, *Rutters of the Sea*, 32.

7 These drawings are the culmination of observation across many media. The immensity of the sea demanded the ability to make "partial observations and then reconcile them," as the literary theorist Margaret Cohen argues; see "Narratology in the Archive of Literature."

8 Boyle, *World of Honourable Robert Boyle*, 3:33. Many members of the Royal Society engaged with the uncertain business of studying the salty, phosphorescent waters that surrounded their island. Christopher Wren pointed out that there were no uniform conditions at sea, except perhaps equally mysterious traits such as salty and phosphorescent. Unlike the stars and the sky, the very depth of the sea remained an unknown topography, mapped by sounding devices and leaded lines. Robert Boyle published "Other Inquiries Concerning the Sea" in 1666, as well as "Relations about the Bottom of the Sea" and "Observations and Experiments about the Saltiness of the Sea." In 1673, Isaac Newton's *Principia* (published in 1687) examined the tides. And in 1691, Robert Hooke gave a series of lectures dedicated to deep-sea research. The study of the sea and its opacity, the inability to draw a line on its surface, and its impenetrable depths became a frequent recourse to metaphors about the process of producing knowledge and about scientific inquiry.

9 Boyle, *World of Honourable Robert Boyle*, 3:473.

10 The translation is from Lago, *Frans Post*, 372–77.

11 It is also likely that Post's ambivalent description of "banished Portuguese" is informed by the complex negotiation around religious identity and race in the Cape Verde islands during this period. Although Iberian authorities attempted to maintain ideas of purity (*limpeça de sangue*, or exclusion of those with Jewish or Moorish blood) in their colonies, the concept became increasingly disconnected from its religious connotations while also offering a destructive structure by which to conceive of divisions according to race (as opposed to religion). See Green, "Building Creole Identity"; and Green, "Building Slavery in the Atlantic World."

12 Amorim, "Salt Trade in Europe"; Emmer, "Dutch Salt and Sugar Trades."

13 For another consideration of salt and its role in African diasporic artistic practice, particularly regarding the Dutch colony of St. Maarten, see McKee, "Salting of Sorts."

14 Sedgwick, *Touching Feeling*, 1–27.

15 On the importance of this type of navigating for the development of maritime painting, see Siegert, "'Chorein' of the Pirate."

16 On this gift, see Van Panhuys, "Recherche des tableaux"; Lemmens, "Die Schenkung an Ludwig XIV"; Vittet, "Jean-Maurice de Nassau-Siegen et Louis XIV"; and C. Anderson, "*Old Indies* at the French Court."

17 Cited in Lago, *Frans Post*, 52.

18 Michiel van Groesen offers an invaluable account of both the "oral archive" and the ephemeral performances staged by Johan Maurits after his return; see Van Groesen, *Amsterdam's Atlantic*.

19 Transcribed and translated in Lago, *Frans Post*, 67.

20 Lago, *Frans Post*, 284.

21 Lago, *Frans Post*, 284.

22 Voltaire, *Candide*, 75.

23 Indeed, Dutch Brazil was a visual model that became consistently emulated across the Dutch Atlantic world, as demonstrated by Fatah-Black in *Sociëteit van Suriname*, 28–234.

24 In Michael Gaudio's recent subtle reading of Post's landscapes, he maintains that they insist on a certain silence that refuses the ability to necessarily connect historical events to the pictorialization of place; see Gaudio, "Frans Post's Silent Landscapes," in *Sound, Image, Silence*, 33–62. The relationship between the inventory and the painting, however, demonstrates a network of actors in which it was considered necessary to give voice to the landscape's silence.

25 For further important studies on the history of landscape and plantation paintings, see Nelson, *Slavery, Geography, and Empire*; and Bagneris, *Colouring the Caribbean*.

26 Chatman, "There Are No Slaves."

27 Hartman, *Scenes of Subjection*, 6.

28 Article XVI of *Le code noir ou Edit du Roy*, March 1685, site de l'Assemblée nationale, https://www.assemblee-nationale.fr/histoire/esclavage/code-noir.pdf.

29 In Emmelyn Butterfield-Rosen's review of "Posing Modernity" and "Black Models," she points out how the discipline of art history, structured around the "archival discovery," often produces a recurrent blindness in the face of certain documents and histories that are extant; Butterfield-Rosen, "Modern Woman," 188.

30 Massing, "Albert Eckhout, Frans Post," 171.

Chapter 3. Monuments and Architectural Painting

1 Steinberg, *Social Construction of the Ocean*, 105. "The sea was fought over not as a space to be possessed, but to be controlled, a special space within world-society but outside the territorial states that comprised its paradigmatic spatial structure" (109).

2 Mack, *Sea*, 16.

3 Bosman, *New and Accurate Description*, 276.

4 Bosman, *New and Accurate Description*, 280–81.

5 Bosman, *New and Accurate Description*, 218–32. The burial practices are

also discussed in De Marees, *Description and Historical Account*, 179–85. On the Akkan terra-cotta statues, see J. Parker, *In My Time of Dying*, 92–106; Vivian, "Sacred to Secular"; and Quarcoopome, "Les portraits funéraires akan."

6 Bosman, *New and Accurate Description*, 232.

7 Smallwood, *Saltwater Slavery*, 152.

8 Loichot, *Water Graves*, 8.

9 Walter C. Rucker, for example, critiques the focus on communal rupture in scholarship, demonstrating the multiple ways in which a continuity of cultural forms is evident across the Atlantic; *Gold Coast Diasporas*. See also Jamieson, "Material Culture and Social Death."

10 Boyle, *Christian Virtuoso*, 150.

11 Boyle, *Hydrostatical Discourse*, 95.

12 Boyle, *Hydrostatical Discourse*, 99–100.

13 Jackson, *Becoming Human*, 3.

14 Boyle, *Hydrostatical Discourse*, 93.

15 Shapin and Schaffer, *Leviathan and the Air-Pump*, 336, 341.

16 Gilroy, *Black Atlantic*; Glissant, *Caribbean Discourse*; Tinsley, "Black Atlantic, Queer Atlantic"; Baucom, *Specters of the Atlantic*; Sharpe, *In the Wake*; King, *Black Shoals*.

17 Sharpe, *In the Wake*, 40–41.

18 R. Walcott, "Black Aquatic," 66. See also Judy, "Unfungible Flow of Liquid Blackness." Omise'eke Natasha Tinsley provides a powerful reading of "fluid" bodies as a means to materialize Black queer experience across the Atlantic, "not as an easy metaphor" but for "concrete, painful, *and* liberatory experience." See Tinsley, "Black Atlantic, Queer Atlantic." For a critique of liquidity in Black studies, see King, *Black Shoals*, 8.

19 Barthes, "World as Object," 4.

20 In Cheryl Finley's use of the term "icon," she demonstrates how the image carried a demonstrative power similar to religious works in its ability to "convert nonbelievers to a cause that was deeply religious, humanitarian, and moral"; *Committed to Memory*, 13.

21 Sekula, *Fish Story* , 43.

22 See Keyes, *Mirror of Empire*; Russell, *Visions of the Sea*; Goedde, *Tempest and Shipwreck*; Giltaij and Kelch, *Praise of Ships and the Sea*; and iconographic readings about the frailty of human life, in which the singular ship in the tempest embodies the uncertainty of the human journey.

23 Amy Knight Powell posits a formal relationship between this genre of drawing, in which ships on parade stand in a limitless expanse of white paper, and the white ground of imported porcelain. She also demonstrates the importance of Grotius's writings for the developing genre of maritime art; see Powell, "Porcelain White."

24 Sekula, "Fish Story," in *Okeanos*, 17. While Sekula attends to the contain-

erization of enemies and commodities, he does not directly grapple with
the inherent presence of enslavement encoded into his reading of maritime space, as demonstrated by Christina Sharpe in a trenchant critique.
As Sharpe makes clear, this visual economy in which goods and labor are
molded into frictionless surfaces cannot be divorced from a simultaneous
trade in humans as chattel property; see Sharpe, *In the Wake*, 25–33.

25 Van Voss, Van Lottum, and Lucassen, "Sailors, National and International."
For an overview of the literature on the Dutch maritime market, and the
differing sectors of the intra-European marine labor force, see Van Lottum
and Lucassen, "Six Cross-Sections of the Dutch Maritime Labor Market."

26 Van Rossum et al., "National and International Labour," 53–54.

27 Van Rossum et al., "National and International Labour," 57.

28 Keyes, "Cornelis Claesz. van Wieringen," 3–4.

29 *Mare liberum*, published as a pamphlet in 1609, was part of a much larger
unpublished manuscript, "De jure Praedae" ("On the law of prize and
booty"), which was not published until the nineteenth century. On this history, see Vervliet, "General Introduction"; and Van Ittersum, "Hugo Grotius
in Context."

30 Grotius, *Mare Liberum*, 85.

31 Grotius, *Mare Liberum*, 85.

32 Fulton, *Sovereignty of the Sea*, 524–25.

33 Meadows, *Observations concerning the Dominion*, 7.

34 Straumann, *Roman Law in the State of Nature*.

35 On the display of armor in church monuments, see Van Swigchem,
Brouwer, and Van Os, *Een Huis voor het Woord*, 264–67.

36 Havener, "Tropaion," 275.

37 Van den Vondel, "*Het lof der zee-vaert*."

38 Lawrence, "Hendrick de Keyser's Heemskerk Monument," 280.

39 Keuning, *Petrus Plancius*; Zandvliet, *Mapping for Money*, 33–49; Noorlander, *Heaven's Wrath*, 11–35.

40 Lawrence, "Hendrick de Keyser's Heemskerk Monument," 267. See also
Lawrence, "Cult of the Seventeenth-Century Dutch Naval Heroes."

41 Sigmond and Kloek, *Zeeslagen en zeehelden*.

42 Vanhaelen, *Wake of Iconoclasm*, 165.

43 The term *citizen* is often aligned with the concept of the *burgher*, which
has been central to scholarship on the Dutch Republic; for example, Simon
Schama noted that "the burgher was citizen first and *homo oeconomicus*
second"; *Embarrassment of Riches*, 7. See also Prak, "Burghers, Citizens,
and Popular Politics." Dutch citizenship was defined by the urban centers,
where individuals could claim citizenship based on birth, marriage,
or purchase.

1 I first encountered this inventory in the collections of Houghton Library at Harvard University, where it is bound with a collection of other seventeenth- and eighteenth-century European travel narratives.

2 Jackson, *Becoming Human*, 49

3 Cook, *Matters of Exchange.*

4 Daston, "Description by Omission," 13.

5 Daston, "Description by Omission," 23

6 Daston, "Description by Omission," 23.

7 Adorno, *Polemics of Possession*; Armitage, "John Locke"; Herzog, *Frontiers of Possession.*

8 For early modern embryological theories, there was a desire to "individuate them [embryos], to grant them coherent, recognizable identities, and even, in one theory, to subjectify them"; Keller, "Embryonic Individuals," 327. There is an accompanying history of the engraved illustrations of the "unborn" in anatomical treatises, yet these representations strip away specificity of geography and race. Many of the anatomists in this period debated generation and development, attempting to describe when the fetus achieved the mark of personhood; Pranghoffer, "Changing Views on Generation." See also Massey, "Pregnancy and Pathology."

9 For a concise overview on views about animality in the early modern period, see Jorink, Woodall, and Wouk, "Humans and Other Animals."

10 Paula Findlen charts how the museum as a public institution emerged as a solution to a "crisis in knowledge" created through early modern encounters, conquests, and religious wars; see Findlen, "Museum," 68. Findlen's establishment of the museum within a "crisis of knowledge" comes full circle today as museums are increasingly called on to recognize their role in structural racism, colonialism, and the knowledge that #museumsarenotneutral. As museums are forced to publicly acknowledge their colonial foundations, Findlen's understanding of the museum as a response to a "crisis in knowledge" is productive in contextualizing the exhibition of an infant in a space attempting to "order knowledge." The side-by-side positioning of infants in jars next to reptiles and birds reveals a crisis over the definition of the human itself.

11 Margócsy, *Commercial Visions.*

12 Otterspeer, *Bastion of Liberty*, 98; Jorink, *Reading the Book of Nature*, 278–89.

13 Hendriksen, *Elegant Anatomy*, 152.

14 One example is in the collection of the Leiden Museum Boerhaave, and its provenance traces to the Leiden anatomist Sebald Justinus Brugmans (1763–1819). This infant is referred to as "African" within the eighteenth-

century catalog and has blue and white beads wrapped around its wrists, ankles, and neck, while placed in a position of prayer and offering. The beads used in this preparation have been traced to the beads used for trade and currency on the coast of West Africa; see Hendriksen, *Elegant Anatomy*, 144–77.

15 Bosman, *Nauwkeurige beschrijving*, 118, cited in Hendriksen, *Elegant Anatomy*, 161.

16 For the term "lightning presences," see Foucault, "Lives of Infamous Men." The concept was also central for Saidiya Hartman in her pathbreaking article, "Venus in Two Acts."

17 The literature on art and science in Dutch picturing is vast; Jorink and Ramakers, *Art and Science in the Early Modern Netherlands*, is a great introduction and an important critique of Svetlana Alpers's description of art and science. See also Jorink and Ramakers, "Undivided Territory."

18 Bosman, *New and Accurate Description*, 118.

19 On Ruysch's display of anatomy within the context of wonder and creation, see Van de Roemer, "Het lichaam als borduursel."

20 Swan, "Birds of Paradise for the Sultan"; Cook, *Matters of Exchange*, 73–74.

21 Often these specific anatomical collections were about studying (and cataloging) rare birth conditions. On this medical history and the collection of Ruysch, for example, see Boer, Radziun, and Oostra, "Frederik Ruysch."

22 On early modern collections and curiosity cabinets, see MacGregor, *Curiosity and Enlightenment*; and Bergvelt and Kistemaker, *De wereld binnen handbereik*. On colonialism and botany, see Casid, *Sowing Empire*; Schiebinger and Swan, *Colonial Botany*; and Crosby, *Columbian Exchange*.

23 The enduring account of Merian's life remains Davis, *Women on the Margins*, 140–202. See also E. Rucker, *Maria Sibylla Merian*; Reitsma, *Maria Sibylla Merian and Daughters*; Neri, "Stitches, Specimens and Pictures: Maria Sibylla Merian and the Processing of the Natural World," in *Insect and the Image*, 139–80.

24 For recent articles addressing her role in colonialism, see Polcha, "Breeding Insects"; Epelbaum, "'Little Atlas,'"; and Kinukawa, "Science and Whiteness as Property."

25 Brown, "Insects," 25. Also discussed in Jackson, *Becoming Human*, 40.

26 Virgil, "The Fourth Book of the Georgics," in *Works of Virgil*, 122.

27 Brown, "Insects," 21.

28 Brown, "Insects," 26.

29 Saxby, *Quest for the New Jerusalem*, 289.

30 Merian, *Metamorphosis*. For an English translation, Merian, *Metamorphosis insectorum Surinamensium—1705*.

31 For more than twenty of her engraved plates, the plant she depicts is not the actual host for the caterpillar and its chrysalis; Reitsma, *Maria Sibylla Merian and Daughters*, 182.

32 Van de Plas, *Metamorphosis insectorum Surinamensium*, 78. The Museum

Wiesbaden holds in its Gerning Collection actual butterfly specimens prepared by Maria Sibylla Merian.

33 Reitsma, *Maria Sibylla Merian and Daughters*, 105.

34 Merian, *Metamorphosis*, 1.

35 Merian, *Metamorphosis*, 1.

36 Merian, *Metamorphosis*, 1.

37 "Clearly, the organs themselves don't produce such ideas, for if they did then the eyes of a man in the dark would produce colours and his nose would smell roses in the winter, whereas in fact nobody experiences the taste of a pine-apple till he goes to India where it is, and tastes it"; Locke, *Essay concerning Human Understanding*, 1. Locke refers to the pineapple several times throughout; see Silver, "Locke's Pineapple."

38 An important exception is Pieter de Wit's *Portrait of Dirck Wilre in the Slave Fort at Elmina* (1669), which pictures the interior of a slave fort in West Africa. On this painting, see Powell, "Life and Death."

39 For an overview of the historiography of the Dutch interior painting genre, see Westermann, "'Wooncultuur in the Netherlands."

40 This genre of painting has a textual counterpart in works such as Jacob Cats's *Houwelyck* (1625) and Petrus Wittewrongel's *Oeconomia Christiana ofte Christelicke Huishoudinge* (1661). See also Franits, *Paragons of Virtue*.

41 Hollander, "Public and Private Life," 286.

42 Powell, "Life and Death," 293.

43 There are exceptions, such as Jan Brandes's drawings from his time in Batavia, although the plantation economy differed between Suriname and Batavia, creating different conditions for "picturing domesticity." On these drawings, see De Bruijn and Raben, *World of Jan Brandes*.

44 Merian, *Metamorphosis*, 60.

45 Merian, *Metamorphosis*, 60.

46 Swammerdam, *Book of Nature*, 46.

47 Remien, "Oeconomy and Ecology."

48 On these debates, see Bowler, "Preformation and Pre-existence"; and Wilson, *Invisible World*, 103–39. More recently, Bowler has clarified the complexity of these two theories, and the preference for "pre-existing germs" as opposed to preformation; see Bowler, "Theories of Generation." See also Henderson, "Doll-Machines and Butcher-Shop Meat."

49 Swammerdam, *Book of Nature*, 104; Jorink, "Beyond the Lines of Apelles."

50 Merian, *Metamorphosis*, 5.

51 Merian, *Metamorphosis*, 45. For the most comprehensive historicization of this passage, see Schiebinger, *Plants and Empire*, particularly 105–49. See also Kinukawa, "Science and Whiteness as Property."

52 Morgan, "*Partus sequitur ventrem*," 17. On the critical role of reproduction and its legal status within American plantation economies and the development of race and enslavement, see Morgan, *Reckoning with Slavery*, 5.

53 Chapman, "Inside Vermeer's Women," 68. See also Chapman, "Women in Vermeer's Home."

54 Wolf, *Vermeer and the Invention of Seeing*, 167. On the role of women within the seventeenth-century Dutch market economy, see Honig, "Desire and Domestic Economy." Most recently, in response to the *Vermeer* exhibition at the Rijksmuseum, Teju Cole wrote a review for the *New York Times* articulating the necessity of contextualizing Vermeer within Dutch colonialism. Cole, "Seeing beyond the Beauty."

55 Morgan, "*Partus sequitur ventrem*," 13.

Conclusion. Historiography and Race

1   Morrison, *Playing in the Dark*. More recently, in the field of art history, Anne Lafont's work has also addressed the central "African presence" in the visual culture of the Enlightenment; see Lafont, *L'Art et la race*.

2   Morrison, *Playing in the Dark*, 5.

3   Barthes, "World as Object," 11.

4   Barthes, "World as Object," 9.

5   Barthes, "World as Object," 8.

6   Barthes, "World as Object," 9.

7   Barthes, "World as Object," 9.

8   Barthes, *Camera Lucida*, 78–79.

9   Barthes, *Camera Lucida*, 79.

10 The umbilical cord reference is discussed extensively by Shawn Michelle Smith in *At the Edge of Sight*, 29–31.

11 Smith, *At the Edge of Sight*, 30

12 Barthes, "World as Object," 9.

13 Barthes, "World as Object," 12.

14 Barthes, "World as Object," 3.

15 Scholars have addressed the formation of whiteness in European portraiture in other artists as well, for example, Angela Rosenthal's canonical essay on British eighteenth-century portraiture, and Nika Elder's work on John Singleton Copley; see Rosenthal, "Visceral Culture"; Elder, "In the Flesh"; and Lafont, *L'Art et la race*, 45–84. For an overview of the literature on whiteness in art history, see Holloway, "Critical Race Art History"; and Knowles, "Making Whiteness."

16 Riegl, *Group Portraiture*, 241.

17 Riegl, *Group Portraiture*, 290.

18 Riegl, *Group Portraiture*, 291.

19 Riegl, *Group Portraiture*, 291.

20 Riegl, *Group Portraiture*, 291.

21 D. Walcott, *Prodigal*.

22 D. Walcott, *Prodigal*, 2.5.

23 D. Walcott, *Prodigal*, 1.2.5.

24 D. Walcott, *Prodigal*, 1.5.2. Walcott also clearly references T. S. Eliot's *Love Song of J. Alfred Prufrock*, in which Eliot writes, "Though I have seen my head (grown slightly bald) brought in upon a platter."

25 B. Anderson, "Creole Pioneers." In one of the more interesting interpretations of Vermeer, Bryan Wolf also connects Vermeer's work to that of the creole pioneer; see Wolf, *Vermeer and the Invention*, 227–52.

26 B. Anderson, "Creole Pioneers," 55–56.

27 D. Walcott, *Prodigal*, 3.18.3.

28 D. Walcott, *Prodigal*, 3.18.2.

29 D. Walcott, *Prodigal*, 3.18.3–4.

BIBLIOGRAPHY

Adorno, Rolena. *The Polemics of Possession in the Native American Narrative.* New Haven, CT: Yale University Press, 2014.

Alpers, Svetlana. *The Art of Describing: Dutch Art in the Seventeenth Century.* Chicago: University of Chicago Press, 1983.

Alpers, Svetlana. *Rembrandt's Enterprise: The Studio and the Market.* Chicago: University of Chicago Press, 1988.

Amorim, Inês. "Salt Trade in Europe and the Development of Salt Fleets." In *The Sea in History: The Early Modern World*, edited by Christian Buchet and Gérard Le Bouëdec, 244–53. Martlesham, UK: Boyell and Brewer, 2017.

Anderson, Benedict. "Creole Pioneers." In *Imagined Communities: Reflections on the Origin and Spread of Nationalism*, 49–68. London: Verso, 2006.

Anderson, Carrie. "The *Old Indies* at the French Court: Johan Maurits's Gift to Louis XIV." *Early Modern Low Countries* 3, no. 1 (2019): 32–59.

Armitage, David. "John Locke, Carolina, and the Two Treaties of Government." *Political Theory* 32, no. 5 (2004): 602–27.

Bagneris, Mia L. *Colouring the Caribbean: Race and the Art of Agostino Brunias.* Manchester: Manchester University Press, 2018.

Balai, Leo. *Slavenschip Leusden: Moord aan de monding van de Marowijnerivier.* Zutphen: Walberg Pers, 2013.

Balkenhol, Markus. "Canonizing De Kom: Sacrality, Blackness, and the Nation in Postcolonial Netherlands." *Small Axe* 27, no. 1 (March 2023): 59–66.

Barbour, Violet. *Capitalism in Amsterdam in the Seventeenth Century.* Baltimore: Johns Hopkins University Press, 1950.

Barlaeus, Caspar. *Rerum per Octennium in Brasilia Siara.* Amsterdam: Ioannis Blaeu, 1647.

Barthes, Roland. *Camera Lucida: Reflections on Photography.* New York: Hill and Wang, 1981.

Barthes, Roland. "The World as Object." In *Critical Essays*, translated by Richard Howard, 3–24. Evanston, IL: Northwestern University Press, 1972.

Baucom, Ian. *Specters of the Atlantic: Finance Capital, Slavery, and the Philosophy of History.* Durham, NC: Duke University Press, 2005.

Bergvelt, Ellinoor, and Renée Kistemaker. *De wereld binnen handbereik: Neder-*

landse kunst-en rariteitenverzamelingen, 1585–1735. Zwolle, Netherlands: Amsterdam Historisch Museum, 1992.

Best, Stephen. *The Fugitive's Properties: Law and the Poetics of Possession*. Chicago: University of Chicago Press, 2004.

Best, Stephen. "On Failing to Make the Past Present." *Modern Language Notes* 73, no. 3 (2012): 453–74.

Blakely, Allison. *Blacks in the Dutch World: The Evolution of Racial Imagery in a Modern Society*. Bloomington: Indiana University Press, 2001.

Boer, Lucas, Anna B. Radziun, and Roelof-Jan Oostra. "Frederik Ruysch (1638–1731): Historical Perspective and Contemporary Analysis of His Teratological Legacy." *American Journal of Medical Genetics* 173, no. 1 (2017): 16–41.

Bosman, Willem. *A New and Accurate Description of the Coast of Guinea, Divided into the Gold, the Slave, and the Ivory Coasts*. London, 1705. Originally published as *Nauwkeurige beschryving van de Guinese Goud-Tand-en Slave-kust* (Utrecht, 1704).

Bowler, Peter J. "Preformation and Pre-existence." *Journal of the History of Biology* 4 (1971): 221–44.

Bowler, Peter J. "Theories of Generation and the History of Life." In *The Secrets of Generation: Reproduction in the Long Eighteenth Century*, edited by Raymond Stephanson and Darren N. Wagner, 79–99. Toronto, ON: University of Toronto Press, 2015.

Boxer, C. R. *The Dutch in Brazil, 1624–1654*. Oxford: Clarendon Press, 1957.

Boyle, Robert. *The Christian Virtuoso*. St. Paul's Churchyard, 1690.

Boyle, Robert. *An Hydrostatical Discourse*. London, 1672.

Boyle, Robert. *The Works of Honourable Robert Boyle*. London: 1774.

Bradley, Rizvana, and Damien-Adia Marassa. "Awakening to the World: Relation, Totality, and Writing from Below." *Discourse* 36, no. 1 (Winter 2014): 112–31.

Brathwaite, Peter. *Rediscovering Black Portraiture*. Los Angeles: Getty, 2023.

Brienen, Rebecca Parker. "Albert Eckhout's 'African Woman and Child' (1641): Ethnographic Portraiture, Slavery, and the New World Subject." In *Slave Portraiture in the Atlantic World*, edited by Agnes Lugo-Ortiz and Angela Rosenthal, 229–55. Cambridge: Cambridge University Press, 2013.

Brienen, Rebecca Parker. "Embodying Race and Pleasure: Dirk Valkenburg's Slave Dance." In *Nederlands Kunsthistorisch Jaarboek: Body and Embodiment in Netherlandish Art*, edited by Ann-Sophie Lehman and Herman Roodenburg, 242–64. Zwolle, Netherlands: Waanders, 2008.

Brown, Eric C. "Insects, Colonies, and Idealization in the Early Americas." *Utopian Studies* 13, no. 2 (2002): 20–37.

Brusati, Celeste. "Pictura's Excellent Trophies: Valorizing Virtuous Artisanship in the Dutch Republic." *Nederlands Kunsthistorisch Jaarboek* 54 (2003): 60–89.

Buck-Morss, Susan. *Hegel, Haiti, and Universal History*. Pittsburgh, PA: University of Pittsburgh Press, 2009.

Burnard, Trevor. "A New Look at the *Zong* Case of 1783." *XVII–XVIII* no. 76 (2019). https://doi.org/10.4000/1718.1808.

Butterfield-Rosen, Emmelyn. "The Modern Woman: Review of 'Posing Modernity' (Wallach Art Gallery) and 'Le modèle noir' (Musée d'Orsay)." *Artforum* 58, no. 2 (October 2019): 188–200.

Campt, Tina M. *Listening to Images.* Durham, NC: Duke University Press, 2017.

Casid, Jill. *Sowing Empire: Landscape and Colonization.* Minneapolis: University of Minnesota Press, 2005.

Cats, Jacob. *Houwelyck.* Middleburgh, 1625.

Chapman, H. Perry. "Inside Vermeer's Women." In *Vermeer's Women: Secrets and Silence*, edited by Betsy Wieseman, 64–123. New Haven, CT: Yale University Press, 2011.

Chapman, H. Perry. "Women in Vermeer's Home: Mimesis and Ideation." *Nederlands Kunsthistorisch Jaarboek* 51 (2000): 237–71.

Chatman, Samuel L. "'There Are No Slaves in France': A Re-examination of Slave Laws in Eighteenth-Century France." *Journal of Negro History* 85, no. 3 (2000): 144–53.

Clifton, Lucille. *Mercy.* Rochester, NY: Boa Editions, 2004.

Cohen, Margaret. "Narratology in the Archive of Literature." *Representations* 108, no. 1 (2009): 51–75.

Cole, Teju. "Seeing beyond the Beauty of a Vermeer." *New York Times Magazine*, May 25, 2023.

Cook, Harold J. *Matters of Exchange: Commerce, Medicine, and Science in the Dutch Golden Age.* New Haven, CT: Yale University Press, 2008.

Corrêa do Lago, Bia, and Pedro Corrêa do Lago. *Frans Post: Catalogue Raisonné.* Milan: Five Continents Editions, 2007.

Crosby, Alfred. *The Columbian Exchange: Biological and Cultural Consequences of 1492.* Westport, CT: Praeger, 2003.

Daalder, Remmelt, Dirk J. Tang, and Leo Balai, eds. *Slaven en schepen en het Atlantisch gebied.* Leiden: Primavera Pers, 2013.

da Silva, Filipa Ribeiro. *Dutch and Portuguese in Western Africa: Empires, Merchants, and the Atlantic System.* Leiden: Brill, 2011.

Daston, Lorraine. "Description by Omission: Nature Enlightened and Obscured." In *Regimes of Description: In the Archive of the Eighteenth Century*, edited by John Bender and Michael Marrinan, 11–24. Redwood City, CA: Stanford University Press, 2005.

Daum, Denise. "Das Privileg des Blicks: Sichtbarkeit und Unsichtbarkeit in Albert Eckhouts 'Kopenhagener Gemäldezyklus.'" In *Die sichtbare Welt: Niederländische Bilder des 16 und 17. Jahrhunderts*, edited by Achim Riether, 221–37. Tübingen: Wasmuth, 1996.

Davis, Natalie Zemon. *Women on the Margins: Three Seventeenth-Century Lives.* Cambridge, MA: Harvard University Press, 1995.

de Bruijn, Max, and Remco Raben, eds. *The World of Jan Brandes, 1743–1808: Drawings of a Dutch Traveller in Batavia, Ceylon, and Southern Africa. Amsterdam: Rijksmuseum, 2004.

de Kok, Gerhard. "Cursed Capital: The Economic Impact of the Transatlantic Slave Trade in Walcheren around 1770." *Tijdschrift voor Sociale en Economische Geschiedenis* 13, no. 3 (2016): 1–27.

de la Vega, Joseph. *Confusion of Confusions.* Translated by Hermann Kellenbenz. Cambridge, MA: Harvard University Press, 1957.

De Marchi, Neil, and H. J. Van Miegroet. "Art, Value, and Market Practices in the Netherlands in the Seventeenth Century." *Art Bulletin* 76, no. 3 (1994): 451–64.

de Marees, Pieter. *Description and Historical Account of the Gold Kingdom of Guinea (1602).* Translated by Albert van Dantzig and Adam Jones. Oxford: Oxford University Press, 1987. Originally published as *Beschrijvinghe ende historische verhael vant gout koninckrijck van Guinea* (Cornelis Claesz, Amsterdam, 1602).

de Vries, Jan, and Ad van der Woude. *The First Modern Economy: Success, Failure, and Perseverance of the Dutch Economy, 1500–1815.* Cambridge: Cambridge University Press, 2011.

Doortmont, Michael R., and Jinna Smit. *Sources for the Mutual History of Ghana and the Netherlands.* Leiden: Brill, 2007.

Ebert, Christopher. *Between Empires: Brazilian Sugar in the Early Atlantic Economy, 1550–1630.* Leiden: Brill, 2008.

Elder, Nika. "In the Flesh: John Singleton Copley's Royall Portraits and Whiteness." *Art History* 44, no. 5 (2021): 949–77.

Eltis, David, Pieter C. Emmer, and Frank D. Lewis. "More than Profits? The Contribution of the Slave Trade to the Dutch Economy: Assessing Fatah-Black and Van Rossum." *Slavery and Abolition: A Journal of Slave and Post-Slave Studies* 37, no. 4 (2016): 724–35.

Elwood, Christopher. *The Broken Body: The Calvinist Doctrine of the Eucharist and the Symbolization of Power in Sixteenth-Century France.* Oxford: Oxford University Press, 1999.

Emmer, Piet C. "The Dutch Salt and Sugar Trades and the Making of the Second Atlantic System, 1580–1650." In *I Seminário Internacional sobre o sal português*, edited by Inês Amorim, 29–40. Porto: Instituto de Historia Moderna de Universidade de Porto, 2005.

Epelbaum, Diana. "'Little Atlas': Global Travel and Local Preservation in Maria Sibylla Merian's *The Metamorphosis of the Insects of Surinam.*" In *Transatlantic Women Travelers, 1688–1843*, edited by Misty Krueger, 23–47. Lewisburg, PA: Bucknell University Press, 2021.

Erickson, Peter. "Invisibility Speaks: Servants and Portraits in Early Modern Visual Culture." *Journal for Early Modern Cultural Studies* 9, no. 1 (2009): 23–61.

Falkenberg, Reindert, and Mariët Westermann. Introduction to *Nederlands Kunsthistorisch Jaarboek* 50 (1999): 6–11.

Fatah-Black, Karwan. *Sociëteit van Suriname, 1683–1795: Het Bestuur van de kolonie in de achttiende eeuw.* Zutphen, Netherlands: Walburg Pers, 2019.

Fatah-Black, Karwan, and Matthias van Rossum. "Beyond Profitability: The Dutch Transatlantic Slave Trade and Its Economic Impact." *Slavery and Abolition: A Journal of Slave and Post-Slave Studies* 36, no. 1 (2015): 63–83.

Fatah-Black, Karwan, and Matthias van Rossum. "A Profitable Debate?" *Slavery and Abolition: A Journal of Slave and Post-Slave Studies* 37, no. 4 (2016): 736–43.

Findlen, Paula. "The Museum: Its Classical Etymology and Renaissance Genealogy." *Journal of the History of Collections* 1, no. 1 (1989): 59–78.

Finley, Cheryl. *Committed to Memory: The Art of the Slave Ship Icon.* Princeton, NJ: Princeton University Press, 2018.

Finley, Cheryl. "Encore." In *Rediscovering Black Portraiture*, by Peter Brathwaite, 148–53. Los Angeles: Getty, 2023.

Foucault, Michel. "Lives of Infamous Men [1977]." In *Archives of Infamy: Foucault on State Power in the Lives of Ordinary Citizens*, edited by Nancy Luxon, 67–84. Minneapolis: University of Minnesota Press, 2019.

Franits, Wayne E., ed. *Looking at Seventeenth-Century Dutch Art: Realism Reconsidered.* Cambridge: Cambridge University Press, 1997.

Franits, Wayne E. *Paragons of Virtue: Women and Domesticity in Seventeenth-Century Dutch Art.* Cambridge: Cambridge University Press, 1993.

Fromentin, Eugène. *The Old Masters of Belgium and Holland.* Translated by Mary C. Robbins. Boston: Hames R. Osgood, 1883.

Fulton, Thomas. *The Sovereignty of the Sea: A Historical Account of the Claims of England to the Dominion of the British Seas, and of the Evolution of the Territorial Waters.* Edinburgh: W. Blackwood, 1911.

Games, Alison. "Conclusion: The Dutch Moment in Atlantic Historiography." In *Dutch Atlantic Connections, 1600–1800: Linking Empires, Bridging Borders*, edited by Gert Oostindie and Jessica V. Roitman, 357–74. Leiden: Brill, 2014.

Gaudio, Michael. *Sound, Image, Silence: Art and the Aural Imagination in the Atlantic World.* Minneapolis: University of Minnesota Press, 2019.

Gelderblom, Oscar, and Joost Jonker. "Completing a Financial Revolution: The Finance of the Dutch East India Trade and the Rise of the Amsterdam Capital Market, 1595–1612." *Journal of Economic History* 64, no. 3 (2004): 641–72.

Gifford, E. Melanie. "Style and Technique in Dutch Landscape Painting in the 1620s." *Historical Painting Techniques, Materials, and Studio Practice*, edited by Arie Wallert, Erma Hermens, and Marja Peek, 140–47. Los Angeles: Getty Conservation Institute, 1995.

Gikandi, Simon. *Slavery and the Culture of Taste.* Princeton, NJ: Princeton University Press, 2011.

Gilroy, Paul. *The Black Atlantic: Modernity and Double-Consciousness.* Cambridge, MA: Harvard University Press, 1993.

Gilroy, Paul. *Black Britain: A Photographic History.* London: Saqi, in association with Getty Images, 2007.

Giltaij, Jeroen, and Jan Kelch. *Praise of Ships and the Sea: The Dutch Marine Painters of the 17th Century*. Rotterdam: Museum Boijmans van Beuningen and the Staatliche Museum zu Berlin, 1996.

Glissant, Édouard. *Caribbean Discourse: Selected Essays*. Charlottesville: University of Virginia Press, 1989.

Go, Sabine. *Marine Insurance in the Netherlands 1600–1870: A Comparative Institutional Approach*. Amsterdam: Amsterdam University Press, 2009.

Goedde, Lawrence O. *Tempest and Shipwreck in Dutch and Flemish Art*. University Park: Penn State University Press, 1989.

Grafton, Anthony, and Thomas DaCosta Kaufmann. "Holland without Huizinga: Dutch Visual Culture in the Seventeenth Century." *Journal of Interdisciplinary History* 16, no. 2 (1985): 255–65.

Green, Tobias. "Building Creole Identity in the African Atlantic: Boundaries of Race and Religion in Seventeenth-Century Cabo Verde." *History in Africa* 36 (2009): 103–25.

Green, Tobias. "Building Slavery in the Atlantic World: Atlantic Connections and the Changing Institution of Slavery in Cabo Verde, Fifteenth–Sixteenth Centuries." *Slavery and Abolition* 32, no. 2 (2011): 227–45.

Grotius, Hugo. *Mare Liberum, 1609–2009*. Edited by Robert Feenstra. Leiden: Brill, 2009.

Hannah-Jones, Nikole. "The Idea of America." *New York Times Magazine*, August 14, 2019.

Hartman, Saidiya. *Scenes of Subjection: Terror, Slavery, and Self-Making in Nineteenth-Century America*. Oxford: Oxford University Press, 1997.

Hartman, Saidiya. "Venus in Two Acts." *Small Axe* 12, no. 2 (2008): 1–14.

Havener, Wolfgang. "Tropaion: The Battlefield Trophy in Ancient Greece and Rome." In *Melammu Symposia 10: Societies at War*, edited by Kai Ruffing, Kerstin Dross-Krüpe, Sebastian Fink, and Robert Rollinger, 267–92. Vienna: Austrian Academy of Sciences Press, 2020.

Hegel, Georg Wilhelm Friedrich, *Aesthetics: Lectures on Fine Arts*. Vol. 1. Translated by T. M. Knox. Oxford: Clarendon Press, 1998.

Helgerson, Richard. *Adulterous Alliances: Home, State, and History in Early Modern European Drama and Painting*. Chicago: University of Chicago Press, 2000.

Henderson, Andrea. "Doll-Machines and Butcher-Shop Meat: Models of Childbirth in the Early Stages of Industrial Capitalism." *Genders* 12 (1991): 100–119.

Hendriksen, Marieke. *Elegant Anatomy: The Eighteenth-Century Leiden Anatomical Collections*. Leiden: Brill, 2014.

Herzog, Tamar. *Frontiers of Possession: Spain and Portugal in Europe and the Americas*. Cambridge, MA: Harvard University Press, 2014.

Ho, Angela K. *Creating Distinctions in Dutch Genre Painting*. Amsterdam: Amsterdam University Press, 2017.

Hochstrasser, Julie. *Still Life and Trade in the Dutch Golden Age*. New Haven, CT: Yale University Press, 2007.

Hollander, Martha. "Public and Private Life in the Art of Pieter de Hooch." *Nederlands Kunsthistorisch Jaarboek* 51 (2000): 272–93.

Holloway, Camara Dia. "Critical Race Art History." *Art Journal* 75, no. 1 (2016): 89–92.

Hondius, Dienke. "Black Africans in Seventeenth-Century Amsterdam." *Renaissance and Reformation* 31, no. 2 (2008): 87–105.

Honig, Elizabeth A. "Desire and Domestic Economy." *Art Bulletin* 83, no. 2 (2001): 294–315.

Horst, W. A. "De peperhandel van de Vereenigde Oostindische Compagnie." *Bijdragen voor Vaderlandsche Geschiedenis en Oudheidkunde* 8, no. 111 (1941): 95–103.

Index to the Indian Closset, An. Which contains severall forreign creatures, and plants swimming in balsamick liquours as if now alive. To be seen in the garden of the Academy of Leyden. London, 1688. https://hollis.harvard.edu/primo-explore/fulldisplay?docid=01HVD_ALMA211970161400003941&context=L&vid=HVD2&lang=en_US&search_scope=everything&adaptor=Local%20Search%20Engine&tab=everything&query=any,contains,index%20to%20the%20indian%20closset&offset=0.

Jackson, Zakiyyah Iman. *Becoming Human: Matter and Meaning in an Antiblack World*. New York: New York University Press, 2020.

James, Erica Moiah. "What Will Blackness Be?" *Callaloo* 38, no. 3 (2015): 589–94.

Jamieson, Ross W. "Material Culture and Social Death: African-American Burial Practices." *Historical Archaeology* 29, no. 4 (1995): 38–48.

Jorink, Eric. "Beyond the Lines of Apelles: Johannes Swammerdam, Dutch Scientific Culture, and the Representation of Insect Anatomy." *Nederlands Kunsthistorisch Jaarboek* 61 (2011): 148–83.

Jorink, Eric. *Reading the Book of Nature in the Dutch Golden Age, 1575–1715*. Leiden: Brill, 2010.

Jorink, Eric, and Bart Ramakers, eds. *Art and Science in the Early Modern Netherlands* (Kunst en wetenschap in de vroegmoderne Nederlanden). Zwolle, Netherlands: WBOOKS, 2011.

Jorink, Eric, and Bart Ramakers. "Undivided Territory: 'Art' and 'Science' in the Early Modern Netherlands." *Nederlands Kunsthistorisch Jaarboek* 61 (2011): 6–33.

Jorink, Eric, Joanna Woodall, and Edward H. Wouk. "Humans and Other Animals in the Low Countries: An Introduction." In "Humans and Other Animals / Mensen en andere dieren," *Nederlands Kunsthistorisch Jaarboek* 71 (2021): 6–31.

Joseph, Celucien L. "'The Haitian Turn': An Appraisal of Recent Literary and Historiographical Works on the Haitian Revolution." *Journal of Pan African Studies* 5, no. 6 (2012). https://www.jpanafrican.org/docs/vol5no6/5.7-AHaitian.pdf.

Judy, R. A. "The Unfungible Flow of Liquid Blackness." *Liquid Blackness* 5, no. 1 (April 2021): 27–36.

Kaphar, Titus. "Can Art Amend History?" TED Talks, April 2017, video, 12:43. https://www.ted.com/talks/titus_kaphar_can_art_amend_history.

Keller, Eve. "Embryonic Individuals: The Rhetoric of Seventeenth-Century Embryology and the Construction of Early Modern Identity." *Eighteenth-Century Studies* 33, no. 3 (2000): 321–48.

Kettering, Alison McNeil. *Drawings from the Ter Borch Studio Estate*. The Hague: Staatsuitgeverij, 1988.

Kerr, Rose. *Asian Ceramics in the Hallwyl Collection*. Stockholm: Hallwyl Museum, 2015.

Keuning, J. *Petrus Plancius: Theoloog en geograaf, 1552–1622*. Amsterdam: P. N. van Kampen and Zoon, 1946.

Keyes, George S. "Cornelis Claesz. van Wieringen." *Oud Holland* 93, no. 1 (1979): 1–46.

Keyes, George S., ed. *Mirror of Empire: Dutch Marine Art of the Seventeenth Century*. Minneapolis: Minneapolis Institute of Arts, 1990.

King, Tiffany Lethabo. *The Black Shoals: Offshore Formations of Black and Native Studies*. Durham, NC: Duke University Press, 2019.

Kingsbury, Susan Myra, ed. *The Records of the Virginia Company of London*. Vol. 3. Washington, DC: United States Government Printing Office, 1933.

Kinukawa, Tomomi. "Science and Whiteness as Property in the Dutch Atlantic World: Maria Sibylla Merian's *Metamorphosis Insectorum Surinamensium* (1705)." *Journal of Women's History* 24, no. 3 (2012): 91–116.

Klooster, Wim, and Gert Oostindie. *Realm between Empires: The Second Dutch Atlantic, 1680–1815*. Ithaca, NY: Cornell University Press, 2018.

Knowles, Marika Takanishi. "Making Whiteness: Art, Luxury, and Race in Eighteenth-Century France." Special issue, *Journal18*, no. 13 (Spring 2022). https://www.journal18.org/issue13/making-whiteness-art-luxury-and -race-in-eighteenth-century-france/.

Kossmann, E. H., and Albert Fredrik Mellink, eds. *Texts concerning the Revolt of the Netherlands*. Cambridge: Cambridge University Press, 1974.

Lafont, Anne. *L'Art et la race: L'Africain (tout) contre l'oeil des Lumières*. Dijon: Les Presses du Réel, 2019.

Lawrence, Cynthia. "The Cult of the Seventeenth-Century Dutch Naval Heroes: Critical Appropriations of a Popular Patriotic Tradition." In *Narratives of Low Countries Histories and Culture: Reframing the Past*, edited by Jane Fenoulhet and Lesley Gilbert, 35–43. London: UCL Press, 2006.

Lawrence, Cynthia. "Hendrick de Keyser's Heemskerk Monument: The Origins of the Cult and Iconography of Dutch Naval Heroes." *Simiolus: Netherlands Quarterly for the History of Art* 21, no. 4 (1992): 265–95.

Leeflang, Huigen, and Pieter Roelofs, eds. *Hercules Segers: Painter, Etcher*. Vol. 1. Amsterdam: Rijksmuseum, 2016.

Lemmens, Gerard Th. M. "Die Schenkung an Ludwig XIV und die Auflösung der brasilianischen Sammlung des Johann Moritz 1652–1679." In *Soweit der Erdkreis reicht: Johann Moritz von Nassau-Siegen 1604–1679*, edited by Guido de Werd, 265–93. Kleve: Das Museum, 1980.

Lesger, Clé. *The Rise of the Amsterdam Market and Information Exchange— Merchants, Commercial Expansion and Change in the Spatial Economy of the Low Countries, c. 1550–1630*. Translated by J. C. Grayson. Burlington, VT: Ashgate, 2006.

Lipsius, Justo. *Epistolario de Justo Lipsio y los Españoles (1577–1706)*. Edited by Alejandro Ramírez. Madrid: Castalia, 1966.

Locke, John. *An Essay concerning Human Understanding*. Vol. 2. London: Printed by Eliz. Holt for Thomas Basset, 1690.

Loichot, Valérie. *Water Graves: The Art of the Unritual in the Greater Caribbean*. Charlottesville: University of Virginia Press, 2020.

Lowe, Kate. "The Black African Presence in Renaissance Europe." In *Black Africans in Renaissance Europe*, edited by T. F. Earle and K. J. P. Lowe, 1–14. Cambridge: Cambridge University Press, 2005.

Lurvink, Karin. "The Insurance of Mass Murder: The Development of Slave Life Insurance Policies of Dutch Private Slave Ships, 1720–1780." *Enterprise and Society* 21, no. 1 (March 2020): 210–38.

Lyon, J. Vanessa, and Caroline Fowler. "Revision and Reckoning: The Legacies of Slavery in Histories of Northern Art." *Journal of Historians of Netherlandish Art* 14, no. 1 (2022). https://jhna.org/articles/revision-and-reckoning -legacy-of-slaveries-in-northern-art/.

MacGregor, Arthur. *Curiosity and Enlightenment: Collectors and Collections from the Nineteenth Century*. New Haven, CT: Yale University Press, 2007.

Mack, John. *The Sea: A Cultural History*. London: Reaktion, 2011.

Margócsy, Dániel. *Commercial Visions: Science, Trade, and Visual Culture in the Dutch Golden Age*. Chicago: University of Chicago Press, 2014.

Marin, Louis. "In Praise of Appearance." *October* 37 (1986): 98–112.

Marx, Karl. *Capital: A Critique of Political Economy*. Vol. 1. Edited and translated by Paul Reitter. Edited by Paul North. Princeton, NJ: Princeton University Press, 2024.

Massey, Lyle. "Pregnancy and Pathology: Picturing Childbirth in Eighteenth-Century Obstetric Atlases." *Art Bulletin* 87, no. 1 (2005): 73–91.

Massing, Jean Michel. "Albert Eckhout, Frans Post and the Imagery of Afro-Americans in Seventeenth-Century Brazil." In *Studies in Imagery*, 2:141–71.

Massing, Jean Michel. *The Image of the Black in Western Art*. Vol. 3, *From the "Age of Discovery" to the Age of Abolition, Part 2: Europe and the World Beyond*, edited by David Bindman, Henry Louis Gates Jr., and Karen C. C. Dalton. Cambridge, MA: Belknap, 2011.

Massing, Jean Michel. "From Dutch Brazil to the West Indies: The Paper Image of the Ideal Sugar Plantation." In *Studies in Imagery*, 2: 172–98.

Massing, Jean Michel. *Studies in Imagery*. Vol. 2, *The World Discovered*. London: Pindar, 2007.

McKee, C. C. "'A Salting of Sorts': Salt, Sea, and Affective Form in the Work of Deborah Jack." *Art Journal* 78, no. 2 (Summer 2019): 14–27.

Meadows, Philip. *Observations concerning the Dominion and Sovereignty of the Seas: Being an Abstract of the Marine Affairs of England*. London, 1689.

Merian, Maria Sibylla. *Metamorphosis insectorum Surinamensium*. Amsterdam: J. Oosterwijk, 1719.

Merian, Maria Sibylla. *Metamorphosis insectorum Surinamensium—1705 = Verandering der Surinaamsche insecten 1705 = Transformation of the Surinamese Insects 1705*. Edited by Marieke van Delft and Hans Mulder. Tielt, Belgium: Lannoo, 2016.

Montias, John Michael. *Art at Auction in Seventeenth-Century Amsterdam*. Amsterdam: Amsterdam University Press, 2000.

Montias, John Michael. *Artists and Artisans in Delft: A Socio-Economic Study of the Seventeenth Century*. Princeton, NJ: Princeton University Press, 1982.

Montias, John Michael. "Cost and Value in Seventeenth-Century Dutch Art." *Art History* 10 (1987): 455–66.

Morgan, Jennifer L. "*Partus sequitur ventrem*: Law, Race, and Reproduction in Colonial Slavery." *Small Axe* 22, no. 1 (2018): 1–17.

Morgan, Jennifer L. *Reckoning with Slavery: Gender, Kinship, and Capitalism in the Early Black Atlantic*. Durham, NC: Duke University Press, 2021.

Morrison, Toni. *Playing in the Dark: Whiteness in the Literary Imagination*. New York: Vintage, 1992.

Nadler, Steven M. "Arnauld, Descartes, and Transubstantiation: Reconciling Cartesian Metaphysics and Real Presence." *Journal of the History of Ideas* 49, no. 2 (1988): 229–46.

Nelson, Charmaine. *Slavery, Geography, and Empire in Nineteenth-Century Marine Landscapes of Montreal and Jamaica*. London: Routledge, 2016.

Neri, Janice. *The Insect and the Image: Visualizing Nature in Early Modern Europe, 1500–1700*. Minneapolis: University of Minnesota Press, 2011.

Nimako, Kwame, and Glenn Willemsen. *The Dutch Atlantic: Slavery, Abolition, and Emancipation*. London: Pluto, 2011.

Noorlander, D. L. *Heaven's Wrath: The Protestant Reformation and the Dutch West India Company in the Atlantic World*. Ithaca, NY: Cornell University Press, 2020.

Otterspeer, Willem. *The Bastion of Liberty: Leiden University Today and Yesterday*. Translated by Beverly Jackson. Leiden: Leiden University Press, 2008. Originally published as *Het bolwerk van de vrijheid: De Leidse Universiteit in heden en verleden* (2008).

Oughtred, William. *The Circles of Proportion and the Horizontal Instrument &c.* Oxford: Printed by W. Hall for R. Davis, 1660.

Parker, Geoffrey. "The Emergence of Modern Finance in Europe, 1500–1750."

In *Fontana Economic History of Europe*, vol. 2, 527–94. London: Collins, 1971–1976.

Parker, John. *In My Time of Dying: A History of Death and the Dead in West Africa*. Princeton, NJ: Princeton University Press, 2021.

Petram, Lodewijk. *The World's First Stock Exchange*. New York: Columbia University Press, 2014.

Phaf-Rheinberger, Ineke. "Von Sklavenhandel und christlichen Vorbehalten: Die Aktualität von Caspar Barlaeus in Amerika und Afrika." In *Sein Feld war die Welt: Johann Moritz von Nassau-Siegen (1604–1679)*, edited by Gerhard Brunn and Cornelius Neutsch, 145–58. Münster: Waxmann, 2008.

Philip, M. NourbeSe. *Zong! As Told to the Author by Setaey Adamu Boateng*. Toronto: Mercury, 2008.

Polcha, Elizabeth. "Breeding Insects and Reproducing White Supremacy in Maria Sibylla Merian's Ecology of Dispossession." *Lady Science*, June 20, 2019. https://www.ladyscience.com/breeding-insects-and-reproducing-white -supremacy/no57.

Ponte, Mark. "Black in Amsterdam around 1650." In *Black in Rembrandt's Time*, edited by Elmer Kolfin and Epco Runia, translated by David McKay, 44–61. Zwolle, Netherlands: wbooks, 2020.

Powell, Amy Knight. "Life and Death according to the 'Episteme' of the Fort: A Picture of the Slave Trader Dirck Wilre in Elmina, 1669." *Nederlands Kunsthistorisch Jaarboek* 72 (2002): 273–304.

Powell, Amy Knight. "Porcelain White." *res: Journal of Anthropology and Aesthetics* 73–74 (2020): 60–75.

Prak, Maarten. "Burghers, Citizens, and Popular Politics in the Dutch Republic." *Eighteenth-Century Studies* 30, no. 4 (1997): 443–48.

Prak, Maarten. "The Golden Age." In *Discovering the Dutch: On Culture and Society in the Netherlands*, edited by Emmeline Besamusca and Jaap Verheul, 109–19. Amsterdam: Amsterdam University Press, 2014.

Prakash, Om. *The Dutch East India Company and the Economy of Bengal, 1630–1720*. Princeton, NJ: Princeton University Press, 2014.

Pranghoffer, Sebastian. "Changing Views on Generation—Images of the Unborn." In *The Secrets of Generation: Reproduction in the Long Eighteenth Century*, edited by Raymond Stephanson and Darren N. Wagner, 167–94. Toronto: University of Toronto Press, 2015.

Price, Leah. *How to Do Things with Books in Victorian Britain*. Princeton, NJ: Princeton University Press, 2012.

Quarcoopome, Nii Otokunor. "Les portraits funéraires akan." In *Ghana: hier et aujourd'hui*, edited by Christiane Falgayrettes-Leveau and Christiane Owusu-Sarpong, 93–134. Paris: Musée Dapper, 2003.

Quilley, Geoff, and Kay Dian Kriz, eds. *An Economy of Colour: Visual Culture and the Atlantic World, 1660–1830*. Manchester: Manchester University Press, 2003.

Ratelband, Klaas, and R. A. M. Basejou. *Nederlanders in West-Afrika 1600–1650: Angola, Kongo en Sao Tomé.* Zutphen: Walburg Pers., 2000.

Reitsma, Ella. *Maria Sibylla Merian and Daughters: Women of Art and Science.* Los Angeles: J. Paul Getty Museum, 2008.

Remien, Peter. "Oeconomy and Ecology in Early Modern England." PMLA 132, no. 5 (2017): 1117–33.

Riegl, Alois. *The Group Portraiture of Holland.* Translated by Evelyn M. Kain and David Britt. Los Angeles: Getty Research Center for the History of Art and Humanities, 1999.

Rivera, Enrique Salvador. "Whitewashing the Dutch Atlantic." *Social and Economic Studies* 64, no. 1 (2015): 117–32.

Robinson, Cedric. *Black Marxism: The Making of the Black Radical Tradition.* London: Zed, 1983.

Robinson, Cedric. "Capitalism, Slavery, and Bourgeois Historiography." *History Workshop* 23 (1987): 122–40.

Rosenthal, Angela. "Visceral Culture: Blushing and the Legibility of Whiteness in Eighteenth-Century British Portraiture." *Art History* 27, no. 4 (2004): 563–92.

Rubiés, Joan-Pau. "Were Early Modern Europeans Racist?" In *Ideas of "Race" in the History of the Humanities,* edited by Amos Morris-Reich and Dirk Rupnow, 33–88. London: Palgrave Macmillan, 2017.

Rubin, Miri. *Corpus Christi: The Eucharist in Late Medieval Culture.* Cambridge: Cambridge University Press, 1991.

Rucker, Elisabeth, ed. *Maria Sibylla Merian, 1647–1717.* Nuremberg: Germanisches Nationalmuseum, 1967.

Rucker, Walter C. *Gold Coast Diasporas: Identity, Culture, and Power.* Bloomington: Indiana University Press, 2015.

Russell, Margarita. *Visions of the Sea: Hendrick C. Vroom and the Origins of Dutch Marine Painting.* Leiden: Brill, 1983.

Saxby, T. J. *The Quest for the New Jerusalem, Jean de Labadie and the Labadists, 1610–1744.* Dordrecht, Netherlands: Martinus Nijhoff, 1987.

Schama, Simon. *The Embarrassment of Riches: An Interpretation of Dutch Culture in the Golden Age.* New York: Knopf, 1987.

Schiebinger, Londa. *Plants and Empire: Colonial Bioprospecting in the Atlantic World.* Cambridge, MA: Harvard University Press, 2004.

Schiebinger, Londa, and Claudia Swan, eds. *Colonial Botany: Science, Commerce, and Politics in the Early Modern World.* Philadelphia: University of Pennsylvania Press, 2005.

Schmidt, Benjamin. *Innocence Abroad: The Dutch Imagination and the New World.* Cambridge: Cambridge University Press, 2001.

Sedgwick, Eve Kosofsky. *Touching Feeling: Affect, Pedagogy, Performativity.* Durham, NC: Duke University Press, 2003.

Sekula, Allan. *Fish Story.* Rotterdam: Richter Verlag, 1995.

Sekula, Allan. *Okeanos*. Edited by Daniela Zyman and Cory Scozzari. London: Sternberg, 2017.

Shapin, Steven, and Simon Schaffer. *Leviathan and the Air-Pump: Hobbes, Boyle, and the Experimental Life*. Princeton, NJ: Princeton University Press, 1985.

Sharpe, Christina. *In the Wake: On Blackness and Being*. Durham, NC: Duke University Press, 2016.

Siegert, Bernhard. "The 'Chorein' of the Pirate: On the Origin of the Dutch Seascape." *Grey Room* 57 (2014): 6–23.

Sigmond, Peter, and Wouter Kloek. *Zeeslagen en zeehelden in de Gouden Eeuw*. Amsterdam: Rijksmuseum, 2007.

Silver, Sean R. "Locke's Pineapple and the History of Taste." *Eighteenth Century* 49, no. 1 (2008): 43–65.

Sint Nicolaas, Eveline, Valika Smeulders, Irma Boom, Pierre Bouvier, and Steve Green. *Slavery: The Story of João, Wally, Oopjen, Paulus, Van Bengalen, Surapati, Sapali, Tula, Dirk and Lokhay*. Amsterdam: Rijksmuseum/Atlas, 2021.

Sluijter, Eric Jan. "Over Brabantse vodden, economische concurrentie, artistieke wedijver en de groei van de markt voor schilderijen in de eerste decennia van de zeventiende eeuw." In *Kunst voor de markt*, edited by Reindert Falkenburg, J. de Jong, and Bart Ramaker, 112–43. Zwolle, Netherlands: Waanders, 1999.

Sluiter, Engel. "New Light on the '20 and Odd Negroes' Arriving in Virginia, August 1619." *William and Mary Quarterly* 54, no. 2 (1997): 395–98.

Smallwood, Stephanie. *Saltwater Slavery: A Middle Passage from Africa to American Diaspora*. Cambridge, MA: Harvard University Press, 2008.

Smith, Shawn Michelle. *At the Edge of Sight: Photography and the Unseen*. Durham, NC: Duke University Press, 2013.

Stedman, John Gabriel. *Narrative of a Five Years' Expedition against the Revolted Negroes of Surinam in Guiana*. London: J. Johnson and J. Edwards, 1796.

Steensgaard, Niels. *The Asian Trade Revolution: The East India Companies and the Decline of the Caravan Trade*. Chicago: University of Chicago Press, 2017.

Steensgaard, Niels. "The Dutch East India Company as an Institutional Innovation." In *Dutch Capitalism and World Capitalism*, edited by Maurice Aymard, 235–57. Cambridge: Cambridge University Press, 1982.

Steinberg, Philip E. *The Social Construction of the Ocean*. Cambridge: Cambridge University Press, 2001.

Straumann, Benjamin. *Roman Law in the State of Nature: The Classical Foundations of Hugo Grotius' Natural Law*. Cambridge: Cambridge University Press, 2015.

Sutton, Elizabeth. "Bittersweet: Sugar, Slavery, and Science in Dutch Suriname." In *Midwestern Arcadia: Essays in Honor of Alison Kettering*, edited by Dawn Odell and Jessica Buskirk. Northfield, MN: Carleton College, 2014. DOI:10.18277/makf.2015.13.

Swammerdam, Jan. *The Book of Nature, or, the History of Insects*. London: C. G. Seyffert, 1758. Originally published as *Bybel der Natuur* (Amsterdam, 1737).

Swan, Claudia. "Birds of Paradise for the Sultan: Early Seventeenth-Century Dutch-Turkish Encounters and the Uses of Wonder." *De Zeventiende Eeuw* 29 (2013): 49–63.

Tavares, Pierre Franklin. "Hegel, critique de l'Afrique: Introduction aux études de Hegel sur l'Afrique." PhD diss., Université Paris I, 1990.

't Hart, Marjolein. "The Merits of a Financial Revolution: Public Finance, 1550–1700." In *A Financial History of the Netherlands*, edited by Marjolein 't Hart, Joost Jonker, and Jan Luiten van Zanden, 11–36. Cambridge: Cambridge University Press, 1997.

Thompson, Krista. "The Sound of Light: Reflections on Art History in the Visual Culture of Hip-Hop." *Art Bulletin* 91, no. 4 (2009): 481–505.

Thornton, John K. "The African Experience of the '20 and Odd Negroes' Arriving in Virginia in 1619." *William and Mary Quarterly* 55, no. 3 (1998): 421–34.

Tinsley, Omise'eke Natasha. "Black Atlantic, Queer Atlantic: Queer Imaginings of the Middle Passage." *GLQ* 14, no. 2–3 (2008): 191–215.

Ufer, Ulrich. "Imagining Social Change in Early-Modern Amsterdam: Global Processes, Local Perceptions." In *Imagining Global Amsterdam: History, Culture, and Geography in a World City*, edited by Marco de Waard, 27–44. Amsterdam: Amsterdam University Press, 2012.

van den Boogaart, Ernst. "Black Slavery and the 'Mulatto Escape Hatch' in the Brazilian Ensembles of Frans Post and Albert Eckhout." In *The Slave in European Art: From Renaissance Trophy to Abolitionist Emblem*, edited by Elizabeth McGrath and Jean Michel Massing, 217–51. London: Warburg Institute, 2012.

van den Vondel, Joost. "*Het lof der zee-vaert* / In Praise of Navigation." Translated by Peter Skrine. *Dutch Crossing: Journal of the Low Countries* 5, no. 13 (1981): 8–33.

van de Plas, Joos. *Metamorphosis insectorum Surinamensium: Eine Entdeckungsreise neu erlebt*. Wiesbaden: Museum Wiesbaden, 2014.

van der Ham, Gijs. *Tarnished Gold: Ghana and the Netherlands from 1593*. Translated by Kevin Cook. Amsterdam: Rijksmuseum, 2016.

van de Roemer, Gijsbert M. "Het lichaam als borduursel: Kunst en kennis in het anatomisch kabinet van Frederik Ruysch." *Nederlands Kunsthistorisch Jaarboek* 58 (2007/2008): 216–41.

Van der Valk, Leendert. "De eerste Afrikaanse Amerikanen werden verhandeld onder de Nederlandse vlag." *NRC Handelsblad*, January 1, 2021.

van der Waals, Jan. *De Prentschat van Michiel Hinloopen: Een reconstructie van de eerste openbare papierkunstverzameling in Nederland*. Amsterdam: Rijksmuseum, 1988.

van Groesen, Michiel. *Amsterdam's Atlantic: Print Culture and the Making of Dutch Brazil*. Philadelphia: University of Penn. Press, 2017.

van Groesen, Michiel. *The Legacy of Dutch Brazil*. New York: Cambridge University Press, 2014.

Vanhaelen, Angela. *The Wake of Iconoclasm: Painting and the Church in the Dutch Republic*. University Park: Penn State University Press, 2012.

van Hoogstraten, Samuel. *Inleyding tot de hooge schoole der schilderkonst-Anders de zichtbaere werelt*. Rotterdam: François van Hoogstraten, 1678.

van Hoogstraten, Samuel. *Introduction to the Academy of Painting; or, the Visible World*. Edited by Celeste Brusati. Translated by Jaap Jacobs. Los Angeles: Getty Research Institute, 2021.

van Ittersum, Martine Julia. "Hugo Grotius in Context: Van Heemskerk's Capture of the 'Santa Catarina' and Its Justification in 'De Jure Praedae' (1604–1606)." *Asian Journal of Social Science* 31, no. 3 (2003): 511–48.

van Kessel, Ineke, ed. *Merchants, Missionaries, and Migrants: 300 Years of Dutch-Ghanaian Relations*. Amsterdam: KIT and Sub-Saharan, 2002.

van Lottum, Jelle. "Labour Migration and Economic Performance: London and the Randstad, c. 1600–1800." *Economic History Review* 64, no. 2 (2011): 531–70.

van Lottum, Jelle, and Jan Lucassen. "Six Cross Sections of the Dutch Maritime Labor Market." In *Maritime Labor: Contributions to the History of Work at Sea, 1500–2000*, edited by Richard Gorski, 13–42. Amsterdam: Amsterdam University Press, 2007.

Van Niekerk, J. P. *The Development of the Principles of Insurance Law in the Netherlands from 1500 to 1800*. Johannesburg: Juta, 1998.

van Panhuys, Louis Constant. "Recherche des tableaux sur le Brésil par le prince Jean Maurice de Nassau au roi Louis XIV." In *Congrès international des Américanistes*, 435–41. Gothenburg: Gothenburg Museum, 1925.

van Rossum, Matthias, Lex Heerma van Voss, Jelle van Lottum, and Jan Lucassen. "National and International Labour Markets for Sailors in European, Atlantic, and Asian Waters, 1600–1850." In *Maritime History as Global History*, edited by Maria Fusaro and Amelia Polonia, 47–72. Liverpool: Liverpool University Press, 2010.

van Swigchem, C. A., T. Brouwer, and W. van Os. *Een Huis voor het Woord: Het protestantse kerkinterieur in Nederland tot 1900*. Zeist: Rijksdeinst voor de Monumentenzorg, 1984.

van Voss, Lex Heerma, Jelle van Lottum, and Jan Lucassen. "Sailors, National and International Labour Markets and National Identity, 1600–1850." In *Shipping Efficiency and Economic Growth, 1350–1800*, edited by Richard Unger, 309–51. Leiden: Brill, 2011.

van Zanden, Jan Luiten. "The 'Revolt of the Early Modernists' and the 'First Modern Economy': An Assessment." *Economic History Review* 55, no. 4 (2002): 619–41.

Vervliet, Jeroen. "General Introduction." In *Hugo Grotius Mare Liberum, 1609–2009*, edited by Robert Feenstra, ix–xxx. Leiden: Brill, 2009.

Vink, Markus. "'The World's Oldest Trade': Dutch Slavery and Slave Trade in the

Indian Ocean in the Seventeenth Century." *Journal of World History* 14, no. 2 (2003): 131–77.

Virgil. *The Works of Virgil: Containing His Pastorals, Georgics and Aeneis*. Translated by John Dryden. London, 1697.

Vittet, Jean. "Jean-Maurice de Nassau-Siegen et Louis XIV: Récit d'une passion partagée pour la vie sauvage du Brésil." In *Exotismus und Globalisierung: Brasilien auf Wandteppichen: Die Tenture des Indes*, edited by Gerlinde Klatte, Helga Prüßmann-Zemper, and Katharina Schmidt-Loske, 59–66. Berlin: Deutscher Kunstverlag, 2016.

Vivian, Brian C. "Sacred to Secular: Transitions in Akan Funerary Customs." In *An African Commitment: Papers in Honour of Peter Lewis Shinnie*, edited by Judy Sterner and Nicholas David, 157–67. Calgary: University of Calgary Press, 1992.

Voltaire. *Candide: Or, All for the Best*. London, 1771.

Walcott, Derek. *The Prodigal*. New York: Farrar, Straus and Giroux, 2004.

Walcott, Rinaldo. "The Black Aquatic." *Liquid Blackness* 5, no. 1 (April 2021): 64–73.

Walsh, Lorena S. *Motives of Honor, Pleasure, and Profit: Plantation Management in the Colonial Chesapeake, 1607–1763*. Chapel Hill: University of North Carolina Press, 2010.

Wandel, Lee Palmer. "Fragmentation and Presence: Reformation Debates and Cultural Theory." In *Cultures of Communication: Theologies of Media in Early Modern Europe and Beyond*, edited by Helmut Puff, Ulrike Strasser, and Christopher Wild, 55–76. Toronto: University of Toronto Press, 2017.

Waters, David W., and Pierre Garcie. *The Rutters of the Sea: The Sailing Directions of Pierre Garcie: A Study of the First English and French Printed Sailing Directions, with Facsimile Reproductions*. New Haven, CT: Yale University Press, 1967.

Westermann, Mariët. "Svetlana Alpers's 'The Art of Describing: Dutch Art in the Seventeenth Century,' 1983." *Burlington Magazine* 153, no. 1301 (August 2011): 532–36.

Westermann, Mariët. "'Wooncultuur,' in the Netherlands: A Historiography in Progress." *Wooncultuur in de Nederlanden / The Art of Home in the Netherlands, 1500–1800; Nederlands Kunsthistorisch Jaarboek* 51 (2000): 6–33.

Westermann, Mariët. *A Worldly Art: The Dutch Republic, 1585–1718*. New York: Harry Abrams, 1966.

Weststeijn, Arthur. *Commercial Republicanism in the Dutch Golden Age: The Political Thought of Johan and Pieter de la Court*. Leiden: Brill, 2012.

Weststeijn, Arthur. "Republican Empire: Colonialism, Commerce, and Corruption in the Dutch Golden Age." *Renaissance Studies* 26, no. 4 (2012): 491–509.

Williams, Eric Eustace. *Capitalism and Slavery*. 3rd ed. 1944. Chapel Hill: University of North Carolina Press, 2021.

Wilson, Catherine. *The Invisible World: Early Modern Philosophy and the Invention of the Microscope.* Princeton, NJ: Princeton University Press, 1995.

Wittewrongel, Petrus. *Oeconomia Christiana ofte Christelicke Huishoudinge.* Amsterdam, 1661.

Wolf, Bryan Jay. *Vermeer and the Invention of Seeing.* Chicago: University of Chicago Press, 2001.

Zandvliet, Kees. *Mapping for Money: Maps, Plans, and Topographic Paintings and Their Role in Dutch Overseas Expansion during the 16th and 17th Centuries.* Amsterdam: De Bataafsche Leeuw, 2002.

INDEX

Note: Page numbers followed by *f* refer to figures. *P* refers to a numbered plate.

48, 132n24; *Planter's House and Village*, P7; *Sugar Mill*, P8

Powell, Amy Knight, 97, 133n23, 137n38

privacy, 103–7, 109; of interior conscience, 97

privateers, 1, 6

property, 19, 50, 97, 103; chattel, 5, 8, 19, 31, 33, 49, 53, 134n24; damage, 94; desecularization of, 6; humans as, 8, 19, 31, 33, 134n24; land as, 47, 68, 85; landed, 22; life as, 3–8, 48–51, 123; lines, 69; mobile, 25; personhood as, 2, 9, 130n36; real, 25, 30; rights, 23, 32, 84

racialization, 2, 114, 121

Reformation, 4, 28, 130n26

Reformed Church, 13, 19, 115; interior, 73, 116; spaces, 73, 76, 109

religion, 5, 131n11; of freedom, 14; wars of, 84

Rembrandt, 25, 30, 32–33; *The Beheading of John the Baptist*, 20, 117–19, 118f; maritime works of, 19; *Syndics of the Drapers' Guild*, 20, 110–13, 115–22, P15; *Two Men of African Descent*, 3, 9, 17–18, 126n10, P1; workshop of, 9, 19, 31–32

reptiles, 81, 88–89, 92, 102, 135n10

republicanism, 15, 19

Riegl, Alois, 20, 116–19

rights, 68, 80, 85, 106–7; property, 23, 32, 84; sovereign, 5

Ruysch, Frederik, 86–87, 90, 136n19, 136n21

Saenredam, Pieter Jansz., 115; *The Interior of the Cunerakerk in Rhenen*, P16

salt, 4, 35, 42–43, 65, 69, 97; African diasporic artistic practice and, 131n13; enslaved labor and, 42; flats, 41; mining, 19, 42; pans, 41–42; production, 44

sea, the, 29, 30f, 34, 57–59, 131n8; Bosman on, 53; Dutch painting and, 18, 60, 65, 67; Grotius on, 68–69, 78–80; level of, 39; monuments and, 122–23; in Post's work, 43, 47, 131n7; surface of, 41; in Ter Borch's work, 77; Walcott on, 52. *See also* Middle Passage; pearl diving

seascapes, 3, 5–6, 13–14, 30, 60, 97, 109, 123

Sedgwick, Eve Kosofsky, 43, 108. *See also* besideness

Segers, Hercules, 19, 25–30, 33; *Rocky Landscape with a Gorge, First Version*, P3; *Landscape with a Waterfall*, 29, P5; *Mountain Valley with the Remains of a Ship*, P4

Sekula, Allan, 64–65, 133n24; *Panorama: Mid-Atlantic*, P10

selfhood, 83–84, 89

shareholders, 11, 23–25

Sharpe, Christina, 59, 134n24

shipbuilding, 22, 129n12

ships, 5, 18, 24, 52, 60, 64–65, 69, 79, 108, 133n23; merchant, 65; raiding of, 1, 125n2; Segers's images of, 26, 28–29; slave, 53, 63f, 95, 128n3; sunk, 11; in Ter Borch's work, 76

silver, 1, 22, 97

slave trade, 5–6, 19, 22, 31, 53, 62, 134n24; development of, 59; Dutch, 32, 73; Dutch art and, 126n8; portraiture and, 126n10; Portuguese, 35; profit margins on, 129n12; stocks and, 25; Verenigde Oost-Indische Compagnie and, 126n14. *See also* transatlantic slave trade

sociality: of insects, 89–90, 92, 108; plantation economy and, 100; of plants, 92; preserved children and, 87; of reproduction, 107

sovereignty, 6, 121

Spain, 14, 23, 31, 67

Spanish, the, 5, 18, 31, 42; in the East Indies, 68; in the West Indies, 25

Spanish monarchy, 2, 4–5, 31

speculation, 6, 23, 27, 30; on commodities, 24; financial, 10–11, 19, 28; precarity of, 29

spice, 23, 28. *See also* mace; pepper

States-General, 69, 72

stock exchange, 4, 8, 22, 25–26, 73

stocks, 7, 23, 25, 30, 33

sugar, 1, 4, 22–23, 30, 45–49, 51, 65, 69, 97, 123; artists and, 16; plantations, 8, 19, 35, 44, 48, 96, 109; trade, 42, 130n4

Suriname, 11, 20, 89–90, 92–95, 97–98, 106–7, 137n43; Indigenous and Afro-diasporic populations in, 102; Stedman's account of, 14. *See also* Merian, Maria Sibylla; plantation economies; plantations

Swammerdam, Johannes, 98–99